f 14-95

SCHOOL OF ORIENTAL AND A

University of L

Th

Spinsters Abroad

Victorian Lady Explorers

Spinsters Abroad

Victorian Lady Explorers

Dea Birkett

Basil Blackwell

First published 1989

Basil Blackwell Ltd
108 Cowley Road, Oxford, Ox4 1JF, UK

Basil Blackwell Inc.
234 Park Avenue South, Suite 1503
New York, NY 10016, USA

British Library Cataloguing in Publication Data

Birkett, Dea,   1958–
  Spinsters abroad : Victorian lady explorers.
  1. Travel by women, history
  I. Title
  910'.88042

    ISBN 0–631–15604–6

Library of Congress Cataloging in Publication Data

Birkett, Dea, 1958–
  Spinsters abroad : Victorian lady explorers/ Dea Birkett
      p.   cm.
  Bibliograpy: p.
  Includes index.
  ISBN 0–631–15604–6
  1. Explorers, Women – Biography.   I. Title
G200.B48 1989
910'.92'2–dc19   88–28252
                                                              CIP

Typeset in 11 on 13 pt Goudy
by Opus, Oxford
Printed in Great Britain by Billing and Sons Ltd, Worcester

Contents

x use for essay

To M

List of Illustrations

List of Maps

Preface

'Adventure', wrote Alexandra David-Neel who trekked through the Tibetan Highlands, 'is my only reason for living'. Her words read as a feminist slogan. A gallery of strong, independent, willful women presented themselves to me: Mary Kingsley breaking free from her life nursing a bedridden mother to canoe up the Ogooué rapids: Marianne North at last escaping the responsibility of looking after an increasingly infirm father to ride sedately in a railway carriage through North America: Mary Gaunt choosing to sway in a hammock along the West African coast rather than wither in widowhood and penury in her London bedsit: Ella Christie freed by the tragic circumstances of her parent's madness and death for the back of a mule in the mountains of Ladakh. What could be more attractive than doing as these women did and daring as these women dared? Breaking free.

So I went to the landscapes which had given these Victorian women their newfound freedom. Mary Kingsley guided me through West Africa; Isabella Bird sailed me through the Yangtze gorges; Marianne North accompanied me on a railway journey across the United States and Canada.

On all my journeys, I took with me their Victorian eyes and images. I looked for dangerous landscapes, intriguing and untouchable people. I looked, of course, for the thing which all of them, Isabella, Mary and Marianne had also sought – I looked for a new identity away from that place called home.

Sometimes I was startled; sometimes shocked; occasionally cradled by the seeming familiarity of all I saw. The home in Quincy where Marianne North had stayed as a guest of the influential Adams family had become Adams National Historic Site ($2.00 Entrance Permit.

Valid For Seven Days); a National Park Service guide dressed entirely in camouflage green took me round a wooden-panelled, empty house. 'By automobile the site can be reached via Exit 24 of the South East Expressway (Mass. 93)' read the brochure. I found no Marianne there.

But in the outskirts of West Manchester, only a few miles up the New England coast, I discovered not only the rockpools in which Marianne had paddled in her new dark blue-grey bathing costume, but the first home of her own. I had packed for my journey her painting of a white wooden house surrounded by water, never imagining its dated seaside splendour would still stand. I found it perched on the same lichen-smothered rocks, the railway sleepers of the nearby station now covered with gravel but with gentle waves still lapping its three seabound sides. 'It is deliciously wild and quiet,' Marianne had recorded in her journal

Other times I explored a landscape disguised, if little changed. I would never have seen the trackers' paths cut into the side of a gorge if Isabella hadn't described, in typically devout detail, how she had sat in her houseboat and been pulled over the cataracts by sixty men: with a huge coil of plaited bamboo up to half-a-mile long attached to each breast strap with a hitch, the trackers tugged barefoot up the narrow flights of stairs chiselled into the rockface at the edge of the Ping-shu gorge. A rapidly beating drum gave them their rhythm as they took tiny steps, swinging their arms and body forward, stooping so low that their hands nearly touched the ground. 'At a distance they look like quadrupeds,' wrote Isabella.

But more than my physical surroundings echoed the women travellers' descriptions in letters and diaries. Their sense of being apart and undeniably privileged also followed me. Isabella had been asked how much she earnt a day writing and sewing, by the Chinese faces who crowded round to witness her horizontal script. 'Where is your husband?' pestered the captain of Mary Kingsley's canoe. My anonymity in London streets was replaced by glowing whiteness. I was different. I was stared at, prodded, continually questioned. As I squatted over the trough in the women's toilet on the ferry taking me through the province of Szechuan, other women's eyes stared on, waiting. In my diary, one day's entry simply read, 'Lack of privacy. I had come to look. I arrived to rows of eyes looking at me. I began to turn those eyes upon myself.'

Why had I been attracted to the women travellers' lives. What had allowed them to roam with the freedom of men in lands so very different and distant from their own? Surprising answers began to emerge, illfitting to those claimed as feminist heroines. They became increasingly unattractive role models; my admiration for them grew awkward.

But if less admirable, I was also discovering more interesting women. In these troubled and contradictory lives lay more than simple portraits of feminist heroines, but women who both were exploited by and exploitative of the prejudices of their time. My journeys with the women travellers had come to an end. My journey in search of them – the writing of this book – was about to begin.

Acknowledgements

There are many people, on many continents, to thank for their hospitality, help and insights during the researching and writing of this book.

In Britain, Julie Wheelwright offered the comment and criticism of a professional writer and the support of a friend. Susan Roast, Sarah Fox, Alison Stephany and Kevin Toolis stood by me. Dorothy Middleton is a source of inspiration to every writer on women travellers.

In Africa, LaRay Denzer, Jane Bryce, Wendy Pittaway, Katherine Frank, Dr Steve Dan Jumbo, Charmian Alexander, Maureen Okonkwo, Mr Efiong Aye, the family of Reverend Onoyom Mbuk, Billy Hawkes and Simon Brownlei all lodged and looked after me. Kenneth Birch of Elder Dempster brought me home.

In America, Amtrak took me around with the style and courtesy Marianne North had found over a hundred years before. Jo Ross believed in and tolerated both of us.

In China, Mr Ding introduced me to a new continent. Travis Wiseman made me laugh.

I am also grateful to the families and friends of the women travellers who shared enthusiasms and memories. I am especially thankful to Mr Robert Stewart of Arndean, the North family at Rougham, Beatrice de Cardi and Mrs Yvonne Fox.

The staff of many libraries provided friendly and efficient answers to my queries. To those at the Royal Botanic Gardens, Royal Geographical Society, Royal Commonwealth Society and John Murray's in particular – thank you.

Dea Birkett,
London.

Part I

The most foreign country is within
Alice Walker

1

The Point of Departure

Sitting by her easel at the window of a small rented room on the edge of the Pyrénées in the early winter of 1859, Marianne North cautiously made her first attempt at capturing a landscape. She peered beyond the river to the foot of the freshly covered mountains, past the distant Port de Vénasque, through the tiny notch in the rugged cliffs to Spain and the great proud Maladeta mountain, 'apparently quite near, but a long journey to reach it. A still blue lake lay close under its snows and rocks and beyond were blue mountains, one over the other, and the plain of Languedoc, like a hazy blue sea, far away.' Once her vision could reach no further, her suggestive imagination moved her hand across the canvas. 'A scrambling descent on the Spanish side leads down to the Trou du Taureau,' she recorded in her journal, 'where the icy torrent from the Maladetta glacier loses itself in a hole of the limestone, to emerge five miles off as the source of the Garonne.'

Her brush had travelled over twenty miles to reach the river's fount, leaping with her imagination, using the hazed tints of her watercolours to incite scenes far beyond the mountain range framed by the window. Until painting this extraordinary visionary landscape, twenty-nine-year-old Marianne had thought she could 'only draw near objects the size of life; but the beauty of the view from our window tempted me.'[1] The manner in which she painted was, she admitted, unorthodox. First she filled in the immediate foreground, slowly lifting her head to the level of the nearby buildings, then, following a chimerical path

---

[1] Marianne North, *Some Further Recollections of a Happy Life selected from the journals of Marianne North chiefly between the years 1859 and 1869: edited by her sister, Mrs. John Addington Symonds*, (London 1893), p. 9.

out of Luchon to the bottom of the mountain, painted the scree tossed down by the glacier. Finally, piece by piece, she reached the snow-capped Pica de Maladeta, the highest summit of the mountain range. But while the imaginary world of her paintings spanned continents and bridged centuries, the world within Marianne's window was edged by the needs of her ailing father whom she accompanied on European tours.

From other sanctuaries, in widely scattered cities, other young female Victorian eyes peered out from windows forced shut against a tempting world. In response to their confinement, they also drew visionary canvasses on which much of their private life was realized, creating wide worlds of the imagination within and forcing a physical and emotional space denied them in reality.

Marianne North's daily life at her parent's Hastings home was girdled by the duties of a conscientious daughter. She had been twenty-four in 1855 when, sitting beside her mother's bed, she had promised the dying woman she would look after her difficult and demanding husband.

During the first few years following his wife's death, Frederick North was accompanied around Europe by his two unmarried daughters while their brother Charley, the eldest sibling, was left to make his own future path. The younger Catherine soon attracted a suitor; scholar John Addington Symonds recorded in his diary first seeing the sisters staying at Mürren in the Alps:

> Both the young ladies were devoted to sketching. The eldest was blonde, tall, stout, good-humoured, and a little satirical. The second was dark and thin and slight, nervous and full of fun and intellectual acumen. The one seemed manager and mother, the other dreamer and thinker. Neither was remarkable for beauty; but the earnest vivacity of the younger grew upon me . . . . Her name was Catherine.[2]

John Addington Symonds' wooing of Catherine was not stirred by love but medical advice; fighting since a teenager against his homosexuality, the surgeon to the Queen's household had recom-

[2] *The Memoirs of John Addington Symonds*, edited and introduced by Phyllis Grosskurth, (New York 1984), pp. 137–8.

mended cohabitation with a hired mistress as a cure – or marriage. When John saw twenty-seven-year-old Catherine, he chose the latter; within six months of spying her from the alpine inn window they were married, and Catherine's sexually and emotionally unfulfilled life with her unresponsive husband, constantly demanding discretion, began. 'I married without passion or feeling,' wrote the new groom. 'I deceived her.'[3]

While the unhappily married couple moved to Davos in the Swiss Alps to avoid the scandal of Symonds' schoolboy affairs, Marianne continued to travel alone with her father, booking in to the mountain inns and tourist hotels as Mr and Mrs North. The canvas of Marianne's life soon became that of housekeeper and chaperone to this increasingly deaf and idiosyncratic man. 'My father hated guides,' wrote his daughter, so Marianne, herself deaf in one ear, shouted out the commentary as they moved around the resorts of Europe and North Africa, constantly on the lookout for sights and sounds that would amuse him. But although she attempted to include Mr North in all her enjoyment, his presence emphasized her role as daughter and female helper, and she was excluded from the more romantic and exotic experiences of their travels. As she watched her father take part in the local festivities at Har Meron mountain, just north of the Sea of Galilee, Marianne 'was permitted to peep through a hole and see the great people eat, all sitting in the usual fashion cross-legged round a "mountain of rice" and other Moslem delicacies, my dear old father trying to look as if he had not got the cramp, and receiving choice morsels tossed into his mouth by the hands of his friends, with a smiling countenance.'[4] Back at home in Frederick North's Hastings parliamentary seat or the family country home of Rougham Hall in Norfolk, she found little to stimulate her in the endless round of balls and parties. 'I hated the dressing up and the stiffness of them, and the perpetual talk of turnips, partridges, or coursing of my partners', she recorded.[5]

Mary Kingsley performed equally arduous and self-effacing duties, catering to the needs of a severely disabled mother and domineering father. Remembering her mother's life at their Highgate home, where

---

[3] Ibid., p. 185.
[4] North, *Further Recollections of a Happy Life*, p. 188.
[5] Ibid., p. 27.

the large frontage winked at the passing traffic with all but one of the windows bricked up, Mary wrote, 'the only thing that ever tempted her to go about her neighbours was to assist them when they were sick in mind, body, or estate. So strongly marked a characteristic was this of our early home life, that to this day I always feel I have no right to associate with people unless there is something the matter with them.'[6] At the age of eighteen the bright young Mary moved with her family to Cambridge, where opportunities for absorption into middle-class academic circles were tantalizingly close. But her mother's creeping illness soon confined her to a wheelchair and Mary to the sickroom as her nurse, for Mrs Kingsley refused to be tended by anyone but her obliging daughter. Days that could have been spent in casual conversation with local Cambridge men and women were consumed in managing the household and daily pushing her mother around Parker's Piece, the green outside the bedroom window. Forced into an unhappy, unrewarding and unequal marriage by pregnancy as her husband's housekeeper, Mrs Mary Kingsley's emotional life was as cramped as her physical existence. Mary's isolation was further enhanced by her mother's social ostracization, for their educated neighbours shunned Mrs Kingsley and labelled the working-class woman in their midst insane, rarely visiting the gloomy grey stone semi-detached at 7 Mortimer Road.

George Kingsley also made demands on his daughter's time of a more stretching, if no less self-effacing, nature. A medical doctor who travelled the world as private physician to titled families, his trips prompted him to dabble in amateur anthropology. His daughter acted as his secretary and research assistant, organizing and compiling his data and backing up his own eclectic and scattered findings with more solid background in the popular German anthropologists.

Isabella Christie and her younger sister Alice also experienced the tragedy of illness and bereavement. Children of a Scottish mineowning family, their father had retired to Cowden Castle, a large rambling grey sandstone house on the southern slopes of the Ochils in Kinrosshire. John Christie's was a late marriage: his wife Alison was forty-two, and the birth of their first child a year later in 1860

---

[6] Mary Kingsley's introduction to George Kingsley, *Notes on Sport and Travel*, (London 1900), p. 203.

Miniature of Mary Kingsley as a child.
Reproduced by kind permission of Beatrice de Cardi.

threatened her life. Her son John lived until twelve, when his two younger sisters were plunged into mourning at his death, wearing their fine black wool dresses for over a year. Their strict elderly nurse Isabella Thorburn, known to the sisters as Baa, suffered acute migraines, making her shut all the nursery blinds and demand absolute silence. In this gloomy atmosphere black-clad eleven year old Ella recited her favourite poem under Baa's stern eye:

> Tell me, Mama, if I must die
> Some day as little Baby died,
> And look so *very* pale and lie
> Down in the pithole by his side.[7]

---

[7] Quoted in Averil Stewart, *Alicella. A Memoir of Alice King Stewart and Ella Christie*, (London 1955), p. 15.

Miss Thorburn put the sisters through rigorous exercises to ensure the maintenance of a fine deportment to compensate for their puppy fat. Alice and Ella took it in turns to sit with a chin resting on a crutch and the end of the stick strapped to their waist, watching the other sister lying flat on a board to straighten her rounded shoulders. Physical uprightness was matched by a training in moral fortitude, and for their childhood reading the young Scottish daughters enjoyed such titles as *The Young Lady's Everyday Book, A Practical Guide in the Elegant Arts, and Daily Difficulties of Domestic Life*; and – to be particularly poignant – stories of the Bird's Nest orphanage in Dublin.

John Christie never wished his daughters to go to school but believed, said Ella, in 'education by travel'.[8] She was only twelve when taken on her first trip abroad to France with the full complement of servants, nurses and too much baggage. Alice, meanwhile, had since barely a teenager been wooed by a young soldier, and at the age of seventeen her parents eventually agreed to their marriage. Her first child was born only ten months later and Alice assumed the position of mistress of Murdostoun Castle in the bleak hills of Lanarkshire. Her mother, continually suffering from poor health and seven years older than her husband, became more and more invalid. Only Ella continued to accompany her father on his summer trips to the Continent.

Gertrude Bell was, like Ella, 'a child of fortune'; born into a prosperous Durham industrial family at a time of expanding middle-class power and prestige, she did not escape the immediacy of confinement and loss. When Gertrude was just two, her mother died bearing her only son. Gertrude immediately assumed maternal responsiblity for the baby Maurice, who remained an ever-present souvenir of the cost of childbirth and the love of men. When Hugh Bell married for a second time in 1876, five years after her mother's death, Florence Olliffe had three children in as many years and Gertrude was reminded once more of the stark contrast between a single and unattached life and that of a married and childbearing woman. As a wealthy middle-class woman, however, her stepmother was freed from many of the daily responsibilities of child rearing, frequently leaving her sons and daughters in the

---

[8] Ella Christie and Lady Alice King Stewart, *A Long Look at Life by Two Victorians*, (London 1940), p. 41.

care of a nurse, governess or trusted servant at their Yorkshire home. But while her economic status allowed her to shed many of the practical burdens of motherhood, the pressures of the maternal role were not diminished. So while Florence Bell accompanied her husband down to London and across to the Continent, the eldest daughter Gertrude unnecessarily assumed responsibility for her young brothers and sisters. At the age of thirteen she was opening ten-year-old Maurice's school report before forwarding it to absent parents.[9]

As a teenager Gertrude, boasting the self-confidence of a wealthy and educated young woman, was in the most privileged of positions to reach beyond her home and out into an unknown world. In 1884, sixteen years old and troubled by puberty, she was enrolled at one of the few exclusive schools for young women, Queen's College in Harley Street, London. Her parents hoped, as had Marianne's in sending her to Madame de Wahl's Norwich school, that a 'lady's education' might quieten a wild disposition and overactive temperament. While acutely homesick for Red Barns' 'delicious autumn smell' and 'the crackly yellow and red leaves', Gertrude began to question the future role that same house and garden held for her. Pleading letters were sent to her stepmother to allow her to stop taking piano lessons – 'I think it a pure waste of time,' she wrote bluntly about the skills which were educating her for the drawing rooms and dinner parties she was witnessing at the Olliffe family's Sloane Street home. 'I'm so consumably bored,' she confessed, finding relief only in immersing herself in reading for her history lessons.[10] By the middle of her second year she was writing, 'I want to know one thing in the world well at least. I'm tired of learning in this sort of diletante way,' and asked her father's permission to apply for university.[11]

In May 1886 Gertrude was one of the handful of women students taking history lectures at Lady Margaret Hall, Oxford under the matronly supervision of Miss Elizabeth Wordsworth, who ran the college on the model of a traditional family, hoping to instil in her students a strong sense of home. As Gertrude sat and argued with knowledge and commitment for Gladstone and the Liberals, or in support of Cromwell at a time when Britain had never had such a

[9] Elsa Richmond, *The Earlier Letters of Gertrude Bell*, (London 1937), p. 11.
[10] Bell to Maurice Bell Summer 1885, Queens College, quoted in ibid., p. 45.
[11] Bell to Hugh Bell Nov. 1885, Queen's College, quoted in ibid., p. 73.

*Christie family at Cowden Castle, 1875. Mr John Christie, (standing). From left
to right: Ella Christie, Dr Lorn, Alice Christie, Mrs Alison Christie and the
Governess, Miss Townsend.*

Reproduced by kind permission of Robert Stewart.

long-reigning and popular monarch, she wound her short auburn fringe round and round her plump fingers. Her teenage stoop, marring an otherwise fine figure, betrayed an inner ferment which all the trappings of a her middle-class education and privilege could not shake off. A talented and hard-working student, Gertrude completed her papers in five terms instead of the customary nine, and passed with first class honours. But although women had been admitted to the Oxford college for the last nine years, they were not awarded a degree. So Gertrude Bell, barely twenty years old, was launched into a world which had little outlet for an educated, excitable and ambitious young woman.

Gertrude's passionate pleas for the underdog, the unpopular, were made at the same time as she resolutely accepted the limits placed upon her own life by rigid, though not unkind, parents. As well as reprimanding her stepdaughter for her loose talk and liberal reading habits, Florence Bell contributed to magazines on the teaching of manners, declaring it was tuition in this aspect which mattered most in the education of future generations.[12] Invitations to visit school-friends at weekends were accepted rashly by her stepdaughter with a childish eagerness and the glad news relayed in unsuspecting detail to scattered parents. The next day the telegram would arrive, forbidding her to go. Reasons were never given, nor were they ever asked for; Gertrude, later pioneer and breaker of so many conventions, always acquiesced. 'I never thought that such good luck was possible as that you would object,' she lied when told to refuse an invitation. 'I can't tell you how relieved I am.'[13]

Mary Gaunt was, of all turn-of-the-century women travellers, the most ready to express her anger and bitterness. She was born and raised in the frontier culture of Australia, surrounded by men who had travelled from far away and hoped to go still further. While her five soldiering and sailing brothers roamed the globe, the first-born Mary and her sister Lucy remained at home in their 'strict, God-fearing old Victorian father' Judge Gaunt's 250 acre farm in south-east Australia,

---

[12] 'A Plea for the Better Teaching of Manners' by Florence Bell, *Nineteenth Century*, vol. 44, (Aug. 1898), p. 281–95.

[13] Bell to Florence Bell Thursday 1885, Queen's College, quoted in Richmond, *Earlier Letters*, p. 38.

edged by a high eucalyptus forest and thick bush.[14] After boarding school, Mary found her approaching and encroaching womanhood acted as another, less tangible but no less keenly felt, border on her world. It was hard to accept, she later wrote, 'that it should be held dangerous that I should walk in the quietest of streets unattended, that I could not be trusted alone with the middle-aged married music-master who held me a first class idiot and suffered under my struggles with C Major. I still feel a sense of wrong about it.'[15] She longed for the carefree time of her youth, before the 'years of discretion' had set in.[16] She succeeded, in 1881, in becoming one of the first women to enter the University of Melbourne, but remained only one year, returning to the small town life of her Ballarat home. She explained,

> When we grew up and went out, my sister, who is a little younger than I am, and is pretty – quite pretty – got plenty of attention, always had heaps of partners at balls, and enjoyed herself everywhere. But I – did not. At the age of twenty I made up my mind that I was not a social success; thought I was getting old, dreadfully old, too old to go to dances any more, and then came a terrible question – what was to become of me?[17]

The sisters' world was 'bordered by our father's lawn and the young men who came to see us and make up picnic parties to the wildest bush around Ballarat for our amusement,' the eldest daughter recorded with irony.[18]

Mary did not step over that garden fence until, at thirty years old, she made her first venture to Europe. Nurturing a strong desire for financial independence which she saw as the key to her freedom, she had been encouraged by the Professor of English at Melbourne University to contribute to local newspapers and magazines; her first review was published in the Melbourne *Age* in 1888. From here her career was launched, and soon she was contributing regularly to the

---

[14] Admiral Sir Guy Gaunt, *The Yield of the Years. A Story of Adventure Afloat and Ashore*, (London 1940), p. 11.

[15] Mary Gaunt, 'Women in Australia', *Empire Review*, vol. 1, (1901), p. 212.

[16] Ibid., p. 214.

[17] 'An Australian Authoress at Home' by E. M. F., *Sydney Mail*, 26 Feb. 1898, quoted in Ian F. McLaren, *Mary Gaunt. A Cosmopolitan Australian: An Annotated Bibliography*, (Melbourne 1986), p. 77.

[18] Mary Gaunt, *Alone in West Africa*, (London 1912), p. 3.

local *Argus* and *Australasian*, and broke into the British market in the *English Illustrated Magazine*. Her most popular stories were those set at sea, inspired by her brothers' seafaring tales and written under the guise of male authorship. But her attempts at and enjoyment of independence were shortlived; one summer's day in 1894, her tiny figured dressed in a pale grey Louis XIV hat and gown and white moiré waistcoat, she walked up the aisle with widowed Dr Hubert Lindsay Miller. The happy couple raced inland to Bright for their honeymoon, away from the sea which would take Mary so far.

Mrs Miller continued to write, but no longer stories as 'Captain of the Maintop Starboard' on life at sea but as 'Mary Gaunt (Mrs H. Lindsay Miller)' on 'The Tribulations of a Charitable Society' and a series on industries for women, including the growing of asparagus and her own poultry breeding. She worked up some old material based on the Australian goldfields of her girlhood into three novels. A persistent journalist soon tracked her down and found her in the surgery where she acted as receptionist. 'I have no writing-room yet, but I mean to have one some day, when I am worth it,' she told the reporter. 'As it is, at present, I find it impossible to work without being interrupted.'[19]

The newly-wed also, however, wrote *Kirkham's Find*, her first novel set in the present and her home town of Ballarat. As she silently battled with her own conflicting desires, she wrote about a young woman struggling to find her way in the world as a beekeeper. In her characteristic confusion between reality and fiction, while completing the novel Mary also contributed a series to the local press on careers for women, including an article on beekeeping. *Kirkham's Find* was deeply autobiographical, the central character Phoebe Marsden as awkward in her tall, lank body as Mary was in her short, stout frame. Phoebe was also, as Mary, the eldest in a large family with only one, younger, prettier sister and a tyrannical father. 'The younger ones looked on [Phoebe] as quite an old maid, and she herself felt her life, as far as any happiness or pleasure to herself went, was nearly over,' wrote the author.[20]

The novelist's content wedded confinement was shortlived; within six years her husband died and she was left 'penniless, homeless and

---

[19] 'An Australian Authoress at Home', quoted in McLaren, *Mary Gaunt*, p. 77.
[20] Mary Gaunt, *Kirkham's Find*, (London 1897), p. 2.

alone'.[21] Mary Gaunt had already established herself as a popular short story writer, but with a guaranteed annual income of only thirty pounds from her husband's estate, her life looked bleak. Turning her back on smalltown life as a doctor's wife, within six months of Dr Miller's sudden death, and with one hundred pounds in her pocket, she sailed to England, hoping to earn a living through her writing. She was never to return.

Taking lodgings in a 'dull and stoney street', she wrote and wrote, and as often as she posted off a story to a prospective editor in the morning, as often one would be returned that same afternoon. 'But how could anyone do good work,' she complained, 'with all the life crushed out of her.' Sitting in her, dull impersonal bedsit, she rarely spoke to anyone and, longing for home, stared through the window at 'the grey skies and drizzling rain.'[22]

The forces which kept these women watching the outside world through closed windows could come as much from within as without. From her couch in a small country parsonage, Isabella Bird looked up at an indifferent and uninspiring world. Born to an Anglican clergyman and a clergyman's daughter in 1831, her young life had been as secure and mundane as possible, but Isa's physical make-up provoked a greater depth of emotional and intellectual thought. From a young age she had been wracked by a spinal disease for which continual operations, the quirkiest of remedies and expert advice could find no cure. Coupled with this disabling illness was the fact that at under five foot – 'four foot eleven and a half inches' she boasted – and with a large long head and an extraordinarily measured way of speaking, she was no beauty. Isa, wrapped in self-pity, was unable to conjure up the emotional strength to move her physical body from its sickbed.

Her father's idiosyncratic fanaticism led him to focus on the observance of Sundays; moving from rural Cheshire to the urban and industrializing environment of Birmingham – ripe for philanthropy and proselytizing – his unpopular and brittle adherence to this creed soon lost him support and he was quickly demoted to a small parish of under three hundred souls. Isa had spent the most formative years,

---

[21] Gaunt, *Alone in West Africa*, p. 4.
[22] Ibid., p. 6.

from eleven to sixteen, in one of Britain's fastest expanding industrial centres. Birmingham in the 1840s was a font for the respectable and respect-seeking middle classes, and as a man of the cloth her father and his family would be drawn into these ambitious and expansive circles. The move to the tiny village of Wyton in Huntingdonshire was not, therefore, matched by a corresponding improvement in Isa's health which the country air might suggest. She pined. In such a small community, there would be few of her perceived social standing to talk to and even fewer to aspire to become like. It was all, as Isabella would later complain, so utterly predictable, 'nothing new, nothing exciting, but the same drudgery day in, day out.'[23]

Isa responded, as did Marianne and so many idle Victorian women, by becoming ill and depressed; soon these conditions aggravated each other to an alarming extent. Summering in the Scottish Highlands, where there were hills to negotiate and turbulent mountain streams to cross, dormant talents were awakened within her which responded to challenge of any kind. Seeing her disability as just another provactive obstacle, she climbed high and leapt across. But on returning to Wyton's rolling plains and well-worn country paths, she sunk back down onto the couch, and from it looked up at a small and enclosed world that demanded nothing from her but to be decorative – and decorative was one thing young Isabella Bird was not.

For a father who was so strict in matters of faith, Edward Bird displayed a singular lack of parental stricture when, in 1854, the doctor suggested his unmarried twenty-three-year-old daughter took a long sea voyage, a common prescription for a woman's ill health and 'restlessness'. Her father gave her one hundred pounds and told her to stay away as long as it lasted, tired of seeing his intelligent young daughter lounge away in the parsonage parlour. Isa went to America, and on returning wrote up an account of her experiences. She had made the important discovery that she could write and people were eager to read what she had written.

Shortly after a second health voyage to the United States her father died, and Isa, her mother, and her devoted younger sister Henrietta were forced to vacate the parsonage and move to Edinburgh. Here the elder sister spent mornings in bed writing morally uplifting articles for *Good Words*, *Leisure Hour* and *Family Treasury*, and afternoons

---

[23] Pat Barr, *A Curious Life for a Lady. The Story of Isabella Bird*, (London 1970).

practising what she preached by doing good works herself. Honouring her father's dying wish, she edited his observations on religion in the United States. But in writing up she named his revival of Christian belief the 'awakening', and in answering the critics of 'sudden conversions' echoed her own emotional resurgence. 'We have not seen the preceeding mental history of those converted persons,' she argues.

> Heavy afflictions in years gone by – no more spoken of, but germinating in each silent reflecting hour – losses, sicknesses, disappointments, chastisements, and mercies – words spoken by voices which speak on earth no more – all these . . . have been working in the soul, until at last one slight outward pressure . . . and man comes out in a decided religious change. We see the change, and, knowing nothing of the previous soul-history, we call it *sudden conversion*.'[24]

Within a year she produced an account of what she herself had witnessed in a separate volume, *Aspects of Religion in the United States*, under 'the author of *The Englishwoman in America*'.

In contrast to their mothers' and sisters' circumscribed lives, the women travellers were impressed with their fathers' freedom of movement and physical space within and without the family home. A Victorian pater could easily demand that a household conform to his peculiar tastes. As a child, Marianne showed great promise as a student of music and felt a passion for classical works later directed into her painting. But Frederick North thought all music 'a horrid noise', so Marianne memorized tunes, humming them silently to herself to avoid upsetting the irritable man.[25] Meanwhile he talked away freely to his paroquet. It was, ironically, her father's ability to assert his own space in the household which made him an even stronger model for his young daughter. 'My first recollections relate to my father,' she wrote. 'He was from first to last the one idol and friend of my life' – an odd and seemingly incompatible combination of attributes.[26]

---

[24] *The Revival in America by an English Eye-Witness*, pp. 41–2.

[25] Marianne North, *Recollections of a Happy Life being the autobiography of Marianne North*, edited by her sister Mrs John Addington Symonds, (London 1891), vol. 1, p. 25.

[26] Ibid., p. 5.

Ella Christie's father cluttered up their large home with pottery, china and silver collected avaraciously on his extensive European tours. A visitor recorded, 'the old house was soon absorbing, in the way that country-houses do, a variety of unrelated objects; floral dadoes in the Italian manner, bronze gasoliers from Brussels, Dutch-tiled fireplaces . . . carpets from the looms of Smyrna, chandeliers from Venice . . . all combined to produce the prodigality beloved of the time, in drawing-room, library and dining-room.'[27] While these exotic objects inspired in the young observers a longing to stretch themselves over the fences of their homes to a greater beyond, they at the same time curtailed and confined the space of their immediate environment.

Dr George Kingsley, although rarely at home from his worldwide travels, also maintained a room of his own in the Cambridge home. The sharp contrast between her father's domestic realm – a book-lined library filled with weapons from the east, Fijian carvings, and whaletooth necklaces gathered on his travels – and her mother's sickroom was stark to the young Mary, and when possible she left the maternal sphere to sit at her father's desk reading from his collection of early travellers' works. Letters from the Rocky Mountains, South Africa and the Pacific islands emphasized Dr Kingsley's freedom. When Mary was ten years old her mother read to her from her sickbed how Dr Kingsley and the young Earl of Pembroke, to whom he was attached as private physician, were 'enjoying very fine sport shooting elk, looking for buffaloes, and leading the life of Red Indians.'[28]

The more absent the father, the more he became an image of escape and freedom from domestic responsibilities and the closer his daughter would be drawn to him. Since his marriage, Dr Kingsley had only spent two to three months of the year at home in London and Cambridge – 'sometimes not at all,' commented his daughter. When he was at home, his quick temper only increased the level of stress and estrangement between the family members and closed the sanctuary of his library to Mary. His sudden and unannounced homecomings meant the little physical autonomy his daughter had was quickly removed. At Highgate, Mary had kept pet fighting cocks which, she recorded, behaved well during her father's long absences but on his arrival did little else but crow. Her favourite cock was called Ki Ki;

---

[27] Stewart, *Alicella*, p. 11.
[28] Mrs Mary Kingsley to Bentley 2 Jan. 1873, Southwood Lane, London.

Mary recalled, 'nothing ever would make that cock realize that the return home of the master of the house entirely altered things.'[29] She was forced to move Ki Ki to the bottom of the garden to avoid Dr Kingsley's volcanic temper as books hurtled out of the window. Mrs Baret, the maid-of-all-works, stopped singing hymns to avoid suffering the doctor's rage. The gardener put off all his plans to nail up creepers or roll the gravel, and Mary retired with her mother to the sickroom. Although never expressing her anger at him, his daughter saw how his freedom at home and abroad depended upon and encouraged her and his wife's confinement. Near her own death she wrote, 'I am fully convinced his taking this view of life really caused the illness which killed my mother . . . . There were months when no letter came . . . her mind was kept in one long nervous strain which robbed her of all pleasure in life outside the sphere of home duty and the companionship of books.'[30]

Women who took to travelling were often influenced by an upbringing which clearly pointed to the way in which the role of wife and mother could injure a women both physically and mentally; happy, stable and long-lasting marriages and family life were rarely within their childhood experience. Their mothers', and sometimes sisters', domestic spheres were associated with cloistered, cramped ambition and human suffering. In response, they created their own sense of stability and belonging in exploring their paternal ancestors, thereby reinforcing their identity with their father and his lineage.

From their students' quarters, sickrooms, bedsits and couches these young women's first imaginary journeys were not to distant lands but in the footsteps of their male forbears. From the dining room walls the stern and imposing faces of the distinguished North lineage stared down at the young Marianne. They were, she wrote, 'the first things which impressed me with childish awe.' She proudly traced her ancestry back through her father's family to Lord Roger North, whose memoirs she would later illustrate. Her maternal heredity is treated briefly. Her mother's life, she wrote bluntly, 'was a dreary one – I do not think she was fond of me, but seemed to like to have me with her when she was ill,' and 'she got more and more into invalid habits.'[31]

---

[29] Kingsley, *Notes on Sport and Travel*, pp. 195–7.
[30] Ibid., pp. 202–3.
[31] Manuscript of autobiography, pp. 59 and 50.

So although her mother came from titled and landed Scottish gentry, who provided the majority of the family income, Marianne did not fully include them in her own forming. Despite this wealthy background, she noted that her mother, in contrast to her father's Harrow and Cambridge training, received no education. 'Her Aunt Marianne taught her the little she did know', her daughter recorded, 'I was called after her in gratitude for that teaching.'[32] So while Marianne's last name allowed her to claim her father's heritage, her first constantly reminded her of the limits placed upon that inheritance as a woman.

Mary Kingsley, in the introduction to her father's memoirs, dwells upon her Kingsley forbears. Giving detailed accounts of her father's two literary brothers Charles and Henry and briefly recording those other sons who died in their youth and childhood, Mary does not once mention their sister Charlotte Chanter, who outlived both brothers and whose daughter was engaged to Mary's younger brother, Charley. Although the Kingsley name was the only family accolade she was allowed to bear – her parents' shotgun wedding only four days before her birth had estranged George Kingsley's family from his godfearing relatives – Mary nevertheless claimed their heritage. Her mother's family, the Baileys, were stationers to the Inns of Court and could not provide her with the status that her mere literary surname could. So while raised entirely by her mother, with her financially embarassed Uncle William and Bailey cousins as her closest relatives, she ignored them in her own written history.

Often finding their inclusion as women in their male heritage uneasy and unsatisfying, these women discovered a more attractive, inclusive history as white people in an age of increasing European intervention in and colonization of distant lands. Raised in a Britain of confidence and Empire, expansion and conquest, they shared common perceptions of a foreign and, as yet, untouchable world. Many of their families were connected, directly or indirectly, with British imperial expansion: Isabella Bird's aunts and cousins were missionaries; the Bell and Christie families had befitted and prospered from British industrial expansion which accompanied an aggressive foreign policy. Women prepared themselves for their journeys by drawing upon the plethora of

[32] North, *Recollections of a Happy Life*, vol. 1, p. 4.

Gertrude Bell and her father, 1876, by Edward Poynter.
University of Newcastle Upon Tyne.

imaginations

visual and written images of exotic places and peoples offered in
Victorian Britain. These provided the ingredients for the imaginary
arenas in which they could act out their most daring dreams and
adventures, and forge a picture of themselves as travellers.

While sharing many common perceptions, women were exposed to, touched by and drew upon different means through which to express these images. For Marianne North, the strokes of a brush always spoke louder than the printed page, and she was able to represent her own feelings and understand those of others better through a visual image. Among the contemporary works she admired were the moralistic biblically-based canvasses of Holman Hunt; when she travelled to Egypt with her father in early 1866, the view of the Red Sea had reminded her of Hunt's *The Scapegoat*. The popular travel diarist and poet Edward Lear, who later gave Marianne letters of introduction for her travels, also provided images of the East. The human presence in Lear's paintings was represented by mere pen outlines, as if at any minute someone might step into the hollow shapes and give them definite form and character. These featureless people stand turned towards a solid dominating backdrop of sky and mountain. On a hillside outside Damascus with her father, Marianne stepped into these ghostly forms: 'From the heights above the city the view was most striking, like an old dream to us, who knew it already from Mr Lear's paintings.'[33]

Marianne took up her brush and began to construct her own exotic world which determined how she later saw, touched and acted in real foreign lands. From the backgrounds of her paintings glimmered hazed mountains and deeply forested valleys, as if viewed through a thin muslin veil and inspired by mythical settings. The foregrounds stood in solid contrast – brilliant, clear and executed with botanical detail, inspired by the tropical plants offered to her by Joseph Hooker of the Royal Botanic Gardens at Kew. When Hooker gave her a hanging bunch of *Amherstia nobilis*, the Queen of Flowering Trees, she excitedly proclaimed, 'it was one of the first that had bloomed in England, and made me long more and more to see the tropics. We often talked of going, if ever my father had holiday long enough.'[34]

Within the circle of her home life, Marianne attempted to realize this backdrop to her dreams. She built three greenhouses in the Hastings garden, recreating the atmosphere in which rare plants flourished – one for orchids, one for temperate plants, and one for vines and cuttings. Here she spent all her unallotted time, ignoring the irritating rash which developed from being shut up all day in such

[33] North, *Further Recollections of a Happy Life*, p. 108.
[34] North, *Recollections of a Happy Life*, vol. 1, p. 31.

humidity and emerging at night into the cold sea winds. 'It was delightful work,' she declared.[35] Gertrude Bell, too, returning from Oxford to Red Barns, planted a small garden outside the meticulously housekept home to play in with her younger sisters and brothers. She called it 'Paradise'.

Other women relied upon the printed world of their childhood books to provide the ingredients with which they could construct, in their own words, their imaginary landscapes. While many did not begin their journeys until the turn of the century, their cultural baggage looked back to an earlier age in which they had been reared. On Sundays, when Ella and Alice Christie were not allowed to play, Miss Thorburn read them stories of the missionary Willie Anderson of Calabar. The only other permitted Sunday reading was *Uncle Tom's Cabin*. Marianne learnt her history from Scott and her geography from *Robinson Crusoe*. Mary Gaunt, always eager explicitly to analyse her motives, attributed her longing to travel to her childhood books. As a girl, she read the story of Carlo, a small boy shipwrecked off the coast of Africa and captured by savages; over fifty years later she remembered, 'from that moment dated my deep interest in West Africa.'[36] Gertrude implored her stepmother 'only books please for my presents from you and Papa' for her seventeenth birthday.[37] In her grandfather's rectory library, Mary Kingsley wrote, her father and uncles had 'found good food for dreamers,' and in reading these tales herself Mary too began to dream. These books had 'roused within them the spirit of adventure, and held their minds in thrall with the glamour of strange lands . . . . Histories of the globes, and lordly folios, on whose maps full many a sturdy coastline dwindled with dots, full many a line of dots went stumbling on to perish at the feet of pregnant nothingness.'[38] Completing her father's memoirs after his death, Mary imparted to his youth the motives of her own: 'George Kingsley's desire to travel grew stronger and stronger in the gloomy atmosphere of Chelsea . . . he was forced to build for himself an ideal world of his own, longing passionately the while for the coming of the days when something like that would stand around him in firm reality.' She

[35] Ibid., p. 69.
[36] Gaunt, *Alone in West Africa*, p. 3.
[37] Bell to Florence Bell June 1885, quoted in Richmond, *Earlier Letters*, p. 44.
[38] Kingsley, *Notes on Sport and Travel*, p. 11.

focused on a letter the young doctor had written to a friend, 'I have been a lonely man all my life . . . only using the external world as a means of getting strands and patches of colour with which to deck my dream palace.'[39]

The family histories, from which women were so often excluded, could nevertheless provide images of travel they would later appro- *images* priate as their own. Mary Kingsley built up her own dreamscape from the tales in her father's library, recreating the exotic worlds described in their pages until they became as real to her as the stifling domestic sphere of her daily existence. 'The whole of my childhood and youth was spent at home, in the house and garden,' she wrote. 'The loving outside world I saw little of . . . . But the truth was I had a great amusing world of my own other people did not know, or care about – that was the books in my father's library.'[40] Her favourite Uncle Henry, responsible for the running and financing of the Kingsley family during his older brother's absences, often sat enveloped in a blue haze of tobacco smoke on the front lawn of their Highgate home under the one unbricked window, relating stories of his travels around the world and his unsuccessful desperate bid to make his fortune as a youngest son in the Australian goldfields of Mary Gaunt's youth.

Foreign lands and peoples were also presented to the young *objects* travellers in objects accumulated by wandering relatives, such as the exotic artefacts in Dr Kingsley's library and the china and pottery of the Christies' jumbled home. When Mary Gaunt visited her grandmother as a child, she was allowed to see but not touch the curios brought by her grandfather from China where he had sailed with the East India Company. 'Beautifully carved ivory chessmen, a model of a Chinese lady's foot about three inches long, dainty mother-of-pearl counters made in the likeness of all manner of strange beasts, lacquer boxes and ivory balls,' were amongst the treasures. Also, 'models of plankeens in ivory, and fans that seemed to me, brought up in the somewhat rough-and-ready surroundings of a new country, dreams of loveliness.'[41] Frederick North imported foreign men and women as temporary servants during the Hastings winters. His daughter's portraits of this diverse group of women were very

[39] Ibid., p. 13.

[40] Mary Kingsley, 'In the Days of My Youth; Chapter of Autobiography', *Mainly About People*, 20 May 1899, pp. 468–9.

[41] Mary Gaunt, *A Woman in China*, (London 1914), p. 1.

different from those she drew of her sister and mother; while her mother remains a shadowy, confined and seldom-mentioned woman in her autobiography, the wife of one season's Italian cook is vividly outlined as a 'brave, Amazon seeming woman'.[42] But while this contact provided images of strong women in foreign lands, their position as servants also imprinted upon the young Marianne her relationship of power over them as a middle-class British woman.

While some escaped in reading books, others developed and elaborated upon their imaginary landscapes by translating and writing them, forging dream worlds into which they would one day roam. American May French-Sheldon initiated herself as a traveller on a psychological journey to the Ancient Middle East as the first translator into English of Flaubert's *Salammbô*, hiding her gender as she had in her earlier romantic novel by signing simply the initial 'M'. Flaubert was one of the most well known mid-century travel writers and his wanderings in Phoenicia in 1850 were the inspiration behind this historical travelogue. As a white woman in the age of colonial expansion, May French-Sheldon could imaginatively cast herself as the hero in this drama of the Orient, thereby including herself as an active participant in a daring history with which the roles offered her as a woman in her home society could provide no comparison.

Amelia Edwards also turned to translation and novels, forced into writing through 'straitened means'. Initially, as Isabella Bird, she had contributed to the pages of women's magazines, providing them with considered articles on music, drama and art criticism. But as Isa had found with her pen and Marianne with her paints, while Amelia's articles began with the concerns of the immediate and familiar in her home life, she soon ventured to include peoples and places far away. In 1858 she chose to translate an unusual account by a young French woman of her captivity at the hands of Chinese pirates. The daring adventuress claimed to have recorded the passing of the days by using the tip of her hairpin to scratch all she could remember on the blank pages of an old German book discovered in the cabin in which she was imprisoned. When her rescuers gallantly sailed over the horizon, she flagged them down by tearing off the white chemise hidden beneath the disguise of her male sailor's outfit. This plucky heroine was

[42] North, *Further Recollections of a Happy Life*, p. 69.

everything a young European woman ought not to be, and the reasons for her undertaking such a long and hazardous round-the-Horn voyage remained cloaked in the catchphrase of 'commercial matters'. Yet that Amelia chose to translate this obscure account is particularly telling, for while her own early physical travel was to familiar European cultures, her psychological journeys took her beyond the safety and comfort of such societies. The heroine's final declaration, in Amelia's words, was:

> I went to seek my fortune, and found only misfortune. Still, with all their troubles, my weary wanderings had not been wholly profitless. I had beheld Nature, bountiful and beautiful Nature, under her most varied aspects; and if I had endured fatigue, privation, and even disease, I had, at least, lived that life of peril which hath its own peculiar charm for the imaginative and the young.
> I have never yet regretted my journey, or its adventures.[43]

At her parents' death within one week of each other in 1860, thirty-year-old Amelia was driven further on to her own financial resources and began prolifically to produce many-volumed one shilling romantic novels, including the bestselling *Debenham's Vow* and *Barbara's History*. Nearly always using the first person, one of her favourite narrators was a mid-century male traveller, wandering around Europe for the purpose of business or pleasure. Long before she had undertaken such journeys herself, she was beginning to write the agenda for her own future life of travel.

Mary Gaunt also consciously erected the scene upon which she would later act out her role as a traveller. Her early novels had been set in the frontier towns of Australia, peopled with heavy-drinking, coarse-living rogues and innocent, pretty, seducible women. All her writing, both fiction and non-fiction, was based on actual events. This was a two-edged relationship between the reality of history and her own wild imagination, for when she wrote about her experiences as a young woman she indiscriminately mixed the stuff of her novels amongst the more mundane truths of her autobiography. Often a character from one of her popular stories spoke in the same words and

[43] Fanny Loviot, *A Lady's Captivity Among Chinese Pirates in the Chinese Seas*, (1858), translated by Amelia Edwards, pp. 139–40.

phrases the writer later used to answer interviewers' questions about her own life. And although inspired by the environment of her Australian girlhood and her father's tales as judge over the unruly settlements, by the time of her teens the rough-and-ready golddiggers had nearly all disappeared and their ramshackle huts been replaced by neatly laid out farms. 'There was no danger from anything but snakes,' she admitted privately.[44]

Yet it was to the violent and unruly past that Mary was attracted and the life at sea which she wrote about through the voice of her sailor brothers, and on arriving in London she found she could draw no inspiration from the 'grey sky and the grey streets and the grey houses, and the well-to-do shivering in their wraps, and the poor shivering in their rags, all the colourless English world.'[45] Mary's rescue came in 'the continent of my dreams'. In 1906, a friend of her brother Guy asked her to Liverpool for Christmas. Mrs Horsfall's family had prospered from the West African trade, and at their home of Larksfield Mary found, 'here it was again presented to me, the land to which I had resolved to go when I was a little child, and everything in the house spoke to me of it.' Under a cedar tree in the garden stood the giant figurehead of an old sailing ship; in the house, rooms were filled with models of West African trading centres, and pictures of tropical rivers and swamps hung enticingly on the walls. 'They reopened a new world of desire,' Mary remembered. 'The vague was taking concrete form.' Widowhood and penury had brought her to London and now, 'the chance had come, through seas of troubles, but still it had come, and I would go to see the great world for myself . . . I should like to see strange places and visit unknown lands.' Declaring she 'had lived my life, that no sorrow or goodness could ever touch me keenly again,' she laid the ground for her voyage to West Africa – 'the trip I had planned years before, when I was a small girl reading about those distant lands.'[46]

Mary began her psychological journey by writing about these new terrains. The stories depicted lands of rampant sexuality, often across race, and 'the really wild Africa' far away from European settlements. She drew on the first-hand experiences of John Ridgewell Essex, who claimed co-authorship, to provide the factual background she found so

---

[44] Gaunt to John Murray 27 Dec. 1922, Bordighera, Italy.

[45] Gaunt, *Alone in West Africa*, p. 9.

[46] Ibid., pp. 5–7.

necessary. Her central figure was the West African trader, resembling the garrulous golddiggers of her earlier novels. In *The Arm of the Leopard* and *Fools Rush In*, she made the myth of West Africa recognizable to both herself and her readers by assimilating it to the frontier culture of the Australian goldfields. As with other less self-conscious creators of their canvasses, Mary blended the familiar and the remote, the known and the unknown. It was this peculiar combination which allowed the reader and author to be at the same time included amongst the gallery of adventurers and safely behave in a manner far outside that of their own societies.

While women travellers were able to paint canvasses on which to exercise their dreams of active and fulfilling lives, theirs was an uneasy inclusion in the myth of exploration and discovery. They were continally torn between the two conflicting landscapes of self-fulfillment and duty. These clashing voices would never be resolved, and their passage from their rooms to the world outside was a troubled one. Often reaching the end of their childbearing years, and long considered unmarriageable, these women had built for themselves roles which were at the same time demanding of feminine attributes of duty, sacrifice and caring and also emphasized their lack of female sexuality. They were often given pet names by their families which highlighted their single status; Marianne was known by the sexually ambiguous name of 'Pop'; Edith Durham was called 'Aunt Dick', and Ella Christie was addressed by the cumbersome title of 'Miss Christie of Cowden' by her estate employees and 'Grandaunt' by her family, while she called her younger married sister Alice 'My Baby'.

Dutiful daughters, loving sisters and maiden aunts would be haunted by a responsibility so heavily felt as young women and demanded of them by the prevailing though often unspoken demands on women of the time. They could only shirk this early load by geographically removing themselves from the society in which it operated. But in shedding the load they acquired the heavy burden of the guilt of its shedding.

From an early age Gertrude Bell was troubled by these conflicting desires. She was painfully aware that her boisterous personality and outspokenness to those deemed her elders and betters vexed her appearance-conscious parents, and was from a young teenager torn between pleasing them and pleasing herself. At sixteen she wrote to her stepmother from Queen's College, 'Dearest mother indeed I have made many resolutions, and I do hope you will find me a better daughter and more obedient, and perhaps a little changed at any rate. It is very difficult to say this sort of thing on paper, you know that the deeper one feels a thing the less one likes to talk about it but you will believe that I am trying to apply the lessons I have learnt to all the bothers and worries.'[47] Her longing to be accepted sat in awkward combination with her fierce need to break all the boundaries of acceptable behaviour. This uncomfortable marriage of desires would force many of the women travellers into espousing a social conservatism in contrast to their personal and increasingly private nonconformity. A fellow student at Lady Margaret Hall described Gertrude as 'half child, half woman' – a need to be approved of and a longing to rebel trapped within the same determined body.[48]

Images from childhood – portrayed as an age of freedom and innocence – were powerful determinants in how the women travellers saw their newfoundlands. When Hunt's *The Triumph of the Innocents* was exhibited for the first time in 1885 at the Fine Arts Society in Bond Street, the flamboyant Anne Ritchie, who had married her godson seventeen years her junior, took the young Gertrude to a viewing. The painting had begun to be executed ten years earlier, while Hunt was resident in Palestine, and depicted a highly visionary landscape of the Middle East. Gertrude, about to enter adulthood at Oxford, was entranced by the image of the children fleeing Egypt:

It is the most wonderful picture I ever saw . . . . [The Innocents] are round and fat and rosy like earth children and yet they are not earth children at all. There is a wonderful something about them that raises them above the ordinary happy child. Their faces are more than happy, there's a divine calm over them . . . . Then behind in the air there are three little ones who are just waking up to the new life and not quite certain whether all the fright and horror is over, not quite certain

[47] Bell to Florence Bell 30 Mar. 1884, Queen's College, quoted in Richmond, *Earlier Letters*, p. 20.

[48] Janet E. Courtney, *An Oxford Portrait Gallery*, (London 1931), p. 51.

whether they will cry or not . . . . It's all so real and yet so supernatural. It sends a sort of shiver right through one.[49]

When Amelia Edwards was asked to contribute to an anthology of poetry and prose on childhood, she submitted three poems mourning lost happiness and innocence. 'The Scramble for Sugarplums' warned:

> Laugh and scramble, shout and play,
> Happy children, while you may;
> Life soon loses its completeness,
> Sugarplums their pristine sweetness,
> Dolls their charm, and nuts their savour,
> And gingerbeer its champagne flavour!
> Laugh, ye little lads and lasses –
> Soon, too soon, your childhood passes . . .
>
> Alas! I wish, but wish in vain,
> That I were a child again.[50]

The women travellers looked on to the far horizon for regions where they could once again celebrate the unfettered freedom of childhood. These continents of their dreams would become both lands of childish imagery and lands where they could be a child.

Gertrude Bell articulated her frustrations as a young woman emerging from childhood. After being stirred by *The Triumph of the Innocents*, she longed to see more: 'I wish I could go to the National,' she wrote to her stepmother, 'but you see there is no-one to take me. If I were a boy, I should go to that incomparable place every week, but being a girl to see lovely things is denied me!'[51] Florence's reply only angered her stepdaughter further; deaf to her teenage demands, she criticized her for talking of 'the National' rather than giving it the full and proper title – the National Gallery. Gertrude responded bitterly, 'Would you have me say when talking of the sovereign: The Queen of England, Scotland, Ireland, Empress of India, Defender of the

---

[49] Bell to Hugh Bell Saturday 1885, quoted in Richmond, *Earlier Letters*, pp. 41–2.

[50] 'The Scramble for Sugarplums' by Amelia Edwards in *Home Thoughts and Home Scenes*, (London 1865), p. 21.

[51] Bell to Florence Bell 26 Oct. 1885, Sloane Street, London, quoted in Richmond, *Earlier Letters*, p. 66.

Faith? . . . My life is not long enough to give everything its full title.'[52] She had written with raw emotion, confessing her feelings of confinement and the barriers put between her and the outside world; the reply had only reinforced what Gertrude sadly already knew – the appearance of propriety must be preserved even in her most personal correspondence. There was no one, she was quickly learning, with whom she could discuss these battling feelings.

Etta Close, with the hindsight of her own painful decision to travel to East Africa, expressed these same conflicting desires:

> It is hard to be content with a few tea-parties and a very few luncheons strictly for 'ladies only', to find it sufficient just to be useful to relations, to meet dear Tommy at the station and take him safely across London . . . . To take care of darling Elsie at the dentists . . . and hardest of all to realize that these things are taken for granted, that the relations are simply saying to each other: 'A single woman, you know, with nothing in the world to do, of course she ought to be glad to be of use to others'.
>
> Looking with a disinterested spinster eye on the world, I notice that even when women have health and the money to be free, they seem to like the feeling of being anchored to somebody, or failing a somebody to something, for those who do not marry a man seem invariably to marry themselves to a garden, or a house, or a dog, and then having forged their own chains say pathetically, 'If only I were free, how I would love to travel and see the world.'[53]

Even Mary Gaunt, a self-determined traveller, felt this pull within her. She wrote: 'I wonder sometimes would I have been contented to lead the ordinary woman's life, the life of the woman who looks after her husband and children. I think so, because it grew to be the life I ardently yearned for. The wonder desire was just pushed a little into the background.'[54]

Like Mary, Gertrude had found as she grew older and the restrictions on her movements only increased, she could push that

[52] Bell to Florence Bell 13 Nov. 1885, ibid., p. 70.

[53] Etta Close, *A Woman Alone in Kenya, Uganda, and the Belgian Congo*, (London 1924), pp. 1–2.

[54] Gaunt, *Alone in West Africa*, p. 3.

particular desire back no longer. Her young cousin Horace Marshall with whom she had played in the garden of Paradise as a child, could now not be seen walking down Piccadilly alone with her. 'I do wish I could be sent promiscuously like a boy to find my own way!' she exclaimed.[55] As she watched the curtailments growing, it was also being made increasingly apparent that the only way to avoid them was by removing herself from this home society. As her half-sister Elsa later wrote, a young female student was not able to walk unchaperoned along a London street, 'where a few clubmen might have looked at her out of the window'.[56]

The work of her college friend Mary Talbot pointed to one way in which Gertrude's movements might be freed from the scrutiny of the clubmen's eyes. Mary had taken up work in a Whitechapel settlement, where she worked alone among women, men and children. On her frequent visits, Gertrude had had to be accompanied by her maid Lizzie Hunt. While Mary Talbot toiled amongst the destitute of the East End of London, her class offered her a protection from accusations of impropriety, while visits to art galleries, dinner party engagements, and walks down Piccadilly could attract the unwelcome and critical attention of those of the same social status as the Bell family. As Elsa pointed out, 'It was one's own class that was taboo.'[57] For Gertrude, acutely aware of these restrictions, relying on the protection of her class afforded in philanthropic work was one possible remedy. But while she was responding to the restrictions shared by many educated middle-class women, her solution was to be more dramatic.

Often women attempted to excuse their desire for travel by claiming it was being undertaken for motives of duty and service to others, seeking to alleviate their sense of guilt for enjoying themselves 'skylarking', 'rambling' and 'puddling around'. Isabella Bird insisted on raising money for missionary hospitals along her routes. She wrote to her close and timid friend Ella Blackie, wife of the Professor of Greek at Edinburgh University, how she 'longed for a cheerful intellect and self-denying spirit which "seeketh not its own and pleaseth not

---

[55] Bell to Florence Bell 16 Feb. 1886, quoted in Richmond, *Earlier Letters*, p. 85.
[56] Ibid., p. 218.
[57] Ibid.

itself"'.[58] When asked why she travelled to West Africa, Mary Kingsley answered she wanted to complete her father's worldwide comparative anthropological survey, a task which in fact she never attempted. Margaret Fountaine, with her usual hint of cynicism, wrote in her diary, 'I suppose it is necessary to one's moral digestion to swallow so many degrees of district visiting, Blind Asylum Fridays, Charity Bazaars, etc., etc., to counteract the delights of roving over foreign lands with a tolerably well-lined purse.'[59]

This conflict between duty and desire was encapsulated by Etta Close in the word 'Victorian'. Even though she did not begin her long journeys until the 1920s, she firmly asserted 'we *were* nineteenth century, there was no getting away from it.'[60] Ella Christie, also waiting until middle age and the Edwardian era before sailing away from Scotland, named the memoirs written with her sister during the Second World War *A Long Look at Life by Two Victorians*. While women travellers often inherited the eyes and imagery of an earlier era, they were also heirs to the constraints it placed upon them as women.

This tight bond of duty was often broken by a sudden event which forced the women travellers to make a drastic and determining choice about their future lives. When all else seemed to collapse around them, their imaginary canvasses held firm and emerged as the only viable direction in which these new paths could lead. The recently widowed Mary Gaunt wrote, 'I think this thought was latent beneath all the misery and hopelessness that made me say I did not care what became of me, was I not free, free to wander where I pleased, to seek those adventures that held such a glamour for me in my girlhood.'[61]

Many of the women experienced an acute sense of depression, loss or radical upheaval which at once broke and freed them. Some, such as Isabella Bird, had been challenged by illness. When Lilian Brown found herself after a serious operation 'condemned by my medical attendant to months of inactivity, combined with the endless though kindly exhortations of my companions to "be careful" my whole soul

[58] Quoted in Barr, *A Curious Life for a Lady*, p. 175.

[59] Margaret Fountaine, *Love Among the Butterflies. The Travels and Adventures of a Victorian Lady*, edited by W. F. Cater, (London 1980), p. 63.

[60] Etta Close, *Excursions and Some Adventures*, (London 1926), p. 1.

[61] Gaunt, *Alone in West Africa*, p. 5.

revolted at the idea . . . . It simply could not be done. Everything under such conditions would be abhorrent to me, and I declined to visualise myself becoming a disagreeable, disgruntled and chronic invalid. Flight was my only salvation.'[62]

For women who had been defined by their relationship with another, the loss of that person was also a loss of part of their own *loss* identity. When Mary Kingsley took her father's letters up to him as usual one winter morning in 1892, she found him lying dead in bed; her mother – too ill to be aware of her husband's death – survived him by only eight weeks. For thirty years Mary's life had been filled with caring for their needs, and now it was empty. Not only her parents had died, but also a part of Mary Henrietta Kingsley, the dutiful daughter. Like Mary Gaunt, she felt she could suffer no greater grief, that nothing could touch her keenly any more. She was grieving of course, not only for her irritable father and utterly dependent mother but for the loss of part of herself. She was grieving, too, in desperation at where to find it again.

Along with many other dutiful daughters, Mary Kingsley attempted to preserve at least a small part of her earlier years by wearing nothing but the black of mourning for the rest of her life in Britain. But this was only .the semblance of continuity, and in fact the break with her former life was radical and far-reaching. Within weeks, the slight thirty-year-old packed her mourning clothes in a long black water-proof sack and sailed for the Canary Islands, rejecting all offers of companionship for the trip. The sea – the way in which distant lands were reached – enraptured her just as the sight of the ship's figurehead had enraptured Mary Gaunt in the Liverpool garden. What enticed her even more, however, were the exotic peoples and wares she saw aboard the ships docked at Las Palmas – West Africa-bound. She wrote to her childhood friend Hatty Johnson:

> I have been very little on Gran Canaria since landing, spending my time mainly on vessels going to and from the coast of Africa and on their way out with iron bedsteads, sperm candles and saltpetre or on their way home with black people of all ages and sexes, monkeys, parrots, snakes, canary birds, sheep, palm oil, gold dust and ivory but mainly and above all with cockroaches,

[62] Lilian Brown, *Unknown Tribes, Unchartered Seas*, (London 1924), p. 3.

such cockroaches as I do not think you have ever met . . . I feel
wonderfully and perfectly well as soon and as long as I am out at
sea but when I get on shore again I find great difficulty in
sleeping but no doubt that will get all right in time. I feel
disgracefully self-indulgent to be lolling about here enjoying
myself and the place is far too beautiful for me to see alone –
Teneriffe – Madeira – Palma and Lanzerote are one series of
lovely pictures and all so different from the beauty of England,
both in form and colour – it is a most entire change.[63]

By the time of her return, her brother had moved their belongings
from the parental home and installed himself and Mary in a small
Kensington upper floor flat, presuming his older sister would now
serve his domestic needs as she had done her parents'. But she stayed
there only twelve months, enough time to make contact with and gain
introductions to men whom she knew, from her careful management
of affairs from a young age, would be useful in West Africa.

Ella Christie's outwardly happy homelife stood in stark contrast to
Mary's stifling background. Living alone with her father in their large
house from her mid-thirties, she wrote chatty letters to friends and
relatives conveying an idyllic and carefree impression of the daily
routine at Cowden Castle. In the summer of 1902, while in
Edinburgh, Ella too found her father dead in bed. With no son to carry
on the family estate, the wealthy mining magnate had bequeathed
everything to an orphanage he patronized. Alice, soon to become a
titled Lady through marriage, could survive, but Ella was penniless
and homeless, and decided to challenge the will. 'The grounds of
reduction are that at the date of both settlements' – Mr Christie had
left two almost identical wills – 'the testator was insane and not of
sound disposing mind,' stated the records bluntly.[64]

In the early months of 1903 Scotland was in a state of national
panic; great floods had swept away the bridges over burns, hurricanes
had felled forests of pine, and at Cowden Castle the wind swept along
the valley and through the heavy wooden door. Ella Christie ordered
the stained glass window erected in honour of her father to be
removed from the local parish church, packed a few practical plain

---

[63] Kingsley to Hatty Johnson 9 June 1892, Las Palmas, Gran Canaria.
[64] *The Evening Despatch*, 6 Mar. 1903, p. 3.

clothes and went to Buckingham Terrace, Edinburgh for the duration of the court case – the same address at which her father had died.

On a dull and cold July morning in 1903, when the rain had not stopped falling on the grey cobbled Edinburgh streets for five days, Ella stood up before the court to give evidence against her father's state of mind. Legal firms had been reluctant to defend the sisters, for it was an unpopular stance for two apparently wealthy young women to challenge a large donation being made to the needy. For women who had been involved in philanthropic work all their lives, it was an uneasy and self-contradictory position in which to find themselves. All their friends implored them not to face the publicity of the courts, but Ella only laughed when she saw her name paraded on the newspaper hoardings as she left the courtroom – THE CHRISTIE WILL CASE. QUARTER OF A MILLION AT STAKE.

Throughout the trial, Ella displayed little emotion, drawing her tall, solid, five foot nine inch figure up to its full imposing height. But for the spinster daughter, life with or without an income from the estate meant the difference between being able to continue her travels or being forced to find work and make her world the parochial Scotland of her girlhood days. In the same year, Mary Gaunt had wryly remarked that money was 'a means of locomotion', and it was the fear of what Margaret Fountaine called 'the small world of poverty' that made Ella pursue the case long after Alice had wanted to concede. Much of the sisters' argument, it was later recorded, 'depended on their testimony of their father's state of mind before his death, and they proved excellent witnesses.'[65]

In court the misery of her last fifteen years gradually seeped out; Mr John Christie, although able to roam about Europe with little effort or discomfort, had, since an attack in 1887 diagnosed as pernicious anaemia affecting the brain, been seriously ill and disturbed. During this eight month long illness, thought to be fatal, Ella described how she sat up through the night nursing him with brandy and egg every two hours. But while declaring he could never express the love and affection he felt in her care, the attendant daughter began to notice small changes in her father. He was given to sudden fits of temper, became a recluse and manifested a 'groundless aversion' to his wife and eldest daughter. When Mrs Christie became severely ill in 1894, her

[65] Stewart, Alicella, p. 90.

husband took little interest. Ella remonstrated with him for his heartless behaviour, telling him such conduct would kill her mother, but he replied simply, 'she won't die before her time.' And indeed at her death he showed no grief, Ella told her cross examiner. He refused to pay for the coffin, so Ella provided the money from her own purse.

In the following years, his condition worsened still further; he became insomniac, suffered attacks of giddiness and extreme paranoia, taking arsenic in an attempt to calm his disquietened mind. To escape his violent temper, Ella often locked herself in her room in fear. In 1895 he was advised, for health reasons, to take a trip to Egypt, and did so under Ella's care. But he abandoned her without warning, returning home suddenly and leaving his daughter to hurry embarrassedly after him. Although in his late seventies, he had grown increasingly vain, dyeing his long moustache and proposing marriage to a woman fifty years his junior. His unpredictability and fanaticism had increased, and in the last years of his life he had been secretive about the simplest things for the smallest reasons, continually changing the locks on even empty cupboards. None of the family had been aware of his patronage of the orphanages.

The security in which Ella had been raised was crushed; she had been forced into exposing her father's intolerable ways for all to see. The home in which she felt so anchored had been given lightly away by the person for whom she had worked at its maintenance. In fighting to retain that home, Ella was fighting to retain two conflicting sides of her own self – the daughter who had created it, the forty-year-old spinster who would never be free to leave it again if her case was lost. When a liberal settlement was agreed, leaving the sisters Buckingham Terrace, forty thousand pounds, Cowden cottages and costs, Ella displayed the victory of her freedom in the most dramatic and extreme way. She sailed for Bombay.

Marianne North was also suddenly released when, in September 1869, on one of their regular trips to Gastein, her father was taken ill. The invalid man blamed his elder daughter for his plight, confiding to his diary that he would never have walked over the mountain but for Pop's enjoyment, and would have returned by the shorter sea route if Pop hadn't wanted to travel overland. Hurriedly returning to London, Marianne, who was accustomed to being a fulltime nurse, stayed by his bedside day and night. 'I am up and down all night as usual, with one to two hours sleep between,' wrote her father in his journal. 'Pop is indefatigable and nurses me like a younger Miss Nightingale. But it is heavy work, and I long for wine with stronger meat than grapes and milk and water.'[66] Within two weeks he died. 'I was left alone indeed,' his exhausted daughter wrote. 'I wished to be so; I could not bear to think of him or of anything else, and resolved to keep out of the way of all friends and relations till I had schooled myself into that cheerfulness which makes life pleasant to those around us. I left the house at Hastings for ever.'[67]

There had been no such grief at her mother's death nearly fifteen years earlier. At that time, with the loss of income from her mother's estate, her father had been forced to let the family home and move to a flat in Victoria Street, London. 'I know not how I shall manage with my girls – the point will be to employ them. As regards money, I shall be short enough, but Pop will help me in economies,' he recorded.[68] But his single daughter enjoyed life up eighty-seven steps in one of London's busiest streets better than the excess of rooms and servants at Hastings Lodge. Victoria Street 'soon became more like home than any other to me', wrote Marianne.[69] For a middle-class unmarried daughter with a mother alive, well and capable, there really was little with which she could meaningfully occupy her time. Household management, the supervision of domestic staff, and the emotional intimacy of the father would be directed towards his wife. But the unmarried daughter to a widower could assume these responsibilities, become useless no longer, and make it feel like *her* real home. Rarely a day would pass without Frederick North mentioning his eldest daughter in his diaries. When Mary Gaunt's young husband died, her parents asked her to move back into the relative comfort of their family house rather than attempt to make a living on her own. She replied, 'Can any woman go back and take a subordinate position when she has ruled?'[70] While the dutiful daughter was confined by her role, she could also revel in it. Isabella Bird, truly redundant while both parents lived, did not have this barbed solace of usefulness.

Like Mary Gaunt, Marianne began her journey from her room not out of liberation but out of despair. Her unnatural grief, which seemed

---

66 Entry in Frederick North's Diary for 22 Sep. 1869.
67 North, *Further Recollections of a Happy Life*, p. 37.
68 Entry in Frederick North's Diary for 17 June 1855.
69 North, *Recollections of a Happy Life*, vol. 1, p. 27.
70 Gaunt, *Alone in West Africa*, p. 3.

unconquerable, is not simply explained by the loss of a loved parent. She had been chaperone, companion and ears to a deaf and ageing man – who was Marianne now? She packed up all the belongings at Hastings and, in the company of her elderly maid Elizabeth, sailed for the Continent. 'For nearly forty years he had been my one friend and companion,' she wrote, 'and now I had to learn to live without him, and to fill up my life with other interests as I best might . . . I went straight to Mentone to devote myself to painting from nature, and try to learn from the lovely world which surrounded me there how to make that work henceforth the master of my life.'[71] But the journey which had begun in the despair of grief became one of self-discovery. Taking a corner room in the attic of a small hotel on the edge of town, Marianne had all her meals sent up to her and devoted herself to painting. It was two months before she left this seclusion, voraciously painting landscapes from her window, tempted by regions which her canvas depicted but her eyes could not see. She began to discover a joy in being alone, finding even the companionship of her maid irksome. She travelled to Italy by road and took a boat across to Sicily. 'All seemed new at last, and novelty was what I longed for after the Anglo-invalidism of the Riviera,' she reflected, in words that had never been spoken in all the years of travel with her father, the Anglo-invalid.[72] Rather than finding a new master in her painting she discovered a fresh way of reaching the world of her imagination. When her sister and brother-in-law joined her at Monte Generoso she was reduced once more to fits of tears; their constant presence was a reminder of that part of her, the dutiful daughter, she had left behind, and threatened the new definition of her life she was beginning to build. 'I had been so long alone that constant conversation tired me,' she explained, 'so they left me to my solitude and I got happier again.'[73]

Throughout the months following her father's death, Marianne's struggles to reach a new sense of her own identity led her to constant turmoil and wild swings of plans for her future. Rejecting the company of a childhood friend who had come to visit her, she found contentment living 'deliciously quiet' in an old wooden boarding house in Northern Austria, where no-one stopped longer than one

[71] North, *Further Recollections of a Happy Life*, p. 231.

[72] Ibid., p. 233.

[73] Ibid., p. 310.

night.[74] The dutiful daughter, however, still rose to the bait when an old friend arranged to lead a party of German nurses to help tend the wounded of the Franco-Prussian war, 'and I wrote, in a fit of weak restlessness, volunteering to help her.'[75] When no reply came, Marianne's path was already beginning to be set in another, more self-fulfilling direction. Returning to the London flat, her father haunted the rooms, empty of all living inhabitants except his green paroquet. Marianne told the bird about her travels, as she had once talked to her parent, but the bird too was deaf to her experiences. 'After a while it found out I was only a woman,' she wrote, 'and liked me no more.'[76]

When women travellers looked back upon their early lives, they recognized the imaginary worlds they had created for the realization of their ambitions. Although tempered by their strong sense of duty and responsiblity to others, they formed a concrete picture of themselves as travellers which later enabled them to step out of the window, over the garden fence and realize their dreams. Lucy Broad, who travelled over 100,000 miles, remembered these early visions. 'There came the blackness of darkness to our home in the death of our loved father, and a while after I moved out of it to successively mother three of my brothers, until each got established with home ties of his own. But all this time I had been fighting a burning desire in my own heart that craved for the whole world.'[77] On the other side of the globe, Mary Gaunt wrote of her and her sister's life 'there was really nothing for a woman but to marry, and accordingly we both married and I forgot in my entrance into that world . . . my vague longings after savage lands.'[78] 'When I was a mere child I had already a strong desire to see the world,' wrote Ida Pfeiffer, released from an unhappy marriage. 'When my son's education had been completed, and I was living in peaceful retirement, the dreams and aspirations of my youth gradually awoke once more. I thought of strange manners and customs, of distant regions, where a new sky would be above me, and new ground beneath my feet . . . I commenced my journey to Palestine with a

---

[74] Ibid., p. 311.

[75] Ibid., p. 312.

[76] Ibid., p. 313.

[77] Lucy Broad, *A Woman's Wanderings the World Over*, (London 1909), p. 12.

[78] Gaunt, *Alone in West Africa*, p. 4.

feeling of perfect rapture.'[79] Amelia Edwards wrote as she approached the Dolomites, 'it was an old longing.'[80] When Marianne North boarded the steamer *Malta* bound for the tropics, she wrote in her journal, 'I had long had the dream.'[81]

As women packed their bags for distant lands, they took with them an awkward load of a deeply-held sense of duty and their wild and roaming imaginary lives. Rising before daylight one morning, Mary Gaunt leant over the flag-dressed rail of the SS *Gando*, straining to see the mouth of the Gambia River, and knew she had reached her destination. 'At last, at last,' she exclaimed, 'I was on the very threshold of the land I had dreamed of years before.'[82] She had reached her point of departure.

---

[79] E. Hobson 'Celebrated Lady Travellers. IV Ida Pfeiffer', *Good Words*, vol. 42, (1901), p. 484.

[80] Amelia Edwards, *Untrodden Peaks and Unfrequented Valleys. A Midsummer Ramble in the Dolomites*, (London 1873), p. 3.

[81] North, *Recollections of a Happy Life*, vol. 1, p. 39.

[82] Gaunt, *Alone in West Africa*, p. 12.

Part II

I am a part of all that I have met;
Yet all experience is an arch wherethro'
Gleams all experience untravell'd world,
whose margin fades
For ever and for ever as I move

2

New Horizons

Whether being lowered in a 'mammy chair' over the side of a West African steamer, climbing down the gangway at Bombay docks, taking a jolly-boat over the river to where her *dahabeeyah* is moored, mounting a carriage at the port of Cattaro heading for the Montenegran mountains, or alighting from the Pacific train at Cheyenne depot on the edge of the Rockies, the woman traveller stepped into a landscape with which she was quite familiar. 'I try to remember what were my first impressions of this my first day in Africa,' wrote Sylvia Leith-Ross, travelling to Northern Nigeria in 1907 to join her Chief Transport Officer husband. 'I can remember no impressions at all except one of complete familiarity . . . all I saw had the imprint of the expected . . . but the echo of what was talked about in our own homes.'[1] On sighting the African coast in August 1893 from the deck of the *Lagos*, Mary Kingsley too exclaimed, 'It was with a thrill of joy that I looked on Freetown harbour for the first time in my life. I knew the place so well.'[2] Journalist Elizabeth Bisland, given the assignment of a journey around the world by her New York editor, reached the shores of Japan in December 1889. 'The enchanting fairy dreams of our childhood . . . have an actual existence, yet more fantastic and delicious than our baby minds could ever have imagined,' she wrote of the islands.[3] Often images culled from books and paintings were applied indiscriminately to foreign landscapes. While the waters of the Red Sea had conjured up Holman

---

[1] Sylvia Leith-Ross, *Stepping Stones. Memoirs of Colonial Nigeria 1907–60*, edited and with an introduction by Michael Crowder, (London 1983), p. 41.

[2] Mary Kingsley, *West African Studies*, (London 1899), p. 36–7.

[3] Elizabeth Bisland, *A Flying Trip Around the World*, (London 1891), pp. 55–6.

Being lowered in a mammy chair on arriving in West Africa, 1908.
Liverpool City Libraries.

Hunt's *The Scapegoat* for Marianne North in 1866, seven years later the Nile made Amelia Edwards remember the same painting.[4] As Mary Hall wandered to the edge of her camp at Nimule on the Ugandan-Sudanese border, as Gertrude Bell reached Ha'il in the Arabian desert, as Marianne North arrived at the palace of Deeg in Northern India, as May French-Sheldon sailed into Aden, and while Edith Durham lodged at the Yugoslavian mountain town of Prizren, they all called *Arabian Nights* to mind.[5]

If the real landscape fell short of the vision of an exotic and distant country imagined at home, dreamscapes were superimposed over them. While Edith Durham travelled to Central Europe, she claimed, 'I do not know where the East proper begins,' drawing her own border to the West of where she stood.[6] By orientalizing the mountains of Yugoslavia and Albania, she retained the images which accompanied her vision of the East – mysterious, exotic, challenging. And when Georgina Mackenzie arrived in Serbia, she saw a land 'as little known to Englishmen as the interior of Tartary or the centre of Africa,' forcing a comparison with a dream of Savage Lands.[7] Gertrude Bell, sailing along the southern shore of the Black Sea, recorded 'memories were our travelling companions'.[8]

While the backdrop was filtered through the accounts they had fed on and elaborated in Edinburgh, New York, London and Yorkshire, the experiences these distant lands offered would differ radically from those available to them as single women in Britain. The discordant blend of familiarity in all they saw and remoteness in all they experienced was described in letters home and copious journals kept of their travels. Gertrude Bell wrote:

By the light of our earliest readings we look upon that other world as upon a fairy region full of wild and magical possibilities; imprisoned efreets and obedient djinns, luckless princesses and fortunate fishermen, fall in their appointed places as naturally as

[4] Amelia Edwards, *A Thousand Miles Up the Nile*, (London 1888 2nd edn; 1877), p. 306.
[5] Mary Hall, *A Woman's Trek from the Cape to Cairo*, (London 1907), p. 377; Bell to Hugh Bell 7 Mar. 1914, Ha'il, quoted in Bell, *Letters*, p. 344; North, *Recollections of a Happy Life*, vol. 2, p. 52; Edith Durham, *High Albania*, (London 1909), p. 273; May French-Sheldon, *Sultan to Sultan. Adventures Among the Masai and other Tribes of East Africa*, (London 1892), p. 48.
[6] Edith Durham, *Through the Lands of the Serb*, (London 1904), p. 1.
[7] Georgina Mackenzie, *Notes on the South Slavonic Countries*, (London 1865), p. 25.
[8] Anon [Gertrude Bell], *Safar Nameh: Persian Pictures*. (London 1894), p. 267.

policemen and engine-drivers, female orators and members of
the Stock Exchange with us; flying carpets await them instead of
railway trains, and the one-eyed Kalender seeks a night's shelter
as readily in the palace of three beautiful ladies as he would hie
him to the Crown Hotel at home. Yet though one may be
prepared in theory for the unexpected, some feeling of bewilder-
ment is excusable when one finds oneself actually in the midst of
it.[9]

Amelia Edwards, after initiating herself into travel gently with a
tour around Belgium, set out for the more rugged and challenging
Dolomites with a woman friend in June 1872. Her first glimpse of the
mountains from the seat of her carriage, was, 'so unfamiliar, and yet so
unmistakable! One feels immediately that they are unlike all other
mountains, and yet that they are exactly what one expected them to
be!'[10] As she began to journey further afield to Egypt a year later, these
conflicting emotions grew even stronger. On gaining her first glimpse
of the giant pyramids outside Cairo, she recorded:

The well-known triangular forms look small and shadowy, and
are too familiar to be in any way startling . . . . It is only in
approaching them, and observing how they grow with every foot
of the road, that one begins to feel they are not so familiar after
all . . . one discovers that it was with the forms of the Pyramids,
and only their forms, that one had been acquainted all these
years past . . . . Standing there close against the base of it;
touching it; measuring her own height against one of its lowest
blocks; looking up all the stages of that vast, receding, rugged
wall, which leads upward like an Alpine buttress and seems
almost to touch the sky, the Writer suddenly became
aware . . . . Now, for the first time, they resolved themselves
into something concrete, definite, real.[11]

Mary Kingsley, who knew Freetown harbour so well, recorded on
her trip from Libreville to the mouth of the Ogooué, 'All day long we
steam past ever varying scenes of loveliness whose component parts

[9] Ibid., p. 187.
[10] Edwards, *Untrodden Peaks and Unfrequented Valleys.* p. 27.
[11] Edwards, *A Thousand Miles Up the Nile*, pp. 13–15.

are ever the same, yet the effect ever different.'[12] The familiar and known elements were the dreamscapes they had constructed and imaginatively lived in from their youths. The unexpected and unfamiliar were the new challenges and experiences the women travellers were to face.

Women travellers found in the Dark Continent, the Orient, the Savage Lands, the stage upon which their new experiences as travellers could be realized and a heady sense of freedom which was – like all opiates – addictive and consuming. Although they had painted, fictionalized, imagined and dreamt of the scenes they saw, these had been but two dimensional pictures on a dabbed canvas or scribbled page. Now they looked out on a tangible world into which they could journey. While the landscape initially conformed to their early dreams, the fact that they could journey into it was entirely new and exhilirating. Standing on the brink of their personal odysseys, teetering on the edge of what Edith Durham called the 'entrance to a world so new and strange,' imbued the women travellers with a drunken vertigo.[13] They felt, many for the first time, irresponsible – the calls and duties of their homes fading away into the greyness with which they depicted the British Isles. Mary Kingsley 'skylarked' on the rapids of the Ogooué river, Amelia Edwards 'rambled' around the Dolomites, and Isabella Bird 'puddled' to Hawaii and the United States. On reaching Estes Park in the Rockies, she wrote back home to her sister of the 'glorious upper world' of the mountains:[14] 'They mean everything that is rapturous and delightful – grandeur, cheerfulness, health, enjoyment, novelty, freedom, etc etc. I have just dropped into the very place I have been seeking, but in everything it exceeds all my dreams.'[15] As Edith Durham stood on the limestone crags bordering the mountainous Montenegran region, 'the world we have always known is left far behind at the foot of the mountain.' The emotional distance she had travelled, and the border between British society and the exotic world she felt she was crossing, were expressed

[12] Mary Kingsley, *Travels in West Africa*, (London 1897), p. 129.
[13] Durham, *Through the Lands of the Serb*, p. 5.
[14] Isabella Bird, *A Lady's Life in the Rocky Mountains*, (London 1880 3rd edn; 1879), p.96.
[15] Ibid., p. 84.

by a simple claim that, 'It is, in fact, easy to travel much farther without being so far off.'[16]

The place to which many women travellers were first drawn was the local market. Here, in the midst of a crowd of unfamiliar bodies, they absorbed the new sensations of the foreign lands. Their senses felt almost assaulted – the vibrancy of the colours, the continual chatter of the bartering, the whispering flow of pouring rice, the damp touch of the strange bodies rubbing past and about them, and that most powerful pungent smell of hot lands. From Ella Christie's Indian bazaars to Mary Gaunt's West African market mammies, it was these overwhelming sensations, awakening in them a physical sensuality long stifled, which filled the pages of their first letters home. 'The market women wear long gowns made either without any waist or with it immediately under the armpits of gay coloured cotton and tie their hair up in bright silk handkerchiefs and look extremely picturesque,' wrote Mary Kingsley on arriving at Freetown. 'Their stalls are as bright as their clothes with chiles, capisicums, Ricketts Blue, pumpkins, pineapples, pawpaws – a thousand things I do not yet know the names of. Indeed I have never spent a more delightful day than that at Sierra Leone.'[17]

As they moved away from their ports of arrival, unanalysed joy at being in open space and on the move informed their impressions of the vast physical landscape which stretched out invitingly before them. Gertrude Bell captured this emotion when she wrote at the eve of her watershed 1905 journey, 'The gates of the enclosed garden are thrown open, the chain at the entrance of the sanctuary is lowered, with a wary glance to right and left you step forth, and, behold! the immeasurable world . . . you feel the bands break that were riveted about your heart as you enter the path that stretches across the rounded shoulder of the earth.'[18] 'Everything was uncertain,' wrote Rosita Forbes in 1920 as she set out from Ajdabiyah on the Gulf of Sirte disguised as a Muslim. 'There were so many difficulties to be surmounted, but we felt that now, at least, the last trace of Europe lay behind us. We breathed more freely.'[19]

[16] Durham, *Through the Lands of the Serb*, pp. 5–6.
[17] Kingsley to Violet Roy 17 Aug. 1873, SS *Lagos*, off Liberia.
[18] Gertrude Bell, *The Desert and the Sown*, (London 1907), pp. 1–2.
[19] Rosita Forbes, *Secret of the Sahara*, (London 1921), p. 10.

For a week, Isabella Bird's Pacific train rolled slowly over the plains towards the Rocky Mountains, from her first glimpse of two tooth-like peaks on the distant horizon to the overpowering vastness of the nearby range. 'They are gradually gaining possession of me,' she wrote home to her sister in her small Scottish highland cottage. 'I can look at and *feel* nothing else.'[20] Edith Durham stood at the top of the pass and looked past the villages to the lake of Shkoder and the Albanian mountains, 'their peaks glittering with snow even in June, show fainter and fainter, and the land of mystery and the unspeakable Turk fades into the sky – a scene so magnificent and so impressive that it is worth all the journey from England just to have looked at it.'[21] Amelia Edwards felt it her first calling on arriving at the forestry centre of Cortina to climb to the top of the tower and gain a view of the surrounding countryside. From here she plotted her future route, peering across the plains of Lombardy at Monte Viso, over 120 miles in the distance. 'It all seemed like a dream,' she wrote. On descending back down to Botzen at the end of her journey, she also descended into 'the hot, dusty, busy, dead-level World of Commonplace again!'[22] On 30 November 1873, Amelia awoke for the first time in a different continent – Africa – and looked through the window of the Shepheard's Hotel in Cairo on to the oriental world:

It was a still, warm morning. Grave grey and black crows flew heavily from tree to tree, or perched, cawing meditatively, upon the topmost branches. Yonder, between the pillared stems, rose the minaret of a very distant mosque; and here where the garden was bounded by a high wall and a windowless house, I saw a veiled lady walking on the terraced roof in the midst of a cloud of pigeons. Nothing could be more simple than the scene and its accessories; nothing, at the same time, more Eastern, strange, and unreal.[23]

As she journeyed into this eastern world the landscape stretched out even further and more temptingly before her. 'We look across a world of desert,' she recorded at the Second Cataract of the Nile, 'and see

[20] Bird, *A Lady's Life in the Rocky Mountains*, p. 34.
[21] Durham, *Through the Lands of the Serb*, p. 15.
[22] Edwards, *Untrodden Peaks and Unfrequented Valleys*, p. 356.
[23] Edwards, *A Thousand Miles Up the Nile*, p. 3

the river still coming from afar. We have reached the point at which
all that is habitable and familiar comes abruptly to an end . . . . But
for the telegraphic wires stalking, ghost-like, across the desert, it
would seem as if we had touched the limit of civilisation, and were
standing on the threshold of a land unexplored.'[24]

Mary Gaunt looked out on to the African continent from the deck
of the SS *Gando*, watching the continent of her dreams come into
view. The surf-edged sand of the West African shore drew a unbroken
yellow line along the perimeter of the grey sea – the line she was to
follow for over three hundred miles. First she stayed cautiously among
colonial society as a guest of Sir George Denton, veteran Governor of
the Gambia, and 'spent most of my time on the verandah outside my
own room, where I had a view not only of the road that ran to the
centre of the town but right across the river. Here I had my breakfast
and my afternoon tea, and here I did all my writing.'[25] The world
which had tempted her from the pages of books now stood before her
in reality, and she would begin to travel into it.

The rooms from which they looked out on to these familiar scenes
which offered such strange experiences were very different from the
parlours, sickrooms, and studies of the suburban semi-detached
middle-class dwellings and solid brick country houses the women
travellers had left behind. Edith Durham's turkish *han* was a
ramshackle shanty with iron bars for windows and earth for a floor.
The only decorations were barrels and bottles, and the only
consumables coffee and *rakia*. Yet here, amongst the peasantry, Edith
claimed to be more comfortable than in any hotel starred by Baedeker.
Amelia Edwards passed her days sitting at her writing table on the
deck of the *Philae*, the flat bottomed barge-like *dahabeeyah* which
floated her up the Nile. As the water ran past and the wind blew on
the sails, she recorded the scenes at the river's bank: a young girl
sauntered down to collect water, a huddle of buffalos dozed in the
moving stream to keep cool, a man lay asleep with his camel in the
shade of a fig tree, and a palm, uprooted by the last flood, balanced its
heavy fronds in the river. They were all, she says, like mirages, passing
by her from the deck.[26]

---

[24] Ibid., p. 320.
[25] Gaunt, *Alone in West Africa*, p. 18.
[26] Edwards, *A Thousand Miles Up the Nile*, p. 98.

Marianne North's first taste of what she simply and without distinction called 'the tropics' came on leaving the United States in December 1871 for Jamaica. Like Mary Gaunt, she first accepted the hospitality of local British residents, but soon jumped at the opportunity to move outside home circles and be by herself. On a drive through the forest, she had spotted a house half hidden among the overgrown tangle of plants in a deserted botanical garden, enmazed by zig-zagging paths. For four pounds a month it was hers and, despite the twenty palatial rundown rooms, she set up her washstand and bed on the upstairs verandah, pinning her sketches around the wall as decoration. She bought a huge bunch of bananas and hung it from the balcony roof in mock imitation of a chandelier. From her windowless, doorless bedroom she could see down to the wooded valley, above to the meadows and hills. Leaving home at daylight, she sought out new subjects to paint, returning at noon when the heat was at its highest to spend a cool afternoon on the verandah finishing half-completed sketches and beginning fresh ones of the morning's collection. Each day, just before sunset, she would choose one of the meandering paths leading up the hill and go exploring, reaching home in the dark. 'I was in a state of ecstasy,' she wrote.[27]

Mary Gaunt also soon sought accommodation away from the colonial crowd. On arriving at Accra in a steamer from Winnebah, halfway through her shoreline journey, she was offered the luxury of the Governor's home at Christianborg Castle, the ex-slave fort. Instead she moved to a tumbledown bungalow just outside the walls of the Governor's compound, opening all the shutters wide to let in the sea air. For, like Marianne, she suffered from claustrophobia, causing her depressive listlessness whenever she was enclosed within walls which looked in rather than out. Soon recovering from the 'langour and weariness' she had felt within the Castle grounds, Mary rose early in the morning before the town awoke and went for long walks, passing bungalows shuttered and barred for the night – the homes of the pallid, white-faced men and women. On her travels Mary insistently, to the consternation of European sentiments, threw feminine scruples aside and set up her old camp-bed on the verandah under the stars. Being physically unfettered was intrinsic to Mary's

---

[27] North, *Recollections of a Happy Life*, vol. 1, p. 83.

emotional health. Physical space gave her, as it did many other women travellers, emotional space to explore herself as well as the landscapes into which she was travelling. This new and strange geography allowed Mary to picture herself in an entirely different environment from middle-class Britain. Geographical location and mental welfare would be dependent upon one another.

Constance Larymore, in 1901 the first woman to be allowed to accompany her Resident husband to Nigeria, wrote of her experiences, 'I had ridden over 3000 miles, learnt a new language, made thousands of new friends in the animal and flower world, as well as valued human ones. I felt as if I had "enlarged my borders mentally", and had certainly begun to know and love Africa with a deep affection that, I think, is never lost by those who once acquire it.'[28] Isabella Bird justified her first major voyage to Hawaii in 1873 in a way startling for one who was considered physically disabled. 'During that time the necessity of leading a life of open air and exercise as a means of recovery, led me to travel on horseback to and fro through the islands, exploring the interior, ascending the highest mountains, visiting the active volcanoes, and remote regions which are known to few even of the residents, living among the natives, and otherwise seeing Hawaiian life in all its phases.'[29] But despite her claims, it was not her back condition that living 'among the natives' and 'visiting the active volcanoes' improved, but her health in a much more general, yet personal and intimate sense. For Isa, forty-one years old, was beginning to find a direction for her energy which had been dissipated on a life of good works and genteel society in Edinburgh.

Gertrude Bell's feelings of freedom in the vastness of the desert began with her first journey, four years after she left Oxford, to Persia as a guest of her uncle Frank Lascelles, recently appointed ambassador to Tehran. Writing up her experiences back in Europe, anonymously and in the masculine, she makes this connection explicit:

> There are moments when the cabined spirit longs for liberty. A man stands a-tiptoe on the verge of the unknown world which lures him with its vague promises; the peaceful years behind lose all their value in his dazed eyes . . . he pines to stand in the great

[28] Constance Larymore, *A Resident's Wife in Nigeria*, (London 1911), p. 54.

[29] Isabella Bird, *The Hawaiian Archipelago, Six Months among the Palm Groves, Coral Reefs and Volcanoes of the Sandwich Islands*, (London 1875), p. vii.

sunlight, the great wide world which is all too narrow for his adventurous energy . . . . He remembers the look of the boundless plain stretching before him, the nights when the dome of the sky was his ceiling, when he was awakened by the cold kisses of the wind that flies before the dawn. He cries for the space to fling out his fighting arm; he burns to measure himself unfettered with the forces of God.[30]

In the constant company of her sixteen-year-old cousin Florence, Gertrude barely escaped the family commitments and demands for propriety which had haunted her at home. But the land to which she travelled – the Persia well founded in myths and legends on which she had been raised – suggested a release from the boundaries of her homelife which the fields surrounding Red Barns had not. 'We arrived on Saturday afternoon in the Garden of Eden,' she wrote home to her stepmother, 'You can't think how lovely it all is.'[31] Within a fortnight, she was writing of the new surge of energy she found after young years of dabbling in philanthropic work, organizing Mothers' Meetings, buttering bread for workers' outings and tame European travel. Riding back from a visit to the Tower of Silence outside Tehran, in the company of the dashing young English Legation secretary Henry Cadogan, she wrote ecstatically, 'Life seized us and inspired us with a mad sense of revelry. The humming wind and the teaming earth shouted "Life! Life!" as we rode. Life! Life! the beautiful, the magnificent! . . . . For us the wide plain and the limitless world, for us the beauty and the freshness of the morning! for us youth and the joy of living!'[32] As her friendship with the poetical, unconventional and unpopular Henry Cadogan turned to courtship, they sat translating romantic Persian poetry together, eating cherries under a waterfall. Together they made an expedition to the banks of the Lar river, sleeping out in a camp; 'the joy is great,' Gertrude wrote home to her stepmother.[33] But still tied to her family, her parents refused to accept Cadogan's offer of marriage to their wealthy, educated twenty-six-year-old daughter, and Gertrude was escorted unceremoniously back to Britain in the care of her junior cousin Gerald

[30] Bell, *Safar Nameh*, pp. 84–5.
[31] Bell to Florence Bell 9 May 1892, Tehran, quoted in Richmond, *Earlier Letters*, p. 266.
[32] Bell, *Safar Nameh*, pp. 26–7.
[33] Bell to Florence Bell 17 Aug. 1892, Lar, quoted in Richmond, *Earlier Letters*, p. 326.

Lascelles. She never saw Henry again; within nine months he had died of pneumonia after falling in the same Lar river by which they had made love.

Looking for exhiliration nearer to home, the long and restless journeys of European travel began again – Switzerland and France with her family, Italy with the older historian Alice Stopford Green, even a Cook's round-the-world trip with her brother Maurice, who bought her a book for the trip on *Manners for Women*, 'with the help of which he hopes to give me some useful advice' – especially in how to sew on his shirt buttons.[34] But Gertrude was continually reminded of the East in all she saw. In the green tubs outside the hotel in Basle, the scarlet flowering pomegranates stirred up memories of those gathered along the Galabet road; even journeying itself reminded her of other journeys eastward. Above and beyond the mystery and charm of the Orient which had been with her since a young student, it now represented her first love. The place itself became that love – the human being now dead – and soon grew to be, for Gertrude, the only place in which to be vibrant, young, in love and alive.

By 1900 she was back in the land of her imagination, staying at the Hotel Jerusalem, but Jerusalem was still too close, in Edith Durham's sense, for her, and within a few days she wrote to ask her father's permission to make her first solo desert journey, 'with no one but Arab-speaking people . . . . If you don't mind.'[35] For Gertrude, this first lone journey was a reconnaissance trip, a confirming instance that the East about which she had so voraciously read could offer the mystery and excitment of her books. 'I shall be back here before long,' she wrote to her father the day before she sailed from Jaffa.[36]

Although over the next four years she established herself as a prominent mountaineer, with many dangerous ascents to her name, the landscape of the Swiss Alps could not provide her with the freedom from home society the image of the exotic East offered. For it was as a *lady* climber that she had earnt fame, not as a simple nomad or traveller, her femininity always haunting her achievements; on climbing down from the mountainside she descended into European

[34] Bell to Hugh Bell [1897/8], quoted in Elizabeth Burgoyne, *Gertrude Bell. From her Personal Papers, 1889–1914*, (London 1958), pp. 56–7.

[35] Bell to Hugh Bell Feb. 1900, quoted in ibid., p. 91.

[36] Bell to Hugh Bell 19 June 1900, quoted in Bell, *Letters*, p. 120.

society, from which she retired early to bed and rose early the next morning with another mountain to climb.

The physical space Amelia Edwards found in the Dolomites also tantalized without satisfying her. Rushing up and down mountainsides with uncontrollable energy and speed, the map of her route spirals around and around the small towns and villages lodged amongst the valleys in a remote region wedged between the fashionable resort of Innsbruck and the glory and culture of Venice. Within a year she had left for Egypt, the Orient of her dreams.

Isabella Bird also began to move farther afield in her travels. After her initial journeys to the United States and Europe, she had attempted to settle back into pious Edinburgh society, living with her sister in the middle-class comfort of the grey stone capital. But life as a cultured spinster could not compare with the flighty, heady sense of freedom felt when she was on the move, and at forty one she boarded a boat for Australia. But finding the heat, glare and gardens of the new continent oppressive, she soon moved on, leaving Auckland harbour on the not quite watertight *Nevada*, California-bound. At once, sailing through storms and confronting hurricanes, she felt enlivened again. 'It is so like living in a new world, so free, so fresh, so vital, so careless, so unfettered, so full of interest that one grudges being asleep,' said the traveller who had spent her Edinburgh mornings abed. 'No door bells, no "please mems", no dirt, no bills, no demands of any kind . . . no conventionalities, no dressing. If my clothes drop into rags they can be pinned together . . . I am often in tempestuous spirits. It seems a sort of brief resurrection of a girl of 21.'[37] Precise destination and route no longer mattered, so Isa, persuaded by a fellow woman passenger, disembarked at Hawaii – intending to remain a few weeks and staying seven months. Hennie, worriedly awaiting her letters, was perhaps astonished at her seemingly reliable middle-aged sister's utter impetuosity.

Travelling from the relative sophistication of the largest island, which housed the main settlement of the American missionary population, to the more remote, rugged and demanding small islands of Kauai and Molokai, Isa was introduced to two accoutrements which would increase her comfort and sense of physical release from her disabled body – the Mexican saddle, on which she rode astride, and

[37] Bird to Henrietta Bird, quoted in Barr, *A Curious Life for a Lady*, p. 22.

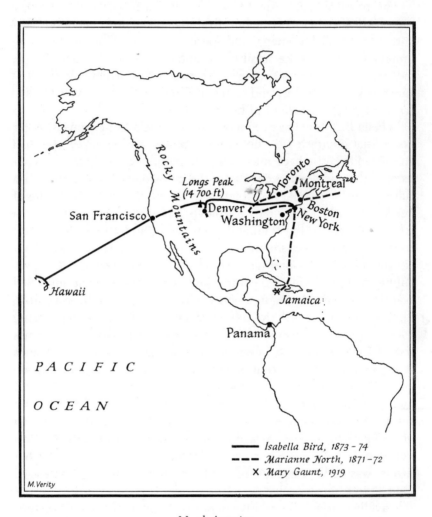

Rocky Mountains

Longs Peak
(14 700 ft)

Toronto
Montreal

San Francisco

Denver
Washington

Boston
New York

Hawaii

Jamaica

Panama

PACIFIC

OCEAN

——— Isabella Bird, 1873 – 74
– – – Marianne North, 1871 –72
✕ Mary Gaunt, 1919

M. Verity

North America

the Hawaiian riding dress, a pair of big baggy trousers gathered at the ankle and covered by a long split skirt. This unconventional mode of fashion combined mobility and comfort with outer propriety, so conforming to the two strands in Isa's character that she would continue to dress thus throughout her travels.

The islands introduced Isa to physical competence not only in mobility but in conquering her fear. In the company of William Green, acting British consul and amateur volcanist, she ascended 14,000 feet up Mauna Loa, an active volcano. Perched on the edge of the crater at 6 p.m. on 6 June 1873, she wrote to her sister, 'Perhaps you are the only person in the world who has ever had a line from this wonderful place . . .'.[38]

Isa revelled in the 'glorious upper world,' towering over the conventionalities of the villages and the verandahed houses which huddled in the valley below. Less than a year later, she looked down from 1,000 feet higher on the summit of Long's Peak in the Rocky Mountains, not in the company of a fledgling consul but the notorious trapper, Rocky Mountain Jim. Since sailing from Hawaii in August 1873, she had made her way by train to San Francisco and cross country to the Rockies. Once the railroad ran out, she had donned her Hawaiian riding dress, mounted her Mexican saddle, and made for the mountain range by horse. At Longmount, Isa and Mountain Jim, together with two student trappers and a mongrel dog, threw their boots over the horns of their saddles, mounted, and made towards the peak through 'the sights and sounds not of the lower earth, but of the solitary, beast-haunted, frozen upper altitudes.'[39] Over hay-coloured fields, plunging into the gloom of great pine forests where 'no lumberer's axe has ever rung' with the illimitable plains lying behind, they rode. On the first day they reached the timber line, unsaddled and built a fire of pine logs to boil the tea drank out of battered tins, and ate roasted strips of beef to chew in their hands. The clear air on the side of the mountain perhaps made these bland tastes as intense and vibrant as the colours of the setting sun on the sealike plains below. In the freezing night, the men sung negro spirituals around the fire, and Isa lay down with her saddle as a pillow and young pine shoots as a mattress, with the dog lying against her back to keep her warm.

[38] Bird, *Hawaiian Archipelago*, p. 32.
[39] Bird, *A Lady's Life in the Rocky Mountains*, p. 101.

Rising with the dawn, they rode as far as the horses could over the boulders, then dismounted and began to walk through 'six succeeding hours of terror'. There were few footholds in the smoothed granite; frozen snow and loose rocks were further obstacles. Roped to Jim, giddy and nauseous from altitude sickness, Isabella was egged on up the mountain by their combined determination, clambering from the shoulders of one man to another. The last five hundred feet – *scaling* not climbing, Isa insisted – took an hour, with only minute footholds, extreme breathlessness and agonizing thirst teased by the surrounding snow and ice, until they arrived at the peak, 'uplifted above love and hate and storms of passion, calm amidst the eternal silences.'[40] So the middle-aged spinster had conquered fear and disability and, in the view from the summit of the waters which 'start for both oceans', found a clearer reflection of herself.

While Isabella Bird escaped the Anglo-American society by climbing to the top of the mountain range, Edith Durham also literally looked down upon Eastern European society from her upper world. Riding from Bridzha through the mountains, she recorded,

> Far away on the left – glowing white in the heat – on a plain at the mouth of the valley was what looked like a large village. The sun caught a white minaret, needle-pointing to the sky.
>
> 'Podgoritza!' I thought of the Hotel Europa – it seemed a little haven below.
>
> I was drenched with sweat, dizzy with heat, had had six days crowded with new events, new knowledge – severe and incessant physical and mental labour and very little sleep. Why suffer torture in an aching wilderness when Podgoritza would receive me joyfully?
>
> I had only to descend the valley, the plain would be easy going. But I could not . . .[41]

For Ella Christie also, travelling upwards was travelling away from the world of Rajah's palaces and Government House which had formed the first few months of her Indian journey. Making her way windingly northwards to Kashmir and higher ground, she abandoned her scottish maid Humphries at the foot of the Ladakh mountains. For

[40] Ibid., p. 114.
[41] Durham, *High Albania*, p. 71.

the journey to the plains of Deosai, at 13,000 feet the highest inhabited region in the world, her 'personal staff' consisted instead of one bearer, Tikaram. The stout Scotswoman rode her small pony over the narrow paths cut into the side of the mountains, often dismounting to walk on the more precarious stony slopes. But as the stones dropped thousands of feet down into the chasm below, she felt no fear; with her indian sandals to protect her feet, smoked glasses against the glare, and cherry brandy to keep her warm, she strode determinedly onwards. 'A long march yesterday of twenty four miles,' she recorded in her distinctive matter-of-fact manner in her diary, allowing herself only the slightest of comment, 'but one never wears of the scenery or the people.'[42]

Women travelled through landscapes whose vastness invoked images of caravans across the desert, expeditions up winding rivers into a distant valley, the ascent of a far-off tempting peak. They were to traverse thousands of miles carried in hammocks, machillas, palanquins, bath chairs, Peking carts and droshkys. They rode – sometimes astride – a mule, camel, horse, elephant or donkey. They floated up rivers in a steamer, sampan, *dahabeeyah*, or, in Ella Christie's case, an inflatable goatskin raft. May French-Sheldon had her specially designed silk-lined rattan palanquin, weighing only seventy pounds, shipped out to East Africa. A few, like Mary Kingsley, even walked. But unlike the long straight lines on the map painted by the male travellers, women often had no definite goal in mind. As Amelia Edwards sailed along the Nile, she noted how the river always wound back on itself, how close the place they were aiming for that night seemed but how long a river voyage it was to reach it. The travellers rarely, if possible, stayed longer than a couple of nights at one station, campsite or trading factory, before moving on to the next. First on Mary Gaunt's agenda after swaying into the capital of the German colony of Togo was, 'Having got into Lomé the question was how to get out of it.'[43]

Since her father's death Marianne North had been continually moving, first gingerly to Europe and the well-known haunts of Cook's tours and Murray's guidebooks, then further and further afield. Unlike many other women travellers who lept with the fearless impetuousity

---

[42] Diary entry 10 Aug. 1904, Kharbo, quoted in Stewart, *Alicella*, p. 168.
[43] Gaunt, *Alone in West Africa*, p. 276.

of their reawakened youth, Marianne trod cautiously. She made sure she was accompanied by someone who was familiar with the route, always arranged to be met at ports and stations, and had letters of introduction to the local English-speaking community. Gradually, moving from the United States to Jamaica and Brazil, from Brazil to Japan, she arrived, as a seasoned traveller, in Ceylon in September 1877. During the last five years she had spent less than one year at the Victoria Street flat, in brief visits broken into one or two months, suffering from what her sister called, as if a diagnosed illness, 'a restless mind'.[44] From Ceylon to India she ran up and down the subcontinent, continually turning back on herself. From the southern tip of Trivandrum to northeastern Darjeeling and northwestern Lahore, in one year she travelled over two thousand miles by ship, mule-car, jampany, garry and train. For Marianne, being trapped in one place was almost as suffocating as being confined to a darkened room and she would soon become ill, developing rheumatism of the thumb which prevented her from holding her palette and pains in her feet which made walking difficult. The cure was simple – moving on.

The absence of a fixed route – that essential ingredient of their childhood planned and packaged European tours – was also vital. 'Just now I am zigzagging, returning on my steps, tripling or quadrupling the distance,' wrote Alexandra David-Neel in the summer of 1922, on her way northwest towards the Gobi desert.[45] When women travellers were asked what had led them to a certain spot, it usually led to a flippant and entirely unsatisfying answer. It was always like Amelia Edwards' reply, 'we had drifted hither by accident . . . without definite plans, outfit, or any kind of Oriental experience, behold us arrived in Cairo on the 29th of November 1873, literally, and most prosaically, in search of fine weather.'[46] When Constance Gordon Cumming was asked on her return to Scotland from Ceylon in the summer of 1874 where she was going next, she replied 'To Fiji', simply, she claimed, 'because that was the most absolutely impossible idea that could suggest itself.'[47] Within a year she was on her way to

[44] Catherine Symonds in introduction to *Further Recollections of a Happy Life*.

[45] Alexandra David-Neel, *Journal de voyage; Lettres à son Mari*, vol. 2, p. 211, quoted in Barbara and Michael Foster, *Forbidden Journey. The Life of Alexandra David-Neel*, (San Francisco 1987), p. 197.

[46] Edwards, *A Thousand Miles Up the Nile*, pp. 2–3.

[47] Constance Gordon Cumming, *Memories*, (London 1904), p. 216.

Marianne North in Ceylon, 1876, photographed by Julia Margaret Cameron.
Royal Botanic Gardens.

those Pacific Isles. Mary Kingsley described the method of choosing
her destination as if sticking a pin into an open map: 'Where on earth
am I to go . . . I got down an atlas and saw that either South America
or West Africa must be my destination, for the Malayan region was

too far off and too expensive. Then I got Wallace's *Geographical Distribution* and after reading that master's article on the Ethiopian region I hardened my heart and closed with West Africa.'[48] 'I daresay you are grumbling that I don't tell you what I am really going to do,' Marianne North wrote to the Sanskrit scholar Dr Arthur Burnell from Begpore. 'I don't know – since my father ceased telling me I have drifted.'[49] Later the same year, having wound her way down from Sehorumpore, she wrote again to the same correspondent, 'I am such an old vagabond that I own to being delighted to be perfectly free again – staying with no one, having no fixed dates for going anywhere, and not even a servant to dog my footsteps.'[50] Isabella Bird, who had spent ten years of her young womanhood in Huntingdonshire, lamented having to stay five days in one forest camp, itching to move onwards and upwards. 'I always fell dil [dull and inactive] when I am stationary. The loneliness is dreadful often,' she wrote to her rooted sister. 'When I'm travelling, I don't feel it, but that is why I can never stay anywhere.'[51]

Drawing women travellers' journeys on a map of world exploration would not add, as might their male counterparts, new spidery routes disappearing into the source of a river or culminating at the summit of an unconquered mountain; their lines would spiral around and around, through forests, up creeks, down canyons, with no goal except the wandering itself. 'There is a peculiar pleasure in riding out into the unknown,' wrote Edith Durham, 'a pleasure which no second journey on the same trail ever affords.'[52] Gertrude Bell again made the most explicit connection. 'My thoughts travelled forward,' she wrote at Tneib, 'and I longed to follow the path they had taken.'[53]

Mary Gaunt followed the white edge of the surf southwards, the palm trees bending over in the wind like choreographed dancers, shaking their fronds free of the light rains at the beginning of the wet season. The footprints of her hammock bearers marked the sand before being washed away by a wave of tiny black crabs. Cutting inland from Accra, she headed for the railway depot of Paliné one

[48] Kingsley, *Travels in West Africa*, p. 1.
[49] North to Arthur Burnell 18 Jan. 1878, Begpore, India.
[50] North to Arthur Burnell 27 July 1878, Nynee Tal, India.
[51] Bird, Sandwich Islands, quoted in Barr, *A Curious Life for a Lady*, p. 172.
[52] Durham, *High Albania*, p. 39.
[53] Bell, *The Desert and the Sown*, p. 44.

hundred miles inside German-ruled Togo, from where she could take a train back down to the coast. From Dodowah she had to strike out twenty-seven miles off route for Akuse on the Volta River – had to, not because of any goal, aim or mission, but because she was travelling, and this was the direction, for the moment, in which she chose to go. She decided on an overnight journey, the humid heat making daytime travel exhausting and uncomfortable even under her protective helmet. She set out at nine o'clock one April night in 1911, her portable furniture born by sixteen carriers. Swaying in her Public Works Department hammock, on loan from her brother, the sudden sounds of the forest and the pad-pad of the carriers feet charmed her through the night. Through areas steeped in mystery and danger in the day, she travelled in the silver-white moonlit darkness, the bearers' chants rising to drown any imminent danger. A leopard cried. They climbed over Krobo Hill – an ancient killing field – the men's feet now splashing through the streams. Mary lay back in her hammock watching the African day dawn, the earth wake up, and the scenery reveal itself in front of her from behind the veil of night. The birds began to speak. 'And still,' she wrote, 'the men went steadily on.'[54]

As well as celebrating being able to pack her bag hurriedly, throw a gingham parasol over her shoulder, and ride away to her new horizon, the woman traveller also kept moving to avoid emotional entangle- ments. On Ella Christie's infrequent returns to Scotland it was often rumoured that she was getting married – and within days she would be again boarding a ship for a distant land. In Ceylon, she was pursued through the streets by an eager Englishman, racing his rickshaw with hers and shouting out flattering compliments as the bearers ran along. Within a week she was on the ferry for India.[55]

As physical boundaries dissolved, so did time and sense of place. 'I do not know when I may reach there or this reach you,' wrote Ella from Shanghai, 'as there is a beautiful uncertainty about everything in this part of the East, and one does feel at the end of the world.'[56] Amelia Edwards lost all track of the time on her Nile journey, and decided to establish her own arbitrary canon; when the sun rose she

[54] Gaunt, *Alone in West Africa*, p. 203.

[55] Stewart, *Alicella*, p. 157.

[56] Christie to Elizabeth Haldane 9 Mar. 1907, Shanghai.

called it seven o'clock, when the sun set six o'clock.[57] Mary Kingsley marked one letter from Calabar to Cambridge, 'July or August' – in the middle of June.[58] Mary Slessor, only thirty miles up the Cross River in her mission station, apologized in a letter back to her Dundee home that she had no idea of the date.[59] Isabella Bird, the precise and organized clergyman's daughter, headed her letter to her sister 'Nameless region, Rocky Mountains, Sept.'[60]

While at home in London, Yorkshire, or Hastings, surrounded by relatives and neighbours, loneliness had haunted the women travellers and was a constant complaint confessed to journals and more intimate friends. But travelling, they began to reinterpret what it meant to be alone, seeing it for the first time as a positive choice rather than an absence of choices. It was not something to be ashamed of or hidden, explained away, but to celebrate and rejoice in. While Mary Gaunt had mourned being left alone at the death of her husband, she entitled her first travel book *Alone in West Africa*, asserting a new identity as a woman by herself and redefining a word which had previously denoted her isolation and despair. Etta Close, cloistered with her mother through her young womanhood, emerged as a traveller late in life and defiantly called her first book *A Woman Alone in Kenya, Uganda and the Belgian Congo*. Ella Christie began her only travel book with the ditty:

> Down to Gehenna or up to the throne,
> He travels the fastest who travels alone.

From Marianne North's loneliness in the resorts of France, Switzerland and Austria arose a need and want to be alone, for it was only when she was by herself that she could, she believed, be herself. Gertrude Bell's 1905 journey marked for her the beginning of long and solo travel in the East. She simply recorded, 'I had a great desire to ride alone.'[61] Mary Gaunt bluntly explained her need to set out from Axim without the company of an European official. 'I found stirring

---

[57] Edwards, *A Thousand Miles Up the Nile*, p. 326.

[58] Kingsley to Hatty Johnson 'July or August' 1895, Consulate, Old Calabar.

[59] Slessor to 'My dear Miss Annie', 'Itu, don't know the date'.

[60] Bird, *A Lady's Life in the Rocky Mountains*, p. 60.

[61] Bell, *The Desert and the Sown*, p. 4.

within me a very masculine desire to be out of leading strings and to be allowed to take care of myself . . . my Freedom was coming.'[62] Alone but not lonely, was how she felt on her journey.

Women travellers imbued the landscape with the emotions they themselves felt and searched for. Edith Durham spoke of the 'rugged loneliness' of the mountains. Looking at Long's Peak, which she was about to ascend, Isabella Bird wrote, 'It becomes invested with a personality,' and Mary Kingsley addressed Mount Cameroon as 'he'.[63] 'Peace and loneliness and beauty' were what Gertrude Bell found in the desert, in sharp contrast to the bustle and society of Sloane Street and Yorkshire country homes.[64] The desert's 'wild free spirit', reflecting the pantheism which infested so many of the women's writing, seeped even into the towns set in its midst. From the balcony on which she stood,

> The great splendid city of Damascus with its gardens and its domes and its minarets, lies spread out before you, and beyond it the desert – the desert almost up to its gates, and the breath of it blowing in with every word, and the spirits of it passing through the city gates with every Arab camel driver. That is the heart of the whole matter.[65]

Danger was an important element in this landscape. In the vast unknownness of the foreign lands it lurked – not usually in the form of a concrete threat but simply as the unknown, the unfettered, the unvanquished. Late Victorian society prided itself in having conquered nature through organizing, explaining and cataloguing it. Weighty compendiums of flora and fauna, to which Edith Durham and Marianne North had both contributed, named and pigeonholed the imperial world, and anthropology was beginning to apply similar techniques to foreign peoples. Railways penetrated through areas of Asia and Africa previously thought inpenetratable because of climate, geography and population. Firearms had conquered the 'noble savage' and reduced him to an ethnographical specimen. The empty spaces of

[62] Gaunt, *Alone in West Africa*, p. 80.
[63] Bird to Henrietta Bird, Estes Park, Colorado, Oct. 1873, quoted in Bird, *A Curious Life for a Lady*, p. 98.
[64] Bell, *The Desert and the Sown*, p. 301.
[65] Bell to Florence Bell 5 Mar. 1905, Ba'albek, quoted in Bell, *Letters*, pp. 199–200.

the early century were being filled in with details, if sketchy and often incorrect, which both pinpointed and named courses of rivers, mountains, and inland lakes. The Dark Continent had been put under the piercing light of Victorian scientific energy, and the Savage Lands tamed by missionary endeavour.

The women whose place within this well-ordered Victorian society was firmly delineated, looked for areas where this Victorian zeal had not yet pierced. The landscapes they found were half imaginary – relying on the accounts of earlier travellers to embellish scenes with dangers long since diminished – and half concrete, seeking areas far removed from the encroaching arm of colonial culture. As Gertrude Bell described her longing for the nomadic life of the desert, it was 'half vision and half nightmare'.[66] She wrote from her oriental world,

> We are not accustomed to finding ourselves face to face with nature. Even the most trivial evidences of the lordship of man afford a certain sense of protection – the little path leading you along the easiest slope, the green bench selecting for you the best view, the wooden finger-post with 'Zum Wasserfall' written up upon it telling you what other men thought worth seeing. Other men have been there before . . . . But here there is nothing – nothing but vast and pathless loneliness, silent and desolate.[67]

Mary Gaunt equated the destruction of West African forests with the advance of 'civilisation', and sought an area where still 'the all-conquering white man is dwarfed' by the majestic trunks of giant trees.[68] Travelling overland from Kumasi to Sunyani through the Gold Coast, the dense forest rose like a cathedral about her. 'No wonder the Ashanti gave human sacrifices,' she wrote, 'sacrifice, we all know, is the basis of all faith, and what lesser thing than a man could be offered in so great a sanctuary?'[69] On sighting Singapore at Christmas 1889, Elizabeth Bisland wrote from the deck of her ship, 'The vegetation is enormous, rampant, violent . . . . It stands round that place like an army with banners, ready to rush in at any breach and destroy. It contests every inch of space with man, and aided by incessant heat

66 Bell, *Safar Nameh*, p. 95.
67 Ibid., pp. 87–8.
68 Gaunt, *Alone in West Africa*, p. 355.
69 Ibid., p. 361.

and moisture constantly wrests from him his conquests and buries them in a fury of irridescence.'[70]

Ironically, the threat or imagined threat of danger enhanced the women travellers' sense of control over their lives: it gave them a situation which in the desert, forest, or mountain range, they had to face up to alone, drawing upon their innermost resources to conquer both the surrounding environment and their own fear. Danger was empowering, because it showed women how strong they could, if called upon, be. 'It would have been no good pointing out the dangers,' wrote Mary Gaunt of setting out to West Africa, 'because dangers at a distance are only an incentive. There is something in the thought of danger that must be overcome, that you yourself can help to overcome, that quickens the blood and gives an added zest to life.'[71] Roumanian writer Elena Ghika often escaped the confines of her role as wife of a Russian prince by ascending to the summit of a mountain. But when the experienced mountaineer expressed the desire to go climbing in the Alps, the treachery of the glaciers and the precipices of the Jungfrau were painstakingly pointed out to her. Rather than scare away her ambition, however, 'my curiosity was so much excited by these accounts, that I burned with impatience to commmence the journey. I could think of nothing except those deserts of snow which crowned the summit of the mountains.'[72] Edith Durham earnt the nickname of 'one that could look death in the eyes' as she tramped on undeterred by the threat of Albanians 'behind every rock, and piff, paff, a bullet in your living heart.'[73] She explained the spur to her courage: 'The danger I did not mind. My two months' liberty each year . . . made the endless vista of grey imprisonment at home the more tolerable. And a bullet would have been a short way out.'[74] 'I have nearly all my life possessed an almost unnatural fearlessness of death,' wrote Margaret Fountaine in her diary. 'Passing from one existence to another seems not much more than passing from one country to another.'[75]

[70] Bisland, A Flying Trip Around the World, p. 116.

[71] Gaunt, Alone in West Africa, p. 2.

[72] Dora D'Istria [pseud.; Elena Ghika], Switzerland. The Pioneer of the Reformation or La Suisse Allemande, translated by H. C., (Edinburgh 1858), p. 307.

[73] Edith Durham, Twenty Years of the Balkan Tangle, (London 1920), p. 87.

[74] Ibid., p. 81.

[75] Fountaine, Love Among the Butterflies, p. 61.

In conquering their fear, women travellers displayed to themselves a strength of mind and purpose which surprised even them. Caught in the bad surf leaving Addah, which crashed against the boat and threw the two steersman from the wheel, Mary Gaunt, the only white passenger, stood firm. Ruminating to herself over the likelihood of dying, she tightened her muscles against the roar and determined not to be afraid. In order to impress upon the German Captain her courage in the face of imminent death by drowning, she reached across and whispered in his distracted ear, 'It's magnificent.'[76]

On her first journey unaccompanied through the desert in 1900, Gertrude Bell employed a soldier as escort at Madeba. Twice on a day excursion they were stopped by the horsemen of the Syrian desert, 'armed to the teeth, black browed and menacing. When they saw our soldier they throw us the salaam with some disgust, and after a short exchange of politeness, proceed on their way.' So she described a simple exchange of greetings with a heightened sense of imminent violence, adding nonchalantly at the end of her letter, 'Don't think I've ever spent such a wonderful day.'[77]

Travelling alone increased the imagined risk of dangers and heightened even further the challenges and outreach of their journeys. While so many women travellers had, in private and unshared, been the physical and mental mainstays of their disintegrating families, their power and strength as spinster daughters had not been recognized. But here, in the distant lands, without the companionship of any other European, no one could challenge their claims to achievement. 'It is good to live in this atmosphere,' recorded Edith Durham. 'Many is the tiny, giddy ledge I have crept round without hestitation, driven forward by the cheery shout: "Go on! It is not *eghel* that you will die here." Which I could not have done had an English friend been screaming: "For God's sake, don't try. You will break your neck!" There are countless advantages in travelling with natives only.'[78] Margaret Fountaine wallowed amongst brigands on the island of Corsica after leaving the cultured resort of Venice in 1893. 'Sometimes in the quieter walks of life I love to look back upon that wild mountain scene, the outlaw and his clan, the savage dogs who prowled about among the grey rocks and the purple heather . . . it

---

[76] Gaunt, *Alone in West Africa*, pp. 306–7.

[77] Bell to Hugh Bell 22 Mar. 1900, Ayan Musa, quoted in Bell, *Letters*, p. 71.

[78] Durham, *High Albania*, p. 100.

makes a sharp contrast to the dull peace of an English home.'[79] Mary
Gaunt mused, 'I am never lonely beside the sea; the murmur of the
waves is company, and I cannot explain it, but I am never afraid.'[80]
Marianne North, alone in her Jamaica home, confessed to her journal
that she 'never for an instant had the slightest fear'.[81]

Danger was such an important element in these half visionary, half
nightmare landscapes that where no real danger existed, threats were
imagined. The more imminent death, the more alive the women felt,
for the proximity of death enhanced the immediacy of life. Mary
Gaunt dwelt upon the 1900 Ashanti war and the violence against
Europeans incurred over ten years before her journey. Travelling
missionary sisters Evangeline and Francesca French and Mildred
Cable, crossing Central Asia in 1928, confronted a contingent of the
vigilante volunteer force which patrolled dangerous passes as they
descended the Lu-Pan mountain. But 'in spite of their declared good
intentions we were glad to see them disappear down the mountain
path, for certain of our party had detected in them too striking a
likeness to Boxer bands of 1900.'[82] As Mary Hall explained, 'it is the
imminent probability of danger, rather than the actuality, that
frightens one, but I was willing to risk the adverse possibilities, and
felt a world of interest and excitement lay before me.'[83]

Overcoming threats and imagined threats enhanced the women
travellers' feeling of physical competence in sharp contrast to the
illnesses and lethargy they often suffered at home. Not only their
minds but their cloistered bodies felt a new release. 'I've never felt so
fit,' Ella Christie confided to her diary at over 10,000 feet after six
days of walking over terrain too difficult for ponies to traverse.[84] May
French-Sheldon found the equatorial heat 'a most felicitous contrast
to the London fog, and conducive to mental exhiliration and physical
exuberance.'[85] Gertrude Bell declared, 'the feeling of physical strength
which lets one do all these things is too delicious.'[86] Mary Kingsley,

[margin annotation: Confidence]

[79] Fountaine, *Love Among the Butterflies*, p. 72.

[80] Gaunt, *Alone in West Africa*, p. 277.

[81] North, *Recollections of a Happy Life*, vol. 1, p. 93.

[82] Evangeline French, Mildred Cable and Francesca French, *A Desert Journal. Letters from
Central Asia*, (London 1939 2nd edn; 1934), p. 30.

[83] Hall, *A Woman's Trek from the Cape to Cairo*, p. 145.

[84] Diary entry 11 Sep. 1904, Skardu.

[85] French-Sheldon, *Sultan to Sultan*, p. 22.

[86] Bell, Aug. 1894, quoted in Burgoyne, *Gertrude Bell, 1889–1914*, p. 39.

painfully thin and with a reluctant if not annorexic attitude towards eating, wrote back to Cambridge how Africa was making her feel fat and young again. Even stocky Alexandra David-Neel began to gain more weight under the many layers of her Tibetan clothing. 'Our appetites, after daily mountaineering, were enormous,' she wrote, tucking into a meal of barley-flour paste and buttered tea.[87]

In the open air, eating and sleeping on mountainsides and pushing their bodies to the limit of physical endurance, a new force was awakened within the women travellers. In a very few, such as Margaret Fountaine in her passionate and long lasting love affair with Khalil, a Syrian dragoman, there arose a sexuality unknown as young women. But for most, the sexuality untapped in youth now found expression as sensuality in their middle age. 'Sensuality is to each in his own way,' wrote Alexandra David-Neel to her estranged husband. 'To me, it is being alone, silence, virgin land not disfigured by cultivation, vast spaces, a rude life under the tent.'[88] Mary Kingsley removed her copious clothing for the first time under the open sky, to bathe naked in a West African river, drying herself on her cummerbund. Constance Gordon Cumming also saw her substantial white and fleshy body in the glare of the tropical light, revelling in its freedom from layers of frills. In 1876 she wrote to a member of her family, wrapped up in the Scottish winter, from an island basking in the Pacific Ocean,

> You can hardly realize what an enchanting feature in our travels is our daily bath. No humdrum tub, filled by a commonplace housemaid, but a quiet place on some exquisite stream, sometimes a clear babbling brook, just deep enough to lie down full length, beneath an overarching bower of great tree-ferns and young palm-fronds, all tangled with trailing creepers, and just leaving openings through which you see peeps of the bluest skies, and tall palms far overhead . . . sometimes I come on such irrestible places when I am scrambling about alone, where the tall reedy grasses are matted with large-leaved convolvuli, and not a sound is heard save the ripple of the storm over the stones, or the rustle of the leaves in the faint breeze, that I just slip in and revel, and go on my way rejoicing.

[87] David-Neel, *My Journey to Lhasa*, p. 137.
[88] David-Neel, *Journal de voyage*, vol. 2, p. 54, quoted in Foster, *Forbidden Journey*, p. 170.

On her way home, she picked ripe oranges from the trees to suck on.[89]

The women travellers followed invisible red lines across a map into a distant unknown. But the pot of gold they were chasing was not the mountain, the source of the river, or the oasis in the desert, but the long shadows, cast by the tropical sunlight and mountain glare, of themselves. They had left behind homes which held either unsatisfactory or shattered answers to their quests for their own identities. In the desert and the mangrove swamps, the tenuous hold they still had on the options available to them as single women in Victorian society were dissolved. First, before looking for concrete models on which to remould and rebuild lives, they lost all sense of who they were. No longer a dutiful daughter or a philanthropic maiden aunt, they were simply nomads, lost in the vastness of the wildernesses through which they travelled. By June 1895 Mary Kingsley had ascended the the Ogooué river as far as Lambaréné, 140 miles from the coast. Here she boarded the small French steamer *Éclaireur*, taking her up to Talagouga, determined to ascend still farther and traverse the rapids. Hiring a crew of eight Galoas, they began their ascent in the dark of night. Stopping at a Fang village to have a map of the route drawn on plaintain leaves, they travelled for seventeen hours until fires guided them to the river bank; following the sound of the drums, they landed for the night on Kembe island. Mary walked away from the camp and sat nestled amongst the rocks:

> In the darkness round me flitted thousands of fireflies and out beyond this pool of utter night flew by unceasingly the white foam of the rapids; sound there was none save their thunder.
>
> The majesty and beauty of the scene fascinated me, and I stood leaning with my back against a rock pinnacle watching it. Do not imagine it gave rise, in what I am pleased to call my mind, to those complicated, poetical reflections natural beauty seems to bring out in other people's minds . . . I just lose all sense of human individuality, all memory of human life, with its grief and worry and doubt, and become part of the atmosphere. If I have a heaven, that will be mine.[90]

[89] Constance Gordon Cumming, 'The Teachers House at Lamiti, Isle Ngau', 27 Apr. [1876], *At Home in Fiji*, (Edinburgh 1881), vol. 2, pp. 5–7.
[90] Kingsley, *Travels in West Africa*, p. 178.

Some women travellers expressed this unfamiliar feeling in the familiar language of religious ecstasy. At a summit of the Alps, Elena Ghika found,

> the image of the infinite presented itself to my mind in all its formidable grandeur. My oppressed heart felt it, as I gazed on the Swiss plains, lost in the mist, and the neighbouring mountains which were covered with golden vapours. I conceived such an idea of God that it appeared to me I had never before that day given him sufficient place in my heart . . . . From that moment my soul was lost in the thought of his incomprehensible power.[91]

Others were simply confused by these unexpected and uncomfortable emotions. Mary Hall, who was accompanied on her 1905 Cape to Cairo trip by a large retinue and rarely left the comfort of European settlements, nevertheless wrote how she experienced in the middle of Lake Tanganyika, 'a feeling of unreality . . . I somehow felt as if I had lost my identity.'[92] At the giant ruins of Karnak, Amelia Edwards recorded, 'The scale is too vast; the effect too tremendous; the sense of one's own dumbness, and littleness, and incapacity, too complete and crushing. It is a place that strikes you into silence; that empties you.'[93]

Soon something unarticulated, almost insubstantial began to trickle into the hollow of their lost identities. 'Are we the same people I wonder when all our surroundings, associations, acquaintances are changed?' Gertrude Bell wrote to her cousin Horace Marshall from Gulahek. 'Here that which is me, which womanlike is an empty jar that the passer by fills at pleasure, is filled with such wine as in England I had never heard of . . . I conclude, cousin mine, that it is not the person who danced with you at Mansfield Street that writes to you today from Persia . . . I remember you as a dear person in a former existence . . . . How big the world is, how big and how wonderful.'[94] Margaret Fountaine wrote in her diary, 'During my short stay abroad I had learnt to enjoy life in a new way. The great void was being filled.'[95]

[91] Ghika, *Switzerland. The Pioneer*, vol. 2, p. 324.
[92] Hall, *A Woman's Trek from the Cape to Cairo*, p. 185.
[93] Edwards, *A Thousand Miles Up the Nile*, p. 148.
[94] Bell to Horace Marshall 18 June 1892, Gulahek, quoted in Bell, *Letters*, p. 25.
[95] Fountaine, *Love Among the Butterflies*, p. 56.

Children in Mandalay, Burma, 1905. Photograph by Ella Christie.
Reproduced by kind permission of Robert Stewart.

Many women began to question who and what they were, and
where they could find a role and meaning for their travels. 'If you
stand up before an audience in a civilised land you know what you are
there for, and you either succeed or fail,' wrote Mary Gaunt. 'But
sitting before a subdued crowd clad in Manchester cotton or simply a
smile, with all eyes centred on you, I at least feel that my role is
somewhat different. What on earth am I to do?'[96] Mary Kingsley wrote
to Lady Macdonald, wife of the Commissioner General of the Oil
Rivers Protectorate with whom she had sailed on her second 1895
journey to West Africa, 'I am really beginning to think that the
traveller – properly so called – the person who writes a book and gets

[96] Gaunt, *Alone in West Africa*, p. 107.

his FRGS [Fellow of the Royal Geographical Society] etc, is a peculiar sort of animal only capable of seeing a certain set of things and always seeing them the same way, and you and me are not of this species somehow. What are we to call ourselves?'[97] On arriving in Cairo, fellow guests at Shepheard's Hotel had wanted to know from Amelia Edwards and her friend three things – 'where these two wandering Englishwomen had come from; why they had not dressed for dinner; what brought them to Egypt.'[98]

Where the women themselves could provide no answers, others proferred them. It was presumed that Beatrix Bulstrode, travelling second class from Peking to Mongolia in 1913, either had a husband in first class and among English people it was customary to treat wives as inferior; or was the wife of a Swedish missionary; or was an obscure scholar because of the number of books she carried. In fact she was travelling, according to her own account, because of her 'fascination of the unknown', and once she had begun 'instead of turning my face homewards, I merely felt the compelling desire for more.'[99] On board ship West Africa-bound, Mary Kingsley was presumed to be a missionary by her fellow voyagers, until she failed to recite her prayers correctly one Sunday service. They then became equally assured of her status as a botanist from the Royal Botanic Gardens at Kew.[100]

After crossing new horizons into a fresh mental and physical world, women travellers looked for a part to play in these foreign landscapes which would at once legitimize and prolong their travels. Options were offered in which they could, as middle-class Victorian women, be included to varying degrees. Those who had initially shared the experience of the freedom on their journeys away from studies, sickrooms and parlours and over the garden fence, now took different paths. Some would look towards the new professions of anthropology and archaeology, others to botanical pursuits. A few would attempt to remain travellers, writing and lecturing on their journeys. They were all to find that though they had crossed one horizon, many more still lay ahead.

[97] Kingsley to Ethel Macdonald quoted in Stephen Gwynn, *Mary Kingsley*, (London 1933), p. 131.

[98] Edwards, *A Thousand Miles Up the Nile*, p. 2.

[99] Beatrix Bulstrode, *A Tour in Mongolia*, (London 1920), p. 1.

[100] Kingsley, *West African Studies*, pp. 12–13.

3

The Borders of Gentility

Although the horizons towards which the women travellers journeyed remained indistinct, mysterious and hazy, what they travelled away from, even in remote lands, was concrete, established and familiar, embodied in the buildings, dress and exaggerated traditions of exiled and colonial communities. These were the centres at which women travellers disembarked on their first day in the continent of their dreams. Here they might meet other white women who had been transplanted from Britain to Africa, Asia and Australasia as wives or sisters of colonial officials and missionaries, whose function was not just to reproduce the homes they had left behind but to reinforce them – to build an English middle-class castle in the desert.

To achieve this, a vast amount of paraphernalia was brought out from Britain in packing cases and trunks containing household goods, clothes and even tinned food. Dress, furniture, forms of address and social activities all assumed a ritualistic importance abroad unnecessary amid the familiar ordering of society at home. Gardens were planted in the heart of arid lands and roses nurtured in soil more fitted to growing tropical flowers.

To maintain the distance from surrounding societies upon which their authority rested, colonial communities had to fortify their own sense of Victorian middle-class identity. While local people dressed in clothing more suitable to their environment, Europeans wrote sweaty letters home asking for flannel underwear, evening gowns and the indispensable hat. The sun itself was an enemy to be combatted and avoided at all costs; preservation of a white skin carried not only racial implications but, for white women, the notion of purity and fragility. Violet Cragg, an administrator's wife in Nigeria in the 1920s, even wore her sun helmet in the bath for fear that the roof of their temporary accommodation might not be fully ray-proof.[1] Constance Larymore, rich with advice for the prospective colonial wife, counselled that apparently hidden and very private symbols of turn-of-the-century British life were still vital. '*Always* wear corsets, even for tête-à-tête home dinner on the warmest evenings; there is something about their absence almost as demoralising as hair in curling-pins!' she wrote, making an explicit connection between maintaining class and race differences through the most intimate dress.[2] When Flora Shaw, colonial editor of the *Times*, became Lady Lugard, wife of the Governor of Northern Nigeria, she gave up her stern professional old-fashioned black dresses for white gowns, and drifted unhappily around the verandah at Zungeru with the outward appearance at least of a colonial woman.[3]

Inside the colonial home, furniture and decoration assumed enormous importance in the rituals of dinner parties and afternoon tea or 'tiffin'. When the first few European nurses arrived in Lagos in 1900, they were well provided for with a quarters equipped with rocking chair, egg poacher, gravy boiler, lime squeezer, crumb brush and sugar tongs.[4] While Marianne North spent cold London winters painting colour into the pen sketches she had hurriedly made on her travels, at Bida Constance Larymore suggested the colonial wife decorate her quarters with pictures of England. 'It is a joy sometimes, when the temperature is unpleasantly high, little worries abounding, and *Africa* asserting itself unduly, to be able to glance occasionally at a sketch of some English woodland, or a corner of a picturesque village,' she explained.[5]

Whether in Hong Kong, Calabar or Simla, colonial residences were perched high above the thriving and thronging bazaars and low-lying huts housing local populations, in the belief that higher living was healthier living. As women travellers looked out from these colonial verandahs, feelings were stirred similar to those experienced while peering from behind the windows of their bedrooms, sickrooms and

---

[1] Helen Callaway, *Gender, Culture and Empire. European Women in Colonial Nigeria*, (London 1987), p. 170.

[2] Larymore, *A Resident's Wife in Nigeria*, p. 300.

[3] E. Moberly Bell, *Flora Shaw (Lady Lugard DBE)*, (London 1947), p. 244.

[4] 'Inventory of Furniture etc. European Nurses' Quarters, Lagos Hospital' (1900), Overseas Nursing Association archives.

[5] Larymore, *A Resident's Wife in Nigeria*, p. 198.

studies at home. The Consul-General's residence in Calabar, where Mary Kingsley was a guest on her second journey, sat high on the hillside overlooking the wide river and settlement of Creek Town, its orange roofs nestling among the rich green vegetation on the opposite bank. A large white two-storey building, the Residency highlighted the occupants' physical and emotional isolation from the surrounding environment. With their wooden shutters, mosquito nets and planned gardens, the colonial communities fought back the encroaching desert, jungle or swamp from their porticoed front doors and erected barriers to block out the African or Asian world.

Determined to maintain and reinforce their difference from the culture which enveloped them, nascent European communities entrenched themselves in manners which reflected styles already outdated in Britain. Even in Australia, Marianne North noticed that, 'the hospitality in Brisbane was of the heavy order, great luncheon-parties, with soup and fish, and four-corner dishes, roast and boiled, etc., as it was forty years ago in England, – and I was glad to escape to the hills.'[6]

In the early development of an exiled and in particular colonial community, there was rarely a well-defined female place, the largely male population resisting the intrusion of white women into the masculine domain of imperial and frontier expansion. At first shunned for appearing to bring the parlours and polite society of Britain with them to the far posts of the Empire, women were gradually drawn into the colonial enterprise. Unable to rely solely on physical and military force in the face of vast outnumbering by local populations, social distance was employed as a tool of control and division between the colonial and the colonized. Wives and sisters were, often reluctantly at first, incorporated into the elaborate and rigid forms of social organization and ceremony through which this distance was expressed. They became embodiments of fossilized Victorian middle-class values abroad, their place within the colonial hierarchies of race and sex as fixed as that of the colonial subjects.

The degree of white women's inclusion differed with the stage of development of imperial control. In India, the 1857 'Indian Mutiny' was a poignant reminder of the limits of British power and the perceived need to bolster might with public displays of wealth and

[6] North, *Recollections of a Happy Life*, vol. 2, p. 111.

prestige, in which women soon played a crucial part. However, in many places in West Africa where British rule was not formalized until the turn of the century, white women's role within colonial culture was not clearly demarcated and their presence proved an embarrassment. Although Mary Kingsley was forbidden to be alone with a single black missionary by her European male fellow passengers on her 1893 voyage down the West African coast, neither was there a place for her within the small white community, still largely consisting of traders and missionaries. Feeling uncomfortably out of place in the 'Society' of the officers, as she called it, Mary would often excuse herself from their company and wander alone around the ports of call. She wrote to her childhood friend Violet Roy from Matadi on the Congo River how she wriggled out of a potentially awkward situation: 'I as usual confined myself to soda water and went off to the *Lagos* – on the plea of being tired – as soon as dessert was served, but I heard sound of revelry by night until I fell asleep and this morning the Captain seems sad and headachy.'[7]

Nearly twenty years later, Mary Gaunt was still writing from West Africa on the incongruity of being a single woman in colonial society. 'The Club may have been a cheerful place if you knew anyone, but it is very doleful and depressing if the only other women look sidelong at you over the tops of their papers as if you were some curious specimen that it might perhaps be safer to avoid,' she wrote in Accra. Although invited to stay at Christiansborg Castle by the Acting Governor, the colonial official was 'inclined to regard a travelling woman as a pernicious nuisance.'[8] Even as late as the 1930s, in Bende in the Niger Delta, colonial wife Aileen Chubb was the only white woman at dinner parties, so 'it was very awkward when it came to the time when ladies had to retire and the men drank their port,' she remembers. 'I used to sit in the bedroom, forgotten by everyone, even my husband, not knowing what to do, whether to go back, stay in the bedroom or what?'[9]

Yet over fifty years earlier, Marianne North had found in the hill resorts of the Raj a well-defined place awaiting white women residents – an inclusion, however, no more attractive than Mary Kingsley's exclusion. She noted how the white men at Simla were accustomed to

---

[7] Kingsley to Violet Roy 10 Oct. 1893, Matadi, Congo River.

[8] Gaunt, *Alone in West Africa*, pp. 190 and 180.

[9] Joan Alexander, *Voices and Echoes. Tales from Colonial Women*, (London 1983), p. 71.

'feminine helplessness', refusing to believe her determination to move on despite the rains.[10] At the time of her visit in 1878, the Lyttons were the viceregal couple who governed Britain's largest possession and had introduced a heightened sense of pageantry and pomp to colonial life. Marianne noted with some distaste this emphasis on form and presentation, commenting that, although living in the same India which she had found teeming with specimens to paint, the vicereine knew little of country life and the viceroy was 'one of the people who look best in a photograph'.[11] He had further courted her disdain by introducing her as 'the accomplished sister of an accomplished brother-in-law', 'rather a poverty of adjectives', she curtly pointed out.[12] For one who had left Britain in search of a new definition of herself, this was a poignant reminder of her relative value in home society and its exaggerated representative – colonial life. This was further confirmed at a Sunday night dinner at the colonial hill resort of Simla, where her enjoyment of the stimulating conversation of Alfred Lyall, a scholar of Indian languages and culture as well as the Governor General's agent in Rajputana, was cut short when discussion did not begin in earnest until 'Mrs Lyall and myself had been replaced by cigars.'[13]

It was while near and living in these strictly ordered colonial communities that the women travellers' single status was most often questioned. While among the Fang peoples in the interior of Gabon Mary Kingsley complained she was always called 'Sir', when she met a bible-reading West African in a canoe returning from Lambaréné island he wanted to know, 'Where be your husband, ma?' 'I no got one,' the spinster answered. 'No got,' he replied with astonishment. 'No got one, ma?' 'No,' replied Mary furiously, and attempted to change the subject – 'Do you get much rubber round here?' But the convert would not be budged: 'Why you no got one?' 'The remainder of the conversation is unreportable,' Mary summed up.[14] Mary Gaunt recorded on her coastal journey, 'When they asked me, as they often did, how my husband was, I always explained that he was very well,

[10] North, *Recollections of a Happy Life*, vol. 2, p. 11.
[11] North to Arthur Burnell 6 June 1878, At Mr Egerton's, Lt. Governor Punjab, Simla.
[12] North to Arthur Burnell 7 Oct. 1878, '14,000 feet above the sea', Sundukju.
[13] North to Arthur Burnell 17 July 1878, At Mrs A. C. Lyall's, Simla.
[14] Kingsley, *Travels in West Africa*, pp. 216–17.

and had gone on a journey; it saved a lot of trouble.'[15] In a Chinese
mission station, the traveller was again asked if she had any sons. She
gently placed her hand on the arm of the young missionary sitting next
to her and lied, 'He is my son.'[16] Before reaching Egypt, Amelia
Edwards found in a territory closer to home, the Dolomites, that she
was greeted with commiserations of 'Alone, and not married!
Poverine! poverine!' when after long interregation it was discovered
she was single.[17] 'They all cry "poverine" in chorus, with an air of
such genuine concern and compassion that we are almost ashamed of
the irrepressible laughter with which we cannot help receiving their
condolences,' Amelia wrote. In Central Europe, Edith Durham was
continually questioned on her marital status. At Cetinje, the traveller
was greeted with cheers of 'Bravo' when it was learnt she had travelled
by train and steamboat just to see the Montenegrans. She must of
course be a very rich lady from a land full of gold – and unmarried,
what luck! A coy youth was immediately thrust forward as a husband.
Edith demurred with a polite, 'No, thankyou.' 'Five offers in twenty
minutes is about my highest record,' she added.[18]

While the single white woman might not have a defined place
within colonial society, one white man could nevertheless constitute
that same society and the restrictions it implied – as Marianne had
found when travelling in the company of her father, and as Mary
Kingsley found with the German official posted in Buea at the foot of
Mount Cameroon. When she arrived at his remote station, splattered
with mud from the rainy-season road, Mary was immediately
concerned with her appearance and reverted to expected social
conventions and attitudes. While she had bathed naked in West
African rivers, with nothing but her cummerbund as a towel, she
refused to wash in his doorless, broken-shuttered house.[19]

When Gertrude Bell returned from her first desert journey through
the Middle East and embarked upon a round-the-world trip with her
brother Hugo in 1903, she too found that just one man could invoke
 rigid observance of divisions between the sexes. On the Irawaddy,
Hugo's arrival immediately altered the way in which she was perceived

[15] Gaunt, *Alone in West Africa*, pp. 289–90.
[16] Gaunt, *A Woman in China*, pp. 318–19.
[17] Edwards, *Untrodden Peaks and Unfrequented Valleys*, pp. 321–2.
[18] Durham, *Through the Lands of the Serb*, p. 10.
[19] Kingsley, *Travels in West Africa*, p. 563.

by her Indian hosts. Asked into a monks' home as she walked along the street, she had been sitting crossed-legged on the floor and, talking through the interpretation of a young member of the order, 'they laughed till their yellow robes fell off their bare shoulders.' But when her brother appeared, 'I was of no account at all . . . Hugo taught the little monk to shake hands when we came away, but he wouldn't shake hands with me. He oughtn't even to have looked at me.'[20] When negotiating with the chief of Lokoja on her Central African journey in the company of the Talbots, Olive Macleod found 'he was courtly in manner, and appeared really interested in Mr Talbot's projects, but Mrs Talbot and I counted for exactly nothing at all.'[21]

women bottom of hierarchy

Men, too, keenly felt the need to conform to social conventions in the presence of just one white woman. When Ella Christie met the first Englishman for a fortnight in the mountains of Ladakh, she recorded in her journal,

> such a nice question for Vanity Fair, when A met B in the wilds of Asia not having been introduced what should he do? This A stopped his pony, then got off and bowed and I asked him if he came from Leh, and if the road were clear. He smiled and asked where I came from, and even attempted to improve his appearance by removing his smoked glasses, but forgot his Turkish bath-towel was hanging down his back, either to dry it or as a spine protector, but these are such trifles in these parts. My dress is of the shabbiest.[22]

The women travellers' first ports of call usually housed the main administrative and political centre of the white community. It was in the heart of the West African colonial society that Mary Kingsley landed in 1895. When she left Liverpool on board the *Batanga* the previous December in the company of Lady Ethel Macdonald, wife of the Consul-General to the Oil Rivers, Mary had embarked on a very different voyage and set of experiences from those of eighteen months previously as the only white woman West Africa-bound. Her 1893

[20] Bell to Florence Bell 2 Mar. 1903, On the Irawaddy, quoted in Bell, *Letters*, p. 159.

[21] Olive Macleod, *Chiefs and Cities of Central Africa, Across Lake Chad by the Way of British, French and German Territories*, (Edinburgh 1912), p. 10.

[22] Diary entry 14 Aug. 1904, Reimm.

Mary Kingsley (centre front) in front of the Residency in Calabar, 1895. To Mary Kingsley's left and right are Lady Ethel and Sir Claude Macdonald, Consul-General of the Oil Rivers. Ralph Locke (left, back row) and Roger Casement (right, back row).
Royal Commonwealth Society.

sailing companions had been merchants and missionaries, and brief forays to trading factories and hulks had been made from the small stations at which they docked on the outlets of the Niger and Gabon rivers. But in 1895 she wrote home, 'I have had a most interesting journey out and being with Lady Macdonald have had great opportunities of seeing a new phase of West African life, namely the Governmental.' This 'new phase' was not what she had had in mind when leaving Britain: 'I must say it is inferior in interest to my former circle of acquaintances – the traders, usually called palm-oil ruffians.'[23] Strolls alone around Freetown markets were replaced by organized tours and introductions to local officials, European and African. 'Going on shore at Accra with Lady Macdonald gave me opportunities and advantages I should not otherwise have enjoyed,' she wrote with a hint of irony, 'such as the hospitality of the Governor, luxurious transport from the landing place to Christiansborg Castle, a thorough inspection of the cathedral in the course of erection,' (which would have delighted the confirmed atheist), 'and the strange and highly interesting function of going to a tea-party at a police station to meet a king, – a real reigning king – who kindly attended with his suite.'[24]

Although she gained audiences with prominent Africans and Europeans, in the company of an official's wife Mary's movements were controlled as a male visitor's would not have been. As a female guest of 'Officialdom', as she called the small British administrative centre at Calabar, she was doubly removed from the African society and culture she had come to the West Coast to observe – as a result of the isolation first of official life itself, and secondly of her status as a woman within it which allowed little room for independent action and absorbed much of her time in social engagements. While Sir Claude Macdonald took reconnaissance trips into the interior and went to Brass in the aftermath of an indigenous uprising against the Royal Niger Company, his wife was kept in residence at Calabar until it was considered safe for her to join her husband. With an unquestioning assumption, which she shared with Gertrude Bell, of immunity in the face of violence, Mary was angered at being prevented from viewing such an important event at first hand. She wrote to her friend Hatty Johnson, 'this affair at Akassa has been a

---

[23] Kingsley to Albert Günther 2 Feb. 1895, Consulate, Old Calabar.
[24] Kingsley, *Travels in West Africa*, p. 30.

horrible one. I feel bitterly disappointed at not having been in it as I should have been had I not come out with Lady Macdonald.'[25]

Ridicule was a form of mute criticism often invoked by women travellers in their portrayals of colonial society. Their keen and critical eyes saw how a nascent colonial community, whose authority depended upon maintaining distance from the surrounding society, could most easily express this difference in buildings, dress and the creation of traditions. With cool detachment, they unflinchingly pointed to many of the inappropriate customs and manners they observed. Mary Kingsley had a particularly cruel vision, and on spotting a strange-looking object in the dining saloon of the steamer taking her down the West Coast, recorded the process by which she deduced its identity:

> I see an apparition on the settee opposite. Is it fever coming on?
> Or does it arise from having got some brain cells permanently
> shaken out of their place by that gun shock this afternoon? I
> don't seem to see it, for fear of exciting their derision, but watch
> it furtively during dinner. It does not move or multiply itself, nor
> has it any phospherescent halo. Good signs, all these, but it still
> cannot be a black silk chimney-pot hat. After all it was, and
> belongs to the Captain. How or why or when he got it, I do not
> know – neither do I exactly know what he and the passengers do
> with it.[26]

Sitting on a hard-backed chair among a row of ladies on the immense verandah of Christiansborg Castle, where Mary Gaunt declined to sleep fifteen years later, Mary Kingsley looked out at the crashing sea which had brought her this far and almost drowned the genteel talk:

> In the middle of January I found conversation with a new-comer
> consisted of 'you should have been here last week.' 'Eh?' 'You
> should have been here last week when we had the races (f) . . .'
> Another individual, whose name you do not catch, is intro-

---

[25] Kingsley to Hatty Johnson 'July or August' 1895, Consulate, Old Calabar.
[26] Kingsley, *Travels in West Africa*, p. 140.

duced. He says something. You say 'Eh?' He says, 'You should have been here last week when we had our races (*ff*).' Then comes the details as before, and so on, *da capo*, throughout the evening.[27]

Amelia Edwards, who never entirely shrugged off conventionality to the extent Mary could, still pointed to the absurdity of maintaining British notions of propriety when attending a festival in the 'Convent of Howling Dervishes' in Cairo:

Being accommodated with chairs among the other spectators, we waited for whatever might happen. More dervishes and more English dropped in from time to time. The new dervishes took off their caps and sat down among the rest, laughing and talking together at ease. The English sat in a row, shy, uncomfortable, and silent; wondering whether they ought to behave as if they were in church, and mortally ashamed of their feet. For we had all been obliged to take off or cover our boots before going in, and those who had forgotten to bring slippers had their feet tied up in pocket-handkerchiefs.[28]

Sometimes women travellers openly ridiculed their own attempts at colonial etiquette. Mary Gaunt described trying to host a dinner party in a cabin at Fatta Tenda, which began with a servant spilling kerosene over the table cloth and ended half way through when their meal was invaded by a swarm of flying ants.

When women travellers met European female residents of distant lands they would contrast rather than compare these expatriate women's lives and attitudes to their own. At the start of the rainy season, Mary Gaunt set out from Sekondi in the company of an English nursing sister. Within a few hours she was regretting her decision, as the young woman was unaccustomed to getting her feet wet even in a tropical downpour. Mary reaffirmed, 'I decided that never again as long as I lived would I travel with another woman. I know my own short comings, but I never know where another woman

[27] Ibid., pp. 34–5.
[28] Edwards, *A Thousand Miles Up the Nile*, pp. 28–9.

will break out.'[29] Gertrude Bell was also keen to distance herself from the newly-arrived British nurses in Baghdad. 'Heaven forbid I should grudge them their entertainments, only I don't want to share them, for they reduce conversation to words of one syllable. I shall therefore go to no more ladies' dinners,' she announced.[30] Like Mary Gaunt, Gertrude looked through male-tinted eyes when portraying the wives of British officials and shared the common prejudice that their presence and manner was to blame for the deterioration of race relations. 'It's the wives that do it, confound them,' she wrote bluntly. 'They take no sort of interest in what's going on, know no Arabic and see no Arabs. They created an exclusive (it's also very second rate) English society quite cut off from the life of the town. I now begin to understand why the British Government has come to grief in India, where out women do just the same thing.'[31]

Women travellers emphasized the supposed femininity of colonial women against their own unfeminine roles, often referring to the colonial women as girls in contrast to their own middle age. From the outset of their time spent together, Mary Kingsley highlighted the difference between 'the very sweet and gracious' Ethel Macdonald, with her family responsibilities, and her own scientific and single status.[32] She also drew unnecessary attention to the fragility of the missionary wives who, although resident in tropical countries, were, in theory at least, conforming to the role of wife and mother. At the Mission Évangélique in Talagouga on the Ogooué river, she noted how Madame Forget, 'is a perfectly lovely French girl, with a pale transparent skin and the most perfect great dark eyes, with indescribable charm, grace of manner, and vivacity in conversation.' Mary contrasted her own looks sharply with those of another missionary wife; Madame Gaçon is 'the lady the planter took me for; and when I saw her, with her sweet young face and masses of pale gold-coloured hair, I felt highly flattered. Either that planter must be very short sighted or the colour of my hair must have misled him, not that mine is pale gold, but hay-coloured. I don't know how he did it.'[33]

[29] Gaunt, *Alone in West Africa*, p. 315.

[30] Bell to Hugh Bell 8 Feb. 1918, Baghdad, quoted in Burgoyne, *Gertrude Bell, 1914–1926*, p. 77.

[31] Bell, 18 June 1921, quoted in ibid., pp. 220–1.

[32] Kingsley, *Travels in West Africa*, p. 12.

[33] Ibid., p. 152.

Similarly, Mary Gaunt, a vociferous critic of pampered colonial women in West Africa, compared her own sunburnt face and small stout figure to that of the idealized colonial woman. When she asked a District Commissioner at McCarthy Island why he didn't bring his wife out to West Africa with him,

> He looked at me a moment, seeking words to show his opinion of a woman who insisted upon going where he thought no white woman was needed.
>
> 'My wife,' he said, with emphasis that marked his surprise; 'my wife? Why, my wife has such a delicate complexion that she has to wash her face always in distilled water.'
>
> It was sufficient. I understood when I looked in the glass that night the reproof intended to be conveyed.[34]

It was also impressed upon Marianne North that her feminine qualities were endangered by her refusal to submit to a sedentary life. While she was staying in a railway hotel at Grahamstown in South Africa in 1882,

> One day I had missed breakfast, and came in hungry and glad to get a cup of tea and bread and butter, three girls forced themselves into my room, with a crowd of others behind them, and began asking me stupid questions till I fairly lost my temper. 'Was I not afraid of spoiling my eyes? I ought to save them.' I asked her in return what eyes were made for, and did she think it would be any use to leave them behind me? Like her beloved diamonds or gold, what good would it do to save them? She thought me mad, and they all fled, and at last I got my breakfast.[35]

Women travellers' relationships with these exiled and colonial communities and the images and options they offered were ambiguous and complex – conditioned both by the time of their journeys, the areas to which they travelled and their own temperament. They were often individually inconsistent in their attitudes towards colonial life;

---

[34] Gaunt, *Alone in West Africa*, p. 34.
[35] North, *Recollections of a Happy Life*, vol. 2, pp. 248–9.

the same traveller could at one time fall back upon the comfort and security it seemed to provide and at another passionately reject its offer of hospitality. Behind the criticism, avoidance, ridicule and contrasts so frequently and emphatically made by the women travellers lay a troubled relationship between their own experiences as travellers and those as colonial women.

However much they appeared to shun the role of the colonial wife and helpmate, all the women travellers embodied, to varying degrees, parts of that same image within themselves. At times of crisis or self-questioning they would fall upon the ritual and familiarity this image offered. In shunning colonial society, many women travellers were also pushing away this part of themselves which they preferred to deny. Marianne North's reaction to colonial company swung from vehement and even violent rejection – 'vegetables suited me better' – to an embrace of its security and comfort.[36] Her scarcely concealed disgust at what she saw as the superficiality and ceremony of colonial life was partly anger at herself for only fitfully being able to break away. When a female member of the Ceylonese colonial community came to 'rescue' her from her blissful solitude, Marianne 'felt like a naughty child being taken back to school, to be punished, I had had such peace at Padura, and had painted so luxuriously and satisfactorily, and hoped to do so much more, but felt quite powerless to resist when the old lady sailed in, with all her flowing drapery and fascinating ways.'[37] Her letters home alternated wildly between pining for colonial comfort and, once embedded in it, writhing in frustration at its cosiness and yearning to break away. 'I am only wasting my time amongst these Anglo-Indian swells,' she wrote from Simla.[38] In Sarawak in 1880, as a guest of the Raja, Marianne literally sat on the border between the two worlds, as behind her chatted the long-gowned white women, supping on a full and formal dinner, and before her a naked man fished:

> I got into disgrace by preferring to sit and look at the moonlight and lights of Kuching reflected on the water, on the cool verandah, instead of joining the dismal circle round the glaring

[36] Ibid., p. 99.
[37] Manuscript of autobiography, p. 711.
[38] North to Arthur Burnell 22 July 1878, At Mrs A. C. Lyall's, Simla.

lamp-lit drawing-room, with its splendid straight-backed ch carved with Rajah-like coats of arms, and leather cushions whi seem to invite white ants. That river always attracted m making me forget all manners. One evening I watched a ma (quite clotheless) throwing his net from the smallest of canoes, and an infant of four years old paddling at the other end. Why did not the thing tip up? I could not understand; or why the man did not throw himself out as well as his net. His movements were so perfectly graceful and secure, far better worth studying than the everlasting Venuses and Apollos of so-called 'High Art'.[39]

But somehow, for a reason inexplicable even to herself, Marianne was never fully able to break the bond between her British and travelling self, causing her much self-destructive anguish. In Japan, the British Minister Sir Harry Parkes and his wife asked if she would join them on the government steamer round the islands on an inspection of lighthouses. Marianne was so unable to decide whether to tear herself away from their company or accept the invitation that she developed, as was often her recourse, 'a terrible attack of pain', and took an injection of morphine which put her to sleep for twenty-four hours. By the time she awoke from her self-induced slumber and recovered from her drowsiness the official launch had sailed, and Marianne set off for Kyoto where she remained apart from the company of other Europeans for three months.[40] Psychosomatic illness would plague Marianne throughout her life, and force a decision which, inevitably denying one or other part of her, was too painful for her to make openly herself.

Many women travellers tried physically to avoid colonial settlements, but they inevitably touched them at every hotel catering for Europeans, every trading post, every colonial residence. Although seeking to shun the confines of their gardens, it was often, to a large extent, their sway and control over local populations which empowered their own travels as white women in colonized or colonizing societies. So while often spurning the restrictions they faced as women within colonial communities, they carried these same trappings as cultural baggage on their lone journeys. Most notably, women

* women promote imperialism

---

[39] North, *Recollections of a Happy Life*, vol. 2, p. 94.
[40] Ibid., vol. 1, p. 216.

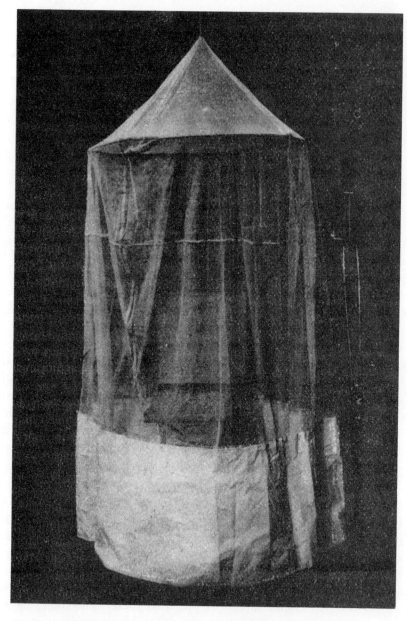

Isabella Bird's mosquito net and photographic equipment.
Bodleian Library, Oxford.

travellers claimed to have dressed with the same fastidious attachment to notions of British middle-class propriety that had been expected of and practised by them at home. Mary Kingsley said she stomped through swamps and tropical forests in a high-necked, muttonchop-sleeved blouse and long black skirt, brandishing an umbrella as a weapon before her. Amelia Edwards wore a 'hideous palm-leaf hat' with green veil and, as added insurance against harmful rays, carried a large white umbrella. Mary Gaunt stares out from the cover of her first travel book enrobed in white lace, her lightly curled hair decorated with dainty ornaments, provoking the reader to wonder just how someone who looked so fragile and so feminine could travel so long and so alone along the West African coast. Even Gertrude Bell wrote home to ask her mother to send her a double-brimmed hat to protect her from the oriental sun. Isabella Bird claimed to wear a construction on her tiny bunned head,

> similar to those worn by the Japanese Jinricksha runners. It consists of two rings of split bamboo round the head, with four uprights, forming a sort of cage. On the top of this is placed the hat, which is an inverted basin of split bamboo, not weighing more than 4oz. This is covered with quilted white cotton. When travelling in the heat, I place under this hat, next to my head, a folded towel, wrung out in water, the end of which hangs down my back. When possible, I keep this damp during the day. As an additional precaution, I have a pad of cotton wool, five inches wide, tacked down the centre seam of my ulster or jacket to protect the spine.

This contraption bears some resemblance to the girdle she once wore for her disability. To protect her face from being scorched by the sun, she 'made a mask of wash leather with holes in it for the eyes, tying it on by tapes round the back of the head. I also had several folds of nuns' veiling outside of this, in front of the face.'[41] As did Marianne North and Mary Kingsley, Isabella wrote of being in excellent health in temperatures well into the hundreds, yet designed her clothing to protect her from the same heat which provided such energy.

[41] 'The Art of Travelling. An Interview with Mrs J. F. Bishop FRGS' (Isabella Bird), *Climate*, vol. 1, (1900), p. 118.

While many women travellers spurned the made-up beds, regular mealtimes and excess of servants in the colonial household, they would also, at times of severe stress, long for the familiarity of the social rituals they had left behind. As in Britain, they were torn by the two voices within themselves – a need to belong and a longing to fly away. These rituals retained a disproportionate importance, becoming the one aspect of their home life to which they would cling. Even Mary Gaunt was not immune from 'breaking out', taking up a pack of cards and playing sole bridge on a portable table dutifully erected by her African travelling companion and cook, Grant. Gertrude Bell lined the path leading up to her Baghdadi summerhouse home with pots of carnations, roses, stock and larkspur, wilting in temperatures of up to 120 degrees. When she ventured into the desert, she took the essential symbols of the culture she was born into with her. Vita Sackville-West recorded meeting Gertrude when 'she had arrived straight out of the desert, with all the evening dresses and cutlery and napery that she insisted on taking with her on her wanderings.'[42] Isabella Bird, in a cabin in the Rockies in which she could see the night stars through a hole in the roof, took out her knitting – another reminder of who and what she was, the woman she could only ever partially leave behind.

Christmas, a ceremony which in their home lives would have provided a rich and certain procedure to follow, proved a poignant test of the women travellers' degree of identification with colonial culture. They often described in great detail their first experience of this festivity away from home. In their different celebrations are revealed the tensions between wanting to leave behind the social manners of home society yet be able to rely upon the ritual and meaning it provided.

On 25 December 1907, Mary Hall awoke at Hoima in Uganda to a Christmas morning 'as different from a Christmas morning at home as it is possible to imagine'. She sat down alone at a table on the broad verandah to eat her lunch. 'I had tinned soup, a scraggy chicken – price twopence – which by a wild flight of imagination I tried to magnify to the proportions of a turkey, and I finished with the *pièce de résistance* in the shape of a tinned plum-pudding.' Nature provided her with the Christmas decorations, for 'the whole was eaten during a

---

[42] Quoted in Bell, *Letters*, p. 751.

magnificent display of lightning.'[43] On her first Christmas on the African continent in 1873, Amelia Edwards was tempted to reflect back to the scene in her Westbury-on-Trym cottage where, 'there are fires blazing at home in every room; that the familiar bells are ringing merrily across the frosty air. Here at midday it is already too hot on deck without the awning.' On their *dahabeeyah* on the Nile, the guests invited from a neighbouring boat did not arrive by carriage but *felucca*, and were summoned not by dinner gong but by a gun, while 'the stars and the crescent moon shone overhead' as fairy lights. But the smallest gesture assumed enormous importance, as Amelia recorded, for not until 'the plum-pudding, blazing demoniacally, appeared upon the scene, did any of us succeed in believing that it was really Christmas Day.'[44]

In December 1904, at the age of forty-three, Ella Christie spent her first Christmas away from home. As she climbed to over 10,000 feet on her way north to Tibet, her sister Alice wrote in minutest detail of the family scene at Murdostoun. She reassured Ella that she had sent presents, in Ella's name, so even in her absence Christmas rituals and duties were duly observed. Marianne North, like Mary Hall and Ella Christie, had dined alone on her first Christmas away, and spent the day wandering around the Jamaican markets with the landlady of her hotel, admiring the black women traders in their best attire and listening to the local band. Six years later, on another distant Christmas on a different continent, Marianne was forcefully reminded of her ambiguous position as a single woman in colonial society. A British artillery battalion, with its tents, guns, camels and elephants, was occupying the compound when she stayed in the guest bungalow. Marianne sketched the busy scene outside her room as the wives prepared the Christmas lunch. She looked up from her easel but remained apart, an observer and outsider to British family life, for fear they might snub 'such a shabby old thing'. She noted the smallest differences between her own world and theirs – how white their skins were under their helmets (Marianne never wore a hat) – how the women cooked for their men (Marianne only ever cooked for herself) – and was relieved when the camp moved on later that same day. 'At last they cleared off, and the great vultures came and picked the bones left by the beef-eating sahibs, and I ate my bit of cold mutton and

[43] Hall, *A Woman's Trek from the Cape to Cairo*, pp. 331 and 335.
[44] Edwards, *A Thousand Miles Up the Nile*, p. 88.

bread, cooked my own tea in my etna, enjoying it as much as most people do mince-pies, plum-pudding, and the "family party" it is part of the English religion to fool with, at Christmas time.'[45] At other Christmasses in exile she simply recorded the date in her diary, as did Mary Kingsley, without comment.

Some women travellers were able to externalize that part of themselves with which they were in constant and often painful conflict through an absent sister. Ella Christie wrote journal-letters every day for more than thirty years back to her married sister, mother of three sons, in Scotland. Alice's daughter-in-law said, 'no-one who knew them can think of one without the other', and called her collection of their letters *Alicella* with this fusion in mind.[46] For Ella, Alice represented the feminine role she could not herself fulfill – the mother, wife and bulwark of upper middle-class society in the Scottish home Alice rarely left. Agnes Smith Lewis took her sister Margaret on her journeys, the younger twin acting as chaperone to the elder Agnes. 'I came into this world as a supplement to my sister and I have always recognised that it was mine to take a second place,' Margaret confessed.[47] When Mary Slessor's sister Janie, to whom she too wrote diary-length letters, died only a few months after her mother, Mary wrote in self-pity, 'I, who all my life have been caring and planning and living for them, am left, as it were, stranded and alone . . . . There is no one to write and tell all my stories and troubles and nonsense to.'[48] Although she had been away from her native Scotland for over a decade, it was not until Janie's death that she claimed, 'Heaven is now nearer to me than Britain.'[49]

Isabella Bird also wrote to her sister at great length from mountain huts, Australian steamers and even the top of an Hawaiian volcano. All her experiences were immediately shared with the younger Hennie, ensconced in their Highland cottage, the ambitious 'Great Perak Letter' scrawling over 116 pages. Only once, at the start of her travelling life, did the elder sister Isa write asking Hennie to come and

---

[45] North, *Recollections of a Happy Life*, vol. 1, p. 61.

[46] Stewart, *Alicella*, p. xix.

[47] Quoted in A. Whigham Price, *The Ladies of Castlebrae. A Story of Nineteenth Century Travel and Research*, (Gloucester 1985), p. 208.

[48] Quoted in Margaret E. Tabor, *Pioneer Women*, (London 1925), vol. 1, p. 111.

[49] Quoted in Carol Christian and Gladys Plummer, *God and One Redhead*, (London 1970), p. 51.

join her so that she could, in a sense, become whole. But it was a wish written in a rash moment, and although Hennie replied with some consideration Isa immediately moved on to speak of other things.[50] At Hennie's death from typhoid in 1880, Isa lost her ability to revel with impunity in her travels now she had no external conscience and duty representing her at home. 'My sister was the inspiration of my letters and neither Hawaii nor the Rocky Mountains would have been anything without her,' she wrote to her publisher.[51] Within a year of her sister's premature death, Isabella at last accepted the persistent offer of marriage from the family doctor, John Bishop, who had nursed Hennie through her final illness. In her letter to Murray informing him of the engagement, the hope that her fiance might take up the role of home conscience that Hennie had so superbly and self-sacrificingly played was barely disguised:

> Dr Bishops's devotion to [my sister] in the last weeks of her life and her great wish that I should accept the care and devotion of one whose character and worth she had thorough trust in have largely helped to make me feel that were I now to decide against him I should be casting away a very precious treasure. We shall be married in the spring and my homes will be Edinburgh and Tobermory. I shall retain in literature the name under which I have gained a fair success. It is an understand that if I again need change, I am to be free for further 'outlandish travelling'.[52]

On her wedding day, the fifty-year-old bride still wore the black of deep mourning. There were no guests. By shrouding herself in grief for her lost sister, Isa may have been able to shirk the physical contact with her husband she so feared. Her vibrant, biting, sensual life was still to be lived on horseback and in the scorching open air.

Other women who had no female relative to live out feminine responsibilities on their behalf attempted to undertake such duties themselves. Edith Durham felt unable to refuse an appeal for help from the Macedonian Relief Committee, but did not hide her impatience with the sick she intended to care for. 'Miss Durham is an artist who went to Turkey in search of the picturesque,' wrote a

[50] Barr, *A Curious Life for a Lady*, pp. 181 and 51–2.
[51] Bird to John Murray 13 Aug. 1891, The Elms, Huntingdon.
[52] Bird to John Murray 9 Jan. [1881], Rutland Square, Edinburgh.

reviewer of her account. 'She found the Bulgarian peasants, who were cowering, broken and stricken, in the ruins of their devastated villages, anything but an attractive spectacle. Starving, downtrodden, hopeless, defeated, they were no subject for romance and but an indifferent foreground to a picture. She scarcely pitied them. She heartily despised them.'[53] Mary Kingsley offered her services as a nurse during a smallpox outbreak at Calabar. She had been up every night for five weeks, she wrote, 'for I did not feel justified in leaving a community to walk about in a state of delirium and pyjamas, with nothing fit to eat and no-one to see after them.' But when, she added, 'Calabar was reduced to its merely normal state of unhealthiness by reason of only too many of its inhabitants dying, and the balance of the rest being carried on board homeward bound steamers, I came up into this forest with the intention of studying the great fetish centre – the long jujus said to be situated in it.'[54] During the Great War, Ella Christie and Gertrude Bell both offered their services; Ella became *Directrice* of a canteen at a rest centre for soldiers in France. Gertrude Bell started working at Clandon Hospital, but soon was relieved to be posted to the bureau in Boulogne for tracing the missing and wounded, where she could continue to seem to serve without having to engage in the feminine activities of nursing and caring for others.

Nowhere was the ambiguity between wanting to be apart from and part of colonial culture expressed more thoroughly than in the women travellers' relationship with the natural world. At the borders of the colonial buildings lay the gardens, the final frontier to the surrounding threatening and encroaching foreign beyond. The garden was an extension of the house and therefore thought a fit domain for women, and in particular colonial wives, to work within. Taming the luxuriant vegetation which often grew around their homes, fencing in the garden and importing acclimatized seeds provided meaningful occupation for many colonial women, a visible display of colonial rule and its conquest of the African and Asian worlds. While Marianne North had nurtured orchids in her tropically-heated greenhouse in the Hastings winters, Constance Larymore saved her soapy bath water each morning for the English potted plants carefully cultivated on her

[53] H. N. Brailsford review of *The Burden of the Balkans*, *The Speaker*, 25 May 1905, quoted in Hodgson, 'Edith Durham', p. 11.

[54] Kingsley to Albert Günther 15 Apr. 1895, Okyon, Upper Calabar River.

verandah, including one tiny prized rose bush. The Resident's wife drew a portrait of her garden as battleground between colonial culture and Africa in all its representations.

> It is said to be very dear to the heart of every Englishman to own a lawn, and it certainly should be double so to John Bull in exile; in a tropical country well-kept turf is much to be desired, there is nothing so cool and refreshing to tired eyes dazzled with the glare of sunshine and baked earth, and, perhaps, nothing gives such a home-like and cared-for look to a West African compound. This demesne is usually reclaimed bush, which in nature grows rank, reed-like, coarse grass, and the ground destined for a lawn must be thoroughly *dug up*. It is worse than useless to attempt to remove it by merely pulling up the grass. After digging and turning, all the roots must be picked out most carefully, for it is indeed heartbreaking to see the enemy reappearing all over your infant lawn.[55]

Although exploiting the image of the colonial woman in the garden, those gardens which tempted the women travellers were not the well-tended beds surrounding colonial houses but the great unpruned beyond. For many the garden symbolized the frontier, the border between European culture and the society past its gates. On an expedition to Lar on her first Middle Eastern journey, Gertrude Bell wrote to her mother, 'I shall be sorry to leave this wonderful freedom and to be back within walls and gardens.'[56] Marianne North wrote to Burnell from Coonor that she wanted to move on from the heights of the European station to, 'the dear old sun and heat again. I fancy it will suit me better than the dressy gardens and trim-shaved roads of this Anglo-Indian Paradise.'[57] She apologized to the Director at the Royal Botanic Gardens at Kew who had asked her for drawings of Australian specimens, 'I fear you will think me very idle in not painting more of the things on your list, but the gardens do not tempt me. They are all so stiff and young.'[58] After spending a week alone climbing Mount Cameroon, Mary Kingsley descended back down to the coast and 'safe into Victoria – sneaking up the Government

[55] Larymore, *A Resident's Wife in Nigeria*, p. 244.
[56] Bell to Florence Bell 17 Aug. 1892, Lar, quoted in Richmond, *Earlier Letters*, p. 326.
[57] North to Arthur Burnell 'Tuesday' 1878, Coonoor.
[58] North to Joseph Hooker 24 Oct. [1880], 'Between Sydney and Melbourne.'

House hill by the private path through the Botanical Gardens.'[59]
Here, from tropical hillside, through tropical garden to colonial
residence, she made an almost symbolic passage from one world to
another. At Ichang gorge on the Yangtze, Isabella Bird left the boat
for a walk:

> By the narrowest of paths I climbed a cleft down which a crystal
> rivulet fell in leaps, pausing to rest now and then in deep pools
> fringed with a profuse growth of maidenhair . . . . Higher rose
> the steep path; more glorious were the mountain views, more
> marvellous the forest of spires and pinnacles, more graceful the
> slender-stemmed palms, finer the contorted *Pinus sinensis*, more
> lush the dense foilage, bluer the sky beyond – not the China we
> picture to ourselves, of water, quaint bridges, curled roofs, and
> flat, formal gardens, but a Chinese Switzerland, subtropical, an
> intoxication, a dream![60]

'We have turned the corner of the road, the Mission House is out of
sight. The adventure begins,' wrote Alexandra David-Neel on setting
out for Lhasa.[61]

The world beyond the garden fence was ever tempting. Etta Close
directly attributed her decision to leave behind European resorts for
East Africa to seeing a gardener in front of the Casino,

> standing over a big semi-tropical-looking plant plunged, pot and
> all, into the grass which always looks such a peculiarly vivid
> green. I stopped and asked him what he was doing. 'Madame,' he
> said, 'the weather is bad, is it not? The flowers will not come out,
> in this garden we must have flowers, I make them come out.' So
> saying, he cut along the edge of a bud and putting in his thumbs
> forced out the reluctant flower inside. 'Voilà,' he exclaimed,
> waving his knife and preparing to continue the process. I felt
> sick, everything artificial, even the flowers not allowed to be
> natural but forced out into the cold air . . . I bade farewell to the

---

[59] Kingsley, *Travels in West Africa*, p. 608.
[60] Bird, *The Yangtze Valley and Beyond*, pp. 108–9.
[61] David-Neel, *My Journey to Lhasa*, p. 1.

black and purple sea, and in my mind said good-bye to the
artificial garden and the green baize tables.'[62]

It was the unfettered, uncultured flora of tropical lands which
attracted the women travellers. Marianne North said the highlands of
Brazil were 'a perfect fairyland':

> The great black and opal Morpho butterflies came flapping their
> wide wings down the narrow lanes close over our heads, moving
> slowly and with a kind of see-saw motion, so as to let the light
> catch their glorious metallic colours, entirely perplexing any
> hold or nets. Gorgeous flowers grew close, but just out of reach,
> and every now and then I caught sight of some tiny nest, hanging
> inside a sheltering and prickly screen of brambles. All these
> wonders seem to taunt us mortals for trespassing on fairies'
> grounds, and to tell us they were unapproachable.[63]

How did this compare to the cultivated flowers her sister painted in
the alpine health resort of Davos? 'My sister had a grand collection of
carnations of various tints,' wrote Marianne, 'which she treated like
pet children, taking them indoors during the winter, and warming
them up through a summer snowstorm with flannels and blankets. She
watered them morning and evening with all kinds of tonics.'[64]

In awkward combination with this enthralment with untamed
countryside was an intense interest in botany and natural history,
which asked for the surrounding natural world to be captured in
words, paint or the identification of scientific species. The mid-
nineteenth century saw a burgeoning of the more casual sciences of
botany, entymology and ichthyology, with the formation of many
clubs and societies designed to consolidate their particular field of
concern. Unlike the so-called learned societies, such as the Royal
Geographical and Linnean, natural history was considered an activity
in which women could, within certain limits, partake. Even in
Britain, seaweed expert Margaret Gatty advised women collectors
that, 'anyone, therefore, really intending work in the matter, must lay

---

[62] Close, *A Woman Alone in Kenya, Uganda, and the Belgian Congo*, pp. 1–2.
[63] North, *Recollections of a Happy Life*, vol. 1, p. 157.
[64] Ibid., vol. 2, p. 282.

aside for a time all thought of conventional appearances,' and must wear no silks, satins, laces, bracelets or jewellery but petticoats above the ankle to stop the hems dragging in the mud and oiled boys' shooting boots. Being slightly unorthodox yet still feminine was thereby sanctioned in naturalist circles, and the emphasis was on comfort. The right attire, Mrs Gatty argued, 'makes you feel free, bold, joyous, monarch of all you survey, untrammelled, at ease, at home!'[65]

Although deemed a suitable pastime for amateurs, these collectors provided much valuable research material to a small group of academics in each field. Women travellers contributed to the late Victorian fashion for collecting which had been displayed by the clutter of their childhood homes. Alexine and Harriet Tinne brought an impressive collection back with them from their Nile journey and published their findings in a weighty tome, *Plantae Tinneanae*. While Mr Amaury Talbot was a member of the prestigious Linnaen Society, Olive Macleod notes that it was his wife who undertook the flower collection as they travelled together inland from the West African coast. Collecting used only primitive technology; Margaret Fountaine needed only her butterfly net, Mary Kingsley her jars and spirits donated by the British Museum of Natural History, and Marianne North her biscuit box filled with damp sand in which to place her cuttings. With these meagre resources, Mary Kingsley collected plants and rocks and had three new species of fish named after her; Marianne North gathered plants and had five new species named after her. Margaret Fountaine simply, dedicatingly collected more than 22,000 butterflies. But despite their discoveries in various fields, naturalist pursuits and collecting were seen to be amateur and women's involvement in these areas did not necessitate them becoming in any way professionals or scientists. Women travellers often emphasized their status as 'mere collector' or 'unscientific visitor'. Even Marianne North, who took on no other disguise than botanist, could call herself 'an amateur collector of a frivolous nature'.[66]

Women travellers took these traditionally feminine areas of concern and subverted them, hoping to defy convention under the cloak of conventionality. They looked for acceptable explanations – both to themselves and to their audiences – why they abandoned

[65] Mrs Alfred Gatty, *British Sea-Weeds*, (manuscript edn, London 1863), pp. viii and xi.
[66] North, *Further Recollections of a Happy Life*, p. 134.

home and domestic life for travel; and found them in the field of natural history. They expropriated the images of the parlour palms of late Victorian society and applied them to the tropical exuberance of their travels. Drawing on the image of the woman in the garden, Marianne wrote of Australia, 'the whole country was a natural flower-garden, and one could wander for miles and miles among the bushes and never meet a soul.'[67] And while she made hasty sketches in her notebooks of the flowers on her travels, when she sent them back to Davos her sister used them as embroidery patterns, converting the imagery back again to its appropriate sphere.

Different women travellers, in different places, both attempted and achieved this uneasy synthesis of woman in the garden and wanderer on the loose to varying degrees. The woman naturalist was a strong enough image for some to make it the core of their identity; others moved in and out of as it suited, and a few relied upon it only when all else momentarily seemed too dangerous, nebulous and unachievable. Some, like Marianne North, sought to challenge openly no further than these borders of gentility allowed. As a result, her propriety was rarely questioned in the way other women travellers' was.

So pervasive was the image of the intrepid woman botanist that fellow passengers on the *Lagos* in 1893 presumed Mary Kingsley, 'was interested in Natural History. "Botany", they said, "They had known some men who had come out from Kew, but they were all dead now."'[68] Alexandra David-Neel, trying to reach the closed-off city of Lhasa incognito, told the villagers she was going on, 'a botanical excursion in the neighbouring mountains,' lending a handy and appropriate cover to her journey.[69]

It was this label of naturalist that Mary Kingsley exploited for most of her first journey, using its guise to provide a legitimate reason for her long excursions into the countryside. In 1895, she answered the French official's objection to her ascent of the Ogooué rapids by explaining, 'that a lady has been up before, Mme. Quinee. He says "Yes, that is true, but Madame had with her a husband and many men" whereas I am alone . . . "True, oh King!" I answer, "but Madame Quinee went right up to Lestourville, whereas I only want to

[67] North, *Recollections of a Happy Life*, vol. 2, p. 149.
[68] Kingsley, *West African Studies*, p. 13.
[69] David-Neel, *My Journey to Lhasa*, p. 2.

Marianne North at her easel, Grahamstown, South Africa, 1882.
Royal Botanic Gardens.

go sufficiently high up the rapids to get typical fish."[70] Her most rigorous collecting of plants and grasses was undertaken around Calabar, providing an acceptable reason to escape from the white society of the administrative centre. Walks and canoe rides inland were ostensibly taken to look for new specimens; she returned from these excursions, however, with less naturalist than ethnographic information, more of the 'fetish' and less of the 'fish' it was her declared combined intention of researching. Marianne North also used her botanical interest to diffuse possible criticism and conflict. When at Ratlam, her interpreter asked her whether she was a member of Miss Carpenter's mission. 'I asked in return if he was,' Marianne retorted. 'He made a face and a shrug and gave a very distinct "no". He then said that the Prime Minister was at the palace close by asking permission to come and see me, so I got out a bundle of sketches to set their minds at rest as to why I had come to India.'[71]

For Marianne, collecting specimens of plants and flowers was, along with illness, an explanation for being so incessantly on the move. 'The flowers I was in search of were still out of bloom, so I left Calcutta again the next morning at 7.30,' she recorded, to begin again on a one thousand mile journey through the subcontinent.[72] Although needed in the arrangements for displaying her paintings in Kew Gardens in 1882, she left Britain hurriedly saying, 'All the continents of the world had some sort of representation in my gallery except Africa, and I resolved to begin painting there without loss of time.'[73] On her 1884 travels around Chile, she repeatedly insisted that her main purpose for being there was to paint the monkey-puzzle tree – even though there were several specimens at Kew which could have served as her subjects.

Along with the knowledge of a certain science went its appropriate presentation, and in the case of natural history this was the sketching with which Marianne North so voraciously filled her travels – jotting down rough outlines of plants even while she was in a train or cart. When she had failed to develop as promised at her singing classes, young Marianne had been given lessons in flower-painting by Miss Van Fowinkel and the flower-painter-in-ordinary to the Queen,

[70] Kingsley, *Travels in West Africa*, p. 167.
[71] North, *Recollections of a Happy Life*, vol. 2, pp. 70–1.
[72] Ibid., p. 27.
[73] Ibid., p. 217.

Valentine Bartholomew. She had borrowed Mrs Husseys two large tomes on funghi from the library and started collecting and painting all the varieties she could gather around Rougham.

This sketching of specimens learnt as young women gave not only cover but also meaning to many women travellers' journeys. Marianne recorded that the Ranee of Sarawak's 'life was monotonous' – so she taught her to paint from nature, thereby giving her some useful purpose.[74] 'It is a blessed provision of nature that [women's] fingers are adapted for knitting, painting and other work to keep them from going mad,' Marianne wrote, in a private display of the anger she publicly masked.[75]

Botanical sketching could also provide some of the comforting ritual often looked for by women in distant lands. As news of the casualties flooded in to Government House at Calcutta during the 1857 'Mutiny', vicereine Charlotte Canning busied her hours, otherwise empty except for troubling thoughts, making 130 sketches in quick succession. For other women, sketching was a reason to be alone, an intrinsically unsociable activity which often required being executed outdoors. Marianne North even suggested that botanical sketching and genteel company were mutually exclusive. 'Singapore was delightful for flower-painting in one's shirt sleeves, but not for so-called society,' she wrote in 1880.[76] Amelia Edwards also found that she could excuse herself from organized excursions around Egyptian ruins by setting up her sketching tent and making detailed ink drawings of the statues and hieroglyphics while her guide and chaperone Salame sat by smoking.

The art to which some women travellers became attracted and soon produced differed radically from the skills in which they had been tutored as young women. Edith Durham had trained at Bedford College of Art and illustrated with careful detailed pictures the *Cambridge Natural History*. On her travels through Albania, however, these delicately executed drawings were replaced by a gradual process of painting through which she built up a picture of this new world. First she would photograph or make a pencil sketch of the scene in front of her – perhaps the Montenegran women gathered in the square at Cetinje, wrapped in embroidered blouses and head scarves. Next

[74] Ibid., p. 99.
[75] North to Joseph Hooker 26 Oct. 1879, Victoria Street, London.
[76] North, *Recollections of a Happy Life*, vol. 2, p. 90.

Edith would make a pen and ink drawing from her initial impression, often shading it in with an ink wash. Finally, she coloured in her distant lands with strong watercolours, dashing them eagerly over the paper. 'Art to be decorative must be barbaric,' she wrote. 'When it becomes "civilised" it become anaemic, and crawls feebly in pallid mauves and greens, with long spindle stalks that lack vitality to throw out more than one or two atrophied leaves. It has lost red blood and the joy of life.'[77]

Marianne North melded the two opposite attractions of the exuberance of the tropical world and the conventional cloak of the woman botanist in her most extraordinary paintings. The rebellious student developed her artistic skills in a different direction from that in which her tutor Valentine Bartholomew had intended, allowing her imagination to intrude powerfully on to the canvas. While British botanists wrote about the 'honest ivy' and the 'modest snowdrop', Marianne portrayed a sensual abundance of blossoming, blooming and cross-fertilizing plants, expressing in vivid strong oils her immediate and unfiltered reaction to the force of colour and vitality in the world about her. While her sister's illustrations were conventional, disembodied, botanically correct specimens floating on a grey sea background, Marianne portrayed all her plants in highly visionary scenes drawn from the surroundings in which she saw them flourish. 'No empty backgrounds or vacant spaces, each picture being as it were a square cut bodily out from nature,' commented one newspaper, for it was the setting of the flora and fauna which attracted her as much as the specimen itself.[78] As Alexandra David-Neel commented wryly, 'Who knows the flower best? – the one who reads about it in a book, or the one who finds it wild on the mountainside?'[79] At Putbus on the Baltic Sea, Marianne had noted 'beautiful jelly-fish floated about, set with stars of all the purest colours, and could easily be caught in the hand, but melted away on dry land. Lovely sea-weed tempted one to collect, but shrank to a formless nothing when captured.'[80] Often she only painted the landscape in which a certain flower flourished; on return to Britain, Kew Gardens would then provide her with the specimen and she would paint it in on top of her canvas. The highly

[77] Durham, *High Albania*, p. 281.
[78] 'London's Hidden Treasures. The North Gallery at Kew', *Morning Post*, 29 Dec. 1905.
[79] Quoted in Foster, *Forbidden Journey*, p. 312.
[80] North, *Further Recollections of a Happy Life*, p. 24.

Montenegran women, Cetinje, 1901, by Edith Durham.

coloured dreamscapes against which the budding and bursting botanical specimens of her paintings were set represented the lands into which she released herself.

While her early pictures had been executed in watercolour, Marianne found the force of colour in tropical vegetation was best conveyed by heavier oils. Oils were also the medium of the professional, male painter, while watercolours remained the material of the amateur, middle-class female dabbler. 'Her methods were unconstitutional and somewhat peculiar,' wrote a woman friend. 'She simply made a rough sketch rapidly in pen and ink of the subject and then worked paint straight on to the canvas and merely squeezed colour out of the tubes and put it on as it was without using any medium. This horrified all artists who knew of it.'[81] Marianne recognized her unconventional style, contrasting her own work with that of the 'real artist'.[82] While her pictures bore no resemblance to her life at home, in Java, she found another European artist

and myself painted the same bit of forest scenery so differently, that no-one would take our productions to have been painted in the same country. His might have been as well done at home in Holland, with some old Dutch pictures as his models, all discoloured by brown varnish. How odd it is that artistic people persist in seeing nature everywhere alike and through smoked spectacles.[83]

Her painting was, like her travels, greedily taken up, as she continually sketched in a notebook when she was unable to take out paints and easel. Running out of materials, she painted on both sides of the canvas. Her autobiography was written as if a catalogue to her paintings, for it was the visual impact of foreign worlds that she experienced most strongly, a reliance enhanced by her deafness. First painting only plants, by the time of her 1878 Indian journey she was sketching buildings and even, occasionally, market scenes. 'Alwar was full of strange sights,' she wrote. 'I used to take my sketching stool and sit at the gate of an evening in the road, making studies of camels and

---

[81] Lady Harriet Thistelton-Dyer to Sir Arthur 12 Mar. 1936.
[82] North, *Recollections of a Happy Life*, vol. 2, p. 93.
[83] Ibid., vol. 1, p. 298.

passing travellers.'[84] The perspective of her paintings was always enormous, stretching back into a hazy distance. If her easel was set up inside a temple, her painting would look out through a small doorway to the hills beyond. In her oil of the 'Street of Blood, Delhi', crowded with people, carts and cattle, a minaret glimmers like a torch on a distant horizon.

Painting outdoors, the natural world often invaded. Ants crawled into Marianne's oil paints; Constance Gordon Cumming's sketches were stained by mildew while the watercolourist herself suffered continual mosquito attacks as she worked. The elements in multifarious forms also plagued Amelia Edwards' attempts at capturing the landscapes of the ancient Egyptian ruins. 'When the wind blows from the north (which at this time of the year is almost always) the heat is perhaps less distressing, but the sand is maddening,' she wrote at the start of 1874 in Abou Simbel.

> It fills your hair, your eyes, your water-bottles; silts up your colour-box; dries into your skies; and reduces your Chinese white to a gritty paste the colour of salad-dressing. As for flies, they have a morbid appetite for water-colours. They follow your wet brush along the paper, leave legs in the yellow ochre, and plunge with avidity into every pool of cobalt as it is mixed ready for use. Nothing disagrees with them; nothing poisons them – not even olive-green.

But, she adds immediately, 'it was a delightful time'.[85]

Natural history and sketching provided, for many women travellers, a mask of decorum which allowed them to travel yet be feminine, blunted criticism and covered unacceptable behaviour with a cloak of gentility. 'My butterflies,' wrote Margaret Fountaine, gave 'a life of wandering beneath summer skies'.[86] And she, like Marianne North, remained content with the security the image of a woman naturalist offered. Yet for many travellers, the dabbling and collecting of an amateur, while quelling the questioning of others, did not entirely satisfy their own. Legitimizing their travels had proved to be only the

[84] Ibid., vol. 2, p. 49.
[85] Edwards, *A Thousand Miles Up the Nile*, p. 310.
[86] Fountaine, *Love Among the Butterflies*, p. 82.

first and easier step. To find greater depth and meaning in their journeys was a much harder quest. As they insatiably moved from one country to another, so they rehearsed different disguises at each port of call – donning them as they approached the colonial verandah, shedding them as they walked down the garden path, through the gate and out into the foreign world. But it was in this foreign landscape itself, away from white settlements, that they were to find their most powerful disguise, which enabled them to cross the border of gentility and strike out a new path of discovery on their own.

4

Over the Garden Gate

'I craved to go beyond the garden gate, follow the road that passed it by, and to set out for the unknown,' wrote Alexandra David-Neel on leaving for the forbidden city of Lhasa.[1] Here, across the border of gentility, the woman traveller found a new identity alluring in the power, authority and self-esteem it promised. Within the colonial compound and white settlements, European women had been defined in relation to the community it housed. But in the setting of a turkish *han*, Fang village or desert camp, those against whom women's worth and role were measured were not white men but foreign and often subjected peoples. In non-European terrain, the sense of achievement they had privately experienced was soon matched by public acknowledgement of their powers and skills.

Their welcome into the heart of foreign landscapes differed greatly from those they had received when stepping down from the ships and carriages into the colonial domain. Sometimes women travellers were attributed with specific skills; at others with general talents and access to authority which was in reality denied them. This new power was often reflected in the titles of honour and respect bestowed upon them by their host societies – titles particularly appealing to the new wealthy industrial middle classes from which many women travellers came. Both Marianne North and Ella Christie soon grew to recognize themselves as 'Your Ladyship'; Gertrude Bell, whose family, like Christie's, had risen to prominence and wealth as mineowners, was inquired after in the following terms: 'Have you seen a queen travelling, a consuless?'[2] She rebuked a too familiar and inquisitive

[1] David-Neel, *My Journey to Lhasa*, p. xviii.
[2] Bell to Hugh Bell 5 May 1900, Jebel Druze, quoted in Bell, *Letters*, p. 96.

Druze guide who fired her with questions: 'Listen, oh you! I am not "thou", but "Your Excellency"'.[3] In Bombay, Christie attended a reception where she was 'salaamed out by the sentries and greeted all along the highway. I bowed like a duchess and you would have died laughing. You will see with what an air I shall do it in Newmains.'[4]

The women travellers' reputations were carried before them, and Edith Durham found herself sung into each new village with cheers of 'She can read and write several languages. She can make pictures without a machine [i.e. draw] She can sing. She can . . .', all endowing her with talents which went unheralded in her home society.[5] She was, she said, generally regarded as 'the champion of the Serbs in England', where no one might have heard of her.[6] Everywhere she went she was greeted with the same accolades: 'To my amazement I found I was celebrated. Some one recognized me as having been in Dechani five years ago. "Ah, it is the Balkan Englishwoman, the friend of the Montenegrins!" The Metropolitan knew all about me – a schoolmistress, lately from Saloniki, retailed my Macedonian career.'[7] Gertrude Bell, despite obtaining first class examination results at Oxford, had been denied the award of a degree on the grounds of her sex. But she could write excitedly to her father from Syria that 'in this country – they all think I was a Person! And one of the first questions everyone seems to ask everyone else is, "Have you ever met Miss Gertrude Bell?"'[8]

General attributes of authority and skill were matched by more specific accolades, and often an extraordinary power of medical healing was presumed of women travellers – a supposed ability which at once flattered and perplexed them. While women were agitating for the recognition of nursing skills as professional and medical in Britain, this forcibly impressed upon the women travellers their more highly perceived value in non-European societies. While Mary Kingsley spoke on platforms throughout England in support of the Colonial Nursing Association and the registration and accreditation of nursing

[3] Bell, *The Desert and the Sown*, p. 80.

[4] Christie to Alice Stewart 26 Jan. 1904, Bombay, quoted in Stewart, *Alicella*, p. 154.

[5] Edith Durham, *Some Tribal Origins, Laws and Customs of the Balkans*, (London 1927), p. 287.

[6] Durham, *High Albania*, p. 275.

[7] Ibid., p. 254. Even today, while Durham is forgotten in the country of her birth, she has streets and squares named after her in Albania.

[8] Bell to Hugh Bell 30 Mar. 1902, Mount Carmel, quoted in Bell, *Letters*, p. 133.

as a profession, in West African villages her medical knowledge was inflated beyond all proportion to its value. On arriving at the small Gabonese town of Egaja, an old woman was brought to her with a severly ulcerated arm. Kingsley cleaned and dressed it, 'then all the afflicted of Egaja turned up, and wanted medical advice. There was evidently a good stiff epidemic of yaws about; lots of cases of dum with the various symptoms; ulcers of course galore; a man with a bit of broken spear head in an abscess in the thigh . . . . It was past eleven before I had anything like done.'[9] In Jordan, Bell was begged to attend to a man whose jaw had been shattered by a bullet and whole face become infected. She gave him an antiseptic, washed the wound and put on fresh bandages. 'This was the first of a long roll of sufferers that must pass before the eyes and catch despairingly at the sympathies of every traveller in wild places,' she wrote. 'Men and women afflicted with ulcers and terrible sores, with fevers and rheumatisms, children crippled from their birth, the blind and the old, there are none who do not hope that the unmeasured wisdom of the West may find them a remedy. You stand aghast at the depths of human misery and your own helplessness.'[10] At Ayserat, outside Cairo, Amelia Edwards was begged by a wife of Ratab Aga, a local notable, for medicines for her little boy. 'It was in vain to tell her that we knew nothing of the nature of his disease and had no skill to cure it,' recorded Edwards. 'She still entreated, and would take no refusal; so in pity we sent her some harmless medicines.'[11] Over ten years before women were able to qualify as medical practitioners in Britain, the steersman of her Nile boat 'chose to fancy I was a doctress,' wrote Marianne North, and 'would uncover his chest and show me with many grimaces that he had a pain there, and I used to give him bits of sugar with camphor on it, after when, whenever I looked at him, he would rub the spot gently, and smile gratefully.'[12]

Many women travellers, like Marianne North, had long years of practical experience tending to an invalid parent – skills which had often been utilized to nurse injured and fevered European residents through whose homes and settlements they passed on their journeys. But amongst Europeans they had been expected to provide moral

[9] Kingsley, *Travels in West Africa*, pp. 283–4.
[10] Bell, *The Desert and the Sown*, pp. 80–1.
[11] Edwards, *A Thousand Miles Up the Nile*, p. 479.
[12] North, *Further Recollections of a Happy Life*, p. 126.

rather than medical care, drawing upon their assumed innate feminine attributes of tenderness, comfort and sympathy. 'Good looks and a cheerful disposition conjoined go a long way in the successful management of cases of illness in this Colony,' wrote the Chief Medical Officer of the Gold Coast in 1896 when consulted as to the employment of European nurses in West Africa. 'I have found that a tender touch, a sympathetic look . . . have done more good to their patients than the drugs, or other therapeutic measures prescribed them.'[13]

The medical power with which women travellers were credited in non-European societies, however, was of an entirely different nature, based not on their feminine aptitudes but their practical power as representatives of a colonial and dominant authority. Medical treatment had been incorporated, first by the missionaries, as a means through which influence, control and allegiance could be wrought from local populations. Realizing this, Lilian Brown intended to win the friendship of the South American peoples by pretending that she and her companion Mitch Hedges were great gods come to cure disease. They administered the highly sophisticated medicament of Epsom salts.

While women were excluded from official positions of power within the colonial administration until the mid-twentieth century, they were nevertheless assumed to hold the sway and influence such posts attracted in foreign lands. 'It is not her wealth, it is not her government or her official representatives that have made Britain's name respected the whole globe round,' wrote one newspaper reporter. 'It is *her unofficial ambassadors*, ordinary men or women who obey the impulse of our race and wander out into the world, and who, wherever they encounter other people . . . learn as much as they can about them, but all the time rigidly hold to their British nationality.'[14] While Alexandra David-Neel was carried in a dandy through the streets of Kalimpong the roadside crowds pointed to a bust of Queen Victoria, of whom they regarded the traveller as an emanation.[15] With a disregard for national boundaries common among white-skinned colonials, in Sikkim she felt like Poincaré – the President of France.[16]

[13] Chief Medical Officer to Acting Colonial Secretary 23 Sep. 1896, Overseas Nursing Association archives.
[14] Article on Flora Sandes in unidentified Australian newspaper 1920.
[15] Foster, *Forbidden Journey*, p. 113.
[16] Ibid., p. 124.

At Lushun, on the coast opposite the Korean peninsula, Ella Christie was greeted with garlands thrown about her neck. 'Is the lady *not* a British general?' asked a perplexed local official.

'Alas, I am not,' replied Christie.

'Perhaps then the lady is *widow* of a British General?' he asked hopefully.

'Not that either – but there is no saying *what I might become*,' she replied, with wry insight into her enhanced role as a traveller in foreign lands.[17]

Durham was endowed with almost superhuman powers and strength of influence in the Albanian region, and 'in spite of my frequent and emphatic denials,' they 'persisted in believing me to be the sister of the King of England come to free them, and addressing me always as Kralitse (Queen).'[18] When the Young Turk Constitution was introduced in 1912 and Durham was drawn into the celebrations, the enormity of the influence attributed to her suddenly became very apparent. 'I myself was the first visible sign of the "Constitution" from the outer world,' she wrote. 'It came on me with a great crash that the simple mountaineers believed largely that I had worked this marvel . . . I denied it vainly. Never before have I been so popular; never in my life shall I be so again,' she scribbled sitting in anonymity in London.[19]

What made Ella Christie 'Your Ladyship', Gertrude Bell 'a Person', Edith Durham 'Kralitse', and Marianne North a 'doctress' in contrast to the 'feminine helplessness' presumed of her at Simla? Outside the limits of European communities, the fact of being female no longer carried the same immediate importance. Sitting supping tea on the colonial verandah or in the lounge of the Shepheard's Hotel in Cairo, the women's appearance and manner had been judged by their relation to fellow Europeans. But in the bush, desert or mountainside, who and what they were was measured against surrounding non-European peoples. They became simply foreign in and to a foreign land.

Gertrude Bell noted the transformation encountered by travellers as they left their home society behind. 'To those bred under an

---

[17] Stewart, *Alicella*, p. 199.
[18] Durham, *High Albania*, pp. 130–1.
[19] Ibid., pp. 228 and 289.

elaborate social order,' she wrote, with a particularly keen eye for women's place within those created hierarchies, 'few moments of exhilaration can come as that which stands at the threshold of wild travel.'[20] 'It can be imagined,' wrote French-Sheldon, 'that a man of activities, who enjoys freedom, and possesses a natural propensity for leadership, should desire to break away from the narrow, cloying environments of civilized society, with all of its set rules, conventionalities, shams, and cant, for just such a life as one might find in Africa.'[21] Bird too noted how, away from the companionship of other Europeans, women travellers could act outside the normal dictates of their sex and class. 'Travellers are privileged to do the most improper things with perfect propriety, that is one charm of travelling,' she wrote.[22] Bird found freedom from class as stimulating and fulfilling as freedom from notions of correct feminine behaviour, enjoying washing her own clothes, baking her own bread, and polishing her own pots and pans, 'taking care that there are no witnesses of my inexperience.'[23] She then turned her hand to farming, and pulled a quarter of an acre of maize at the foot of the Rockies. 'I much prefer field work to the scouring of greasy pans and to the wash-tub, and both to either sewing or writing,' she wrote to her sister.[24]

But for most women travellers, the newfound sense of achievement and authority rested on the dissolving of barriers not of class but of gender. At the turn of the century being British in Africa and Asia meant more than simply being an outsider – it meant being a visible representative of a colonial power. Colonialism stressed the importance of physical appearance and racial characteristics which were used to form an absolute distinction between the ruler and the ruled. To a greater extent than other systems of control of one people by another, British colonialism rested upon the embodiment of power in individual colonial officers and informal representatives, displayed through dress, housing and, most simply and importantly, the colour of their skin. This was a display of authority in which white women, on the grounds of their white faces, could share.

[20] Bell, *The Desert and the Sown*, p. 1.
[21] French-Sheldon, *Sultan to Sultan*, p. 65.
[22] Bird quoted in Barr, *A Curious Life for a Lady*, p. 54.
[23] Bird, *A Lady's Life in the Rocky Mountains*, p. 6.
[24] Ibid., p. 79.

As women travellers journeyed alone through lands which had been or were under threat of colonization and subjection, it was the colour of their skin, their dress, their identity as Europeans which held importance. When in all-white societies, where gender was an important element of their identity, women travellers had silently rejected the trappings of colonial life. Outside of the colonial compound, however, they exploited and exaggerated these same trappings to their own advantage, donning in the bush the symbols of colonialism they had shunned amongst Europeans. They used them to stress their difference, based on race, from the local populations – differences on which their status as white rulers rested. For here, they recognized, lay their freedom and prestige; here lay their newfound power.

Women travellers journeyed through areas whose relationship with their home governments differed, and it was this relationship which to a large extent affected their own daily experiences. In politically volatile Albania, where many different forces were vying for control, there was initially some debate as to how Durham should be treated by her hosts. When she arrived in the Prokletija, the head of the house received the three-person party of the guide Marko, a padre and the traveller courteously, but 'of course it was not etiquette for him to take notice of me. I sat on the floor in a corner as bidden, held my tongue, and looked on.'[25] But when it came to the time to eat, Durham was asked to sit with the men; as the day progressed, the subject of where she should sleep also had to be broached. Although she had expected to be sent to the women's quarters, she found herself put to bed in a corner with the six men of the house in a row on the opposite side of the room.[26] 'I am always classed with the buck herd,' she was soon writing confidently.[27]

In a British West African colony, however, Gaunt's position and the masculine authority it wielded were more clear cut:

It is very curious how soon one gets an idea of one's own importance. In England, if I came across a crowd of shouting, furious, angry men, I should certainly pass by on the other side, but here in Africa when I was by myself I felt it my bounden duty

[25] Durham, *High Albania*, p. 138.
[26] Ibid., p. 142.
[27] Ibid., p. 64.

to interfere . . . Here was I, alone, unarmed, only a woman, and yet immediately I heard a commotion I attended at once and dispensed justice to the very best of my ability. I fully expected village elders to bow to my decision, and I am bound to say they generally did.[28]

In East Africa, French-Sheldon just had to 'put my head outside of my tent flap any hour of the day or night and call "Boy!" constantly back would come the answer, "Sabe!" (Sir)', clearly displaying the relationship of power between herself and her carriers. 'They never could seem to reconcile my sex with my position, which, in their eyes, indubitably belonged to a man,' she explained.[29] When Lilian Brown arrived in Central America in the early 1920s, she said simply, 'I was not the same being – sex had disappeared.'[30]

Sex hadn't simply disappeared – it had been transformed. Assuming different aspects of masculinity was one way in which women travellers could also assume power. A very few, such as Ménie Dowie on her journey through the Karpathians in 1890, dressed in male attire, but the vast majority relied upon constructions of racial difference which accompanied and justified colonial development to endow them with this white male status. In Peking, Gaunt was simply called 'gentleman' by her servants, whereas Gordon Cumming was addressed respectably as 'Aged Sir'.[31] As Olive Macleod and Mr and Mrs Amaury Talbot made their way northwards from the swampy West African coast to the dry and dusty interior in 1910, they were described as 'three biggest white men'.[32]

Bell explained at greater length how the fact of her colour was of overriding importance to the people amongst whom she travelled. It was no good her trying to make friends and gain access to powerful families through the women, she wrote to her stepmother: 'If the women were allowed to see me they would veil before me as if I were a man.'[33] From being a genderless 'Person', Bell had developed into an *effendi*, a Turkish title of respect given to professional men. When

[28] Gaunt, *Alone in West Africa*, p. 162.
[29] French-Sheldon, *Sultan to Sultan*, p. 38.
[30] Brown, *Unknown Tribes, Unchartered Seas*, preface.
[31] Gaunt, *A Woman in China*, p. 22; Constance Gordon Cumming, *Wanderings in China*, (London 1886), p. 260.
[32] Macleod, *Chiefs and Cities of Central Africa*. p. 124.
[33] Bell to Florence Bell 14 Mar. 1920, Baghdad, quoted in Bell, *Letters*, p. 484.

writing to her father and boasting of this new honour, she was quick to reassure him that she continued to conform to home standards of femininity. Although admitting she had taken to riding astride, she comforted that she still wore 'a most elegant and decent divided skirt'. But, Bell added, as only her eyes showed from behind her bedouin headscarf and 'all men wear skirts of sorts too, that doesn't serve to distinguish me.'[34] Her chosen style of dress could at the same time appease her British audience that she was acting with due feminine propriety yet endow her with male appearance, and therefore prestige, in the foreign societies through which she travelled. Although Kingsley claimed to dress in nothing but her long skirts and high-necked blouses while travelling in West Africa, she still found cause to complain, 'I am a most lady-like person and yet get constantly called "Sir"'.[35]

Women exaggerated the trappings of their home culture to reinforce this genderless white power. Sylvia Leith-Ross wrote how, 'when you are alone, among thousands of unknown, unpredictable people, dazed by unaccustomed sights and sounds, bemused by strange ways of life and thought, you need to remember who you are, where you come from, what your standards are. A material discipline represents – and aids – a moral discipline.'[36] But as French-Sheldon elaborated, it was not only for the benefit of the traveller herself that such displays of material culture were necessary. 'The observances of little ceremonies and indulgence in certain refinements, as well as some few luxuries, conduced not only to my prestige in the natives' eyes, but to my personal comfort and self-respect.'[37]

Dress was an important element in these displays of authority and difference, and one in which French-Sheldon, with her heightened sense of the dramatic, loved to indulge. While refusing to don masculine attire, she took with her to East Africa a white sequinned evening gown, a long blonde wig, a ceremonial sword and an excessive amount of sparkly jewellery. On approaching a village, she donned this costume and made a staged entrance, heralded by her guides as 'the White Queen'. The colour, extravagance and fake wealth of her disguise, together with her assumed title, laid claim to

[34] Bell to Hugh Bell 30 Apr. 1900, Deraa, quoted in ibid., p. 84.
[35] Kingsley, *Travels in West Africa*, p. 502.
[36] Leith-Ross, *Stepping Stones*, p. 69.
[37] French-Sheldon, *Sultan to Sultan*, p. 199.

power and prestige over a recently conquered land which French-Sheldon, a Bostonian, could share on the grounds of her white skin.

In a very different landscape, David-Neel also assumed a disguise with the purpose not of claiming authority but diffusing any suspicion of being a threat to the societies through which she had to pass. As she repeatedly noted in the account of her journey to the city of Lhasa, closed to foreigners, she had to *disguise* herself as an oriental and as a woman. She lengthened her plaits with strands of jet black yak's hair, rubbed a wettened stick of Chinese ink on her brown roots, powdered her face with a mixture of cocoa and crushed charcoal, wrapped herself up in the dress of a female *arjopa* – the peasant pilgrims who made the long trek to the holy city – and 'with a humility suitable to my part of an Oriental woman', the former actress played her role in 'a comedy of admiration and stupidity'.[38] She was, David-Neel constantly reminds her readers, pretending to be something she was not – poor, female and powerless. When out of her 'disguise', alone except for her young male Sikkimese companion Yongden, she could be her true, powerful (male) self. While in the company of others, Yongden called her his old mother and treated her with the disdain that relationship earnt; but in private he addressed her as *Jetsunma*, a title of respect meaning reverend lady. At night, when everyone else was asleep, David-Neel 'whispered in my young companion's ear what he was to do', and when day broke he obeyed her instructions under the pretence of being in charge himself.[39]

Beneath her Tibetan disguise, David-Neel carried an automatic pistol – another symbol of masculine power. While women travellers often denied both having and using firearms to home audiences, in fact they almost all carried a gun and employed it, not to injure, but as a display of their authority. Gaunt had a small pistol and thirteen cartridges; Kingsley slept with a gun under her makeshift pillow; French-Sheldon swung two 'baby guns' in holsters about her waist as she marched through East Africa. If her carriers were rowdy, she would gallantly draw and shoot a vulture overhead or, with both pistols cocked, walk through a crowd of worried men pointing the barrel at each quietened face. As she boarded the SS *Ortana* bound for the East, Bell stored one revolver in her pocket and had another

[38] David-Neel, *My Journey to Lhasa*, pp. 44 and 272.
[39] Ibid.. p. 152.

Studio portrait of Lady Dorothy Mills, traveller in West Africa, 1920s.
Reproduced by permission of Duckworth.

buried amongst her petticoats. At Berisha, Durham appeared as 'a strange woman, with a new kind of weapon' with a Browning stuck in her belt, encouraging the villagers to offer the very best of their hospitality.[40] When David-Neel was tempted into using her automatic pistol in a threatened robbery, she realized her disguise as a poor elderly pilgrim was put in danger and she would be assumed to possess the position and power suggested by carrying arms. 'It was annoying to be identified as carrying a revolver, for only chiefs and rich traders own these. Of course they thought it was Yongden who had fired,' she recorded.[41]

Soon women travellers learnt to rely upon and then emphasize these expressions of racial difference and celebrate the newfound authority attributed to them as 'white men', enabling them to create a fiction of themselves utterly unavailable within the confines of their home society or the colonial communities. They rejected the title of 'tourist', which held none of the assumptions of racial privilege or masculine power. While Edwards had called herself a 'stray foreign tourist' while rambling in the Dolomites where she had ridden sidesaddle among Western Europeans, when she reached North Africa less than two years later she was distancing herself and her role from that of Cooks' clients.[42] Gaunt was being continually questioned as to the purpose of her journey: '"A tourist on the coast", a surprised ship's captain called me, and I disclaimed it promptly,' she declared.[43] Instead she chose to travel to areas 'untrodden by the tourist, or indeed any white man'.[44] On the road to Jericho, Bell stopped at a wayside inn where three Germans 'were writing on picture-postcards . . . and bargaining with the khanji for imitation Bedouin knives. I sat and listened to their vulgar futile talk – it was the last I was to hear of European tongues for several weeks, but I found no cause to regret the civilisation I was leaving . . . I desired eagerly to leave the tourists behind, and the hotels and the picture-postcards.'[45]

In places where race was a more powerful social determinant than gender, women travellers strove to include themselves amongst white

---

[40] Durham, *High Albania*, p. 183.
[41] David-Neel, *My Journey to Lhasa*, p. 212.
[42] Edwards, *Untrodden Peaks and Unfrequented Valleys*, p. 110.
[43] Gaunt, *Alone in West Africa*, p. 120.
[44] Gaunt, *A Broken Journey*, p. 76.
[45] Bell, *The Desert and the Sown*, p. 10.

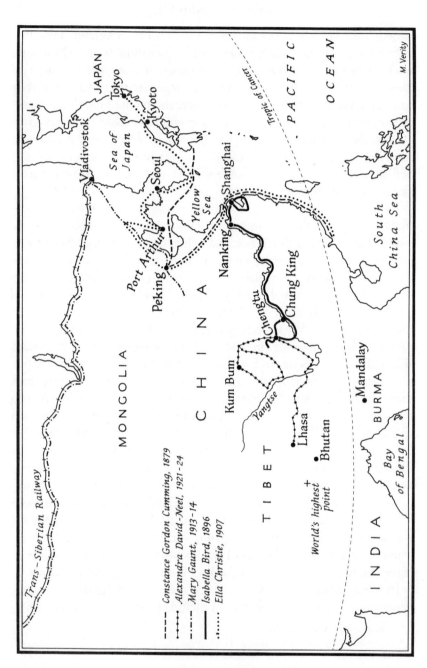

China and Japan.

male travellers. Their claims to identity and continuity with th
tradition of male exploration were displayed in many ways – through
images, language, practical achievements and attitudes. Like an
unwritten letter of introduction, they would often initially explain
themselves to foreign societies with explicit reference back to these
earlier male travellers. Although Bell had found Max von
Oppenheim's book of little practical use as guidance for her journey,
she showed the illustrations and maps to those who remembered him
and was thereby herself seen as a successor and inheritor of his role.[46]
Kingsley talked with much admiration of 'the school of travellers of
which Du Chaillu, Dr Barth, Joseph Thomson, and Livingstone are
past masters, and of which I am a humble member.'[47] Edwards sat at
her table on the roof of her *dahabeeyah* reading travellers' tales – then
took up her pen and began writing one herself. At Tashkent, in
Central Asia, Christie silently recited the explorer Richard Burton's
poetry to herself as she moved along.

While Bell only looked back a few years to Oppenheim's Middle
Eastern journeys, other women claimed a much longer heritage of
European travel, thus embedding themselves firmly in a tradition
which stretched over not mere decades but centuries. Kingsley
consciously presented herself as the successor to Pierre de Brazza who
had travelled in the Gabon region twenty years earlier. Lilian Brown
could picture herself 'living in the days of Drake and Sir Henry
Morgan – the days of the buccaneers,' as she sailed into the
Carribean.[48]

These claims of heritage paid as scant regard to differences of
nationality as they did to the years which divided them. Kingsley
claimed Du Chaillu, Stanley and de Brazza as her predeccesors –
travellers who themselves had all assumed nationalities different from
those of their birth. The Australian Gaunt, in the company of a
British Forestry Officer, met a German trader at Beyin who was
'somewhat difficult to understand at times when he grew excited; but
he stood on the same side of the gulf as we other two, while the black
people, those who served us, and those who stared at us, were apart on
the other side.'[49] The community of racial status surpassed all other
divisions of gender, class and nationality.

[46] Ibid., p. 102.
[47] Kingsley, *Travels in West Africa*, p. 368.
[48] Brown, *Unknown Tribes, Unchartered Seas*, p. 6.
[49] Gaunt, *Alone in West Africa*, pp. 99–100.

This claim to a place in the heritage of white male exploration not only enforced their authority on alien societies but also enabled women travellers to explain and legitimize, in their own minds, the purpose of their travels. Their celebration of this newfound authority and their arrogance as unquestioned members of the white colonial world led them to internalize their role as white men, and references to themselves in their journals and letters were made in the male gender. 'I know all the mysteries of camping life, can find a blind trail with something of Indian instinct, and I have the character of a very expert horseman,' wrote Bird from the Rockies. 'I write horseman, because I have been living for ten months where sidesaddles are not recognized, and if you saw me on my mustang, and a peaked Mexican saddle with great wooden stirrups and Mexican spurs, if you did not say it was "neither brute nor human", you would say "neither man nor woman." '[50] Often the internalization of this role was so complete that references to themselves as masculine would be made quite unwittingly. 'I have given into temptation and am the third Englishman to ascend the Peak,' wrote Kingsley in her diary after climbing Mount Cameroon.[51] Gaunt could unselfconsciously count Government House at Bathurst as 'womanless' as she sat in it, which led her to hire a male servant to take care of domestic chores.[52] At Udjidji, where Stanley's poignant meeting with Livingstone occurred, Hall sat back and imagined herself as the young American greeting the old man, creating a vivid and detailed picture of the encounter.[53] On the other side of the world, Lilian Brown sat amongst the San Blas Indians of Central America and again imagined herself as Stanley and Livingstone, surrounded by dark peoples. Christie's sister Alice wrote to her in Asia, 'one deplores Stanley's death, as now there is no one to go look for you.'[54]

As with their images of the foreign worlds, the women travellers took scant account of specific time or place in their identification with the tradition of white male exploration. While the lands and peoples were dissolved into the Exotic, the Savage, the Unknown, the women's roles were simplified into the Adventurer, the Discoverer,

[50] 'Lady Travellers', *Blackwood's Edinburgh Magazine*, vol. 160; (1896), p. 60.
[51] Kingsley, *Travels in West Africa*, p. 550.
[52] Gaunt, *Alone in West Africa*, p. 18.
[53] Hall, *A Woman's Trek from the Cape to Cairo*, p. 164.
[54] Quoted in Stewart, *Alicella*, p. 103.

the Explorer. It was a pervasive image which could be used to assert their authority over many different foreign peoples in many different exotic lands.

As women travellers frequently pointed to the continuities and similarities with earlier European male travellers, the supremacy of distinctions of race above those of sex allowed them to take little account of their one obvious difference from these forbears – the fact they were female. But while their racial status was the most essential element of their inclusion into the gallery of explorers, there were other qualifications needed. One was the achievement of a 'first' – a new route, an unconquered summit, a region and people no European had witnessed before. Accordingly, women travellers stressed, sometimes to the point of fabrication, their unique achievements and the strangeness, to European eyes, of the lands through which they travelled. 'I daresay you have never heard of Shala,' commented Durham, 'the wild heart of a wild land.'[55] When deciding upon her route, of prime importance was its foreignness to Western Europeans; 'I did not want to go through the Christian tribes by the Ura Vezirit, like other travellers. What I wanted was something new – through Moslem lands, which, perhaps, when the *besa* was over, would again be closed.'[56] Although she had travelled thousands of miles, Kingsley drew the attention of her audience to her two 'firsts' – the short overland journey from the upper Ogooué to the Remboué in Gabon, a journey of little more than fifty miles and lasting less than a week. 'I think I may say no region in Africa, certainly no region of equal importance, is so little known in England,' she claimed.[57] Her second achievement was to climb Mount Cameroon by a route previously unattempted by Europeans, perhaps because it was a relatively easy and unchallenging path.[58] Bell boasted that she had reached the very

[55] Durham, *High Albania*, p. 118.

[56] Ibid., p. 302.

[57] Kingsley, *Travels in West Africa*, p. 353.

[58] To put Kingsley's claims into perspective, it is interesting to compare present-day climbing of Mount Cameroon. It is now necessary to acquire a visa from the tourist office, and be accompanied by an official guide. Visas are not issued during the rainy season – from April until November – as it is considered too difficult and dangerous. Kingsley made her ascent in September. Strictly speaking, the ascent of the mountain is not a climb at all, but a stiff walk. There are no rock climbing or vertical ascents. Walkers today are usually able to reach the summit in a day. The route via Buea, which Kingsley pioneered, is now the most popular because of its ease.

edge of the Palestine Exploration Map and was about to ride over it.
As with their claims to power and prestige, these 'firsts' were racially
specific and relied upon emphasizing, often through display and dress,
the difference between the women travellers and their surroundings.
In the Prokletija, 'the Forbidden Land', Durham noted she 'was said to
be the first foreign female and the first female dressed *alla franga* in
Vuthaj; and the first foreigner of any sort that had come right into
Vuthaj.'[59]

In attitude as well as achievement, women travellers sought to
emulate the white male explorers they had so avidly read as young
women in their homes. In addition to the commonly used derogatory
titles which denoted the relationship between the colonizer and the
colonial subject – Christie's 'lacqueys', North's 'monkeys' – women
travellers adopted the practice of giving their porters, bearers, cooks,
and guides names which reflected idiosyncratic physical characteristics
or mannerisms. Among Kingsley's companions on the Ogooué were
those she called Gray Shirt, Pagan and Duke, thereby reducing their
power and humanity in contrast to her own accentuated sense of
individuality which in her frequent claims to be 'first' and 'only' she
always stressed. Close named one of her guides 'Baboon' on her
East Africa safari. From India, North wrote that she had nicknamed
her 'ill countenanced savage' servant 'Calaban'.[60] The uniqueness of
the white-skinned traveller amongst a dark-skinned people was often
highlighted. While Gaunt claimed 'a black man was a black man to
me, and he had no individuality about him,' Gordon Cumming wrote
from Canton that 'all these men and all these women are extraordinarily alike. The same features, the same yellow skin, the same black
hair, dark eyes, and, at first sight, even the same expression.'[61]

Women travellers also claimed status and position over foreign male
peoples by infantilizing them. As adults, the travellers described the
Arabs as 'babies', Albanians as a 'child-people', and Tibetans as 'wild
children of the wild heights!'[62] David-Neel accentuated her role as
mother to her companion Yongden, reducing the adult man to the
status of a dependent young boy. Later in life she candidly admitted

[59] Durham, *High Albania*, p. 138.
[60] North to Arthur Burnell 24 Aug. 1878, Doora Hath.
[61] Gaunt, *Alone in West Africa*, p. 176; Gordon Cumming, *Wanderings in China*, p. 40.
[62] Edwards, *A Thousand Miles Up the Nile*, p. 166; Durham, *High Albania*, p. 223; David-Neel,
My Journey to Lhasa, p. 142.

the purpose behind her maternal attitude: 'I consider [Yongden] to be the fourteen-year-old kid that I took close to me in bygone days. But the years have passed and the kid will be thirty-nine at Christmas. Happily he has remained a child in many ways, perhaps because of the manner in which I have directed him. I acknowledge my egotism. I wanted to have someone useful to me no matter the circumstances and who would bend to my desires. This has been to the detriment of the boy's development . . . I preferred to keep him dependent.'[63] But the most extreme expression of power through language was when the women travellers, who themselves adopted and accepted male titles, gave male attenders female names. Bell, as *effendi*, called the 'obliging gentleman in a fez who brings me my hot bath in the morning and is ready at all times to fly round in my service' in Jerusalem, 'my housemaid'.[64]

The women travellers learnt to develop colonial temperaments to match their colonial status – the very same temperaments they had rejected when turned on themselves and exercised in attributing them with a supremely feminine role. Outside the colonial compounds, however, women travellers revelled in their control over people, and in particular adult men, which this same attitude realized. Climbing over the rocks from Sekondi to Shama, Gaunt exercised this authority with undisguised glee:

> My hammock-boys stopped, and I got out and watched my men with the loads scrambling over the rocks, and one thing I was sure of, on my own feet I could not go that way. I mentioned that to my demurring men, and insisted that over those rocks they had to get me somehow, if it took eight hammock-boys to do it. And over those rocks I was got without setting foot out of my hammock, and I fairly purred with pride, most unjustly setting it down to my own prowess and feeling it marked a distinct stage on my journey Eastwards.[65]

[63] David-Neel, *Journal de voyage*, vol. 2, p. 347, quoted in Foster, *Forbidden Journey*, pp. 293–4.

[64] Bell to Hugh Bell 13 Dec. 1899, Hotel Jerusalem, quoted in Bell, *Letters*, p. 65. Jane Hunter, *The Gospel of Gentility. American Women Missionaries in Turn-of-the-Century China*, (New Haven 1984), p. 250, points out that women missionaries gave their Chinese male servants female names.

[65] Gaunt, *Alone in West Africa*, pp. 126–7.

Mary Gaunt at the Ming Tombs, 1912.
Reproduced by kind permission of Yvonne Fox.

Bell took great pride in directing 'a well-trained and well-organized camp, where the work goes as regularly as Big Ben, and the men have cheerful faces and willing hands.'[66] For Bell, setting up tent meant simply ordering others to do it for her, as for Gaunt conquering the summit of a stiff hill meant her bearers carrying her to the top. In Edwards' account of digging the sand away from the entrance to an unexcavated momument at Abou Simbel, which she claimed as a discovery and scratched her name on like graffiti, she but barely mentions that she had the assistance of one hundred Arab labourers. Bell wrote to her stepmother, 'You would be suprised to see the scene in the middle of which I am writing. Thirty one Turks are busy with picks and spades clearing out a church and monastery. At intervals they call out to me "Effendim, effendim! is this enough?"'[67] While women claimed to fish, excavate, collect butterflies and other specimens on their travels, often this work was undertaken by one of their vast retinue. French-Sheldon's morning roll call listed 153 paid attendants, plus forty more volunteers, slaves and hangers on. When Gaunt was asked how few carriers she could cope with on the short Sekondi-Shama route, she replied seventeen, plus two servants. Travelling *Alone in West Africa* meant only alone from other Europeans. Hall hired twenty-five porters for her machilla alone; her total caravan numbered forty-two. While the women still claimed these achievements as their own, their real and as important success was in exercising power over large numbers of non-European peoples, and in particular adult men.

The size of the women travellers' retinues, equipment and baggage did not, however, in any way compare with the hundreds of men and women employed by the male travellers. Lack of resources and access to sponsorship made the reality, if not the rhetoric, of their experiences in the foreign lands very different from those of their male rolemodels. Stanley took on three hundred porters with his newspaper backers' money, and de Brazza by his third mission commanded 770 men and forty-four canoes, as Kingsley herself points out. Although she would claim de Brazza as her predecessor, her own crew and guides never numbered more than nine. Bell was angry at being given two escorts to Kerak, which she felt was 'quite unnecessary, but this is the penalty of my distinguished social position! and also, I think, of my

[66] Bell, *The Desert and the Sown*, p. 271.
[67] Bell to Florence Bell 14 June 1907, Daile, quoted in Bell, *Letters*, p. 243.

nationality, for the Turks are much afraid of us and he probably thinks
I have some project of annexation in mind.'[68] Durham simply hired
one local guide, loading her belongings on to her pack animal.
Although Gaunt employed a score of carriers, her baggage, she
insisted, consisted modestly of a folding table and chair, enamel
plates, two glasses, a knife and fork, kitchen utensils, bedding,
cushions and rugs. She forgot to mention that she also carried a hefty
typewriter.

In addition to the size of retinue and equipment, the nature of the
routes of women travellers was also curtailed by financial restrictions.
All showed constant concern about the financing of their trips, and
costs per mile would be meticuously calculated and plans made with
the minimum of expenditure in mind. Kingsley budgeted one pound
for every five miles in West Africa. As a result, the length of time and
distance of her 'first' route bore little resemblance to Stanley's three
thousand mile journey. This did not, however, prevent her from
pointing out that she stayed in the same hut at Kabinda as the
transcontinental traveller. Ten years later, it cost Gaunt eighteen
pounds to hire muleteers, four mules and one donkey to take her 1,000
miles through West Africa. Yongden and David-Neel between them
spent only one hundred rupees on their four months' journey to Lhasa
in 1923. 'One need not be rolling in riches to travel in the blessed
lands of Asia!' she observed.[69] Edwards noted how the cost of running
the *Philae*, including wages and food for passengers and crew, was ten
pounds per day. Bird, who soon financed her travels entirely by her
writing, found she could live in her own peculiar style for ten pounds a
month on the Sandwich Islands.

Even those travellers who financed their trips through inherited
wealth shared an insecurity in their income. Christie could support
her own journeys through the settlement agreed after her father's
death, but even she felt cautious about spending; as her father's will
had so clearly demonstrated, it was hers as a privilege, not a right. Her
married, and therefore more financially secure, sister Alice was
appalled at Christie's parsimony. The coat she wore in 1912 was 'still
in active service' over twenty years later, which caused Alice to
order her chauffeur to drive on past her in an Edinburgh street.[70] Other

[68] Bell to Hugh Bell 23 Mar. 1900, 'from my tent', quoted in Bell, *Letters*, p. 72.
[69] David-Neel, *My Journey to Lhasa*, p. 116.
[70] Related by Ava Stewart (niece-in-law) to John Murray 12 Sep. 1955.

travellers were, initially at least, provided for by their family, whose pull was often felt on the purse strings – one reason why even in middle-age Bell would ask her parents' permission before embarking on a new journey. Gordon Cumming's landed background did not save her from being, as the youngest and unmarried daughter, made homeless on the death of her father. The family property went to her brothers, and for the remainder of her life in Britain she was shuttlecocked from one relative to another relying on their hospitality and perhaps, their pity.

Acutely aware of the relatively short lines they could draw across the terrain they had travelled, women were often reluctant to include maps in their published accounts. David-Neel did not put one in *My Journey to Lhasa* and displayed a vagueness over dates and plans which alarmed reviewers. Kingsley's *Travels in West Africa* included only a vague outline of the area in which she travelled and did not show her Gabon route. While Du Chaillu boasted of the quantative achievements of his travels – an 8000 mile journey, in which he shot 2000 birds, 1000 quadrupeds, and suffered 50 attacks of fever for which he took 14 ounzes of quinine – women became defensive about their decision to cover only a short distance, often holding no particular goal in sight. 'The "arm-chair explorer" may be impressed by the greatness of length of the red line route of an explorer,' wrote Kingsley, 'but the person locally acquainted with the region may know that some of those long red lines are very easily made . . . . In other regions a small red line means 400 times the work and danger, and requires 4,000 times the pluck, perseverance and tact.'[71] Edwards explained how her route through Egypt, however mundane and cursory it may appear, gave her the most privileged view of the country and its people. 'The traveller on the Nile really sees the whole land of Egypt,' she wrote. 'Going from point to point in other countries, one follows a thin line of road, railway, or river, leaving wide tracts unexplored on either side.' But in the mountain waste through which the Nile ran Edwards could 'survey the entire face of the country from desert to desert.'[72]

For many women travellers, the short distance of their journeys was not merely a necessary result of restricted finances. The decision not to imitate the long red lines of earlier male travellers, while still

[71] Kingsley, *Travels in West Africa*, p. 35.
[72] Edwards, *A Thousand Miles Up the Nile*, p. 167.

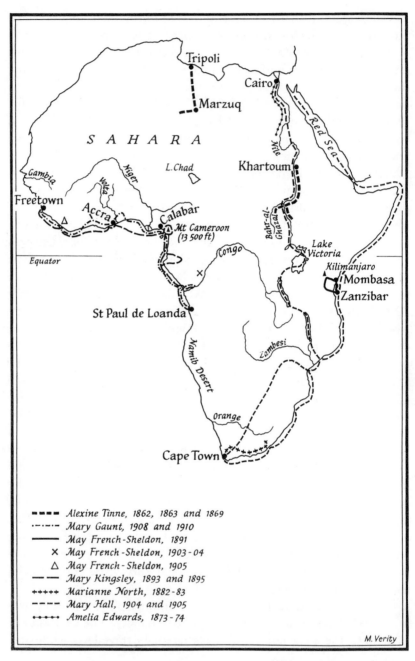

▪▪▪▪	Alexine Tinne, 1862, 1863 and 1869
▪·▪·▪	Mary Gaunt, 1908 and 1910
─────	May French-Sheldon, 1891
✕	May French-Sheldon, 1903-04
△	May French-Sheldon, 1905
─ ─ ─	Mary Kingsley, 1893 and 1895
+++++	Marianne North, 1882-83
─── ───	Mary Hall, 1904 and 1905
••••••	Amelia Edwards, 1873-74

M. Verity

Africa.

relying upon the image of the European traveller and the authority this gave them, was at least in part a positive choice. Gaunt explained her own particular style of travelling: 'setting out on a long journey by road, moving along slowly, at the rate of thirty miles a day, I find I do not have the end in view in my mind all the time . . . I take a point a couple of days ahead and concentrate on getting there. Having arrived so far, I am so pleased with the performance I can concentrate on the next couple of days ahead. So I pass on, comfortably, with the invigorating feeling of something accomplished.'[73] Unable to achieve her original plan of following the caravan route through China eastwards to Central Asia, she simply forges a new journey by the Trans-Siberian railway instead. Riding on the back of a camel from Amman, Bell recorded, 'We march slowly, for they eat as they go, but I don't mind. I never tire of looking at the round gold landscape and wondering at its amazing desolation. I like marching on through it and sometimes I wonder whether there is anywhere that I am at all anxious to reach.'[74] Kingsley assures her readers that she 'did not want to go across the continent, and I do not hanker after Zanzibar but only to go puddling about obscure districts in West Africa after raw fetish and fresh-water fish.'[75]

The contrived tradition of exploration, expressed in such ceremonies as flag planting and the naming of geographical features, was also seldom exercised by women travellers. There is no Kingsley River flowing through West Africa, no Bird Peak in the Rockies, no Durham Lake in Albania. *Les Chutes Macleod* were so named on the insistence of Olive Macleod's male travelling companion. While the American travellers May French-Sheldon and Fanny Bullock Workman both carried flags, Workman's read 'Votes for Women' as she waved it at 21,000 feet on the Silver Throne plateau of the Karakorams – an appropriation and inversion of the symbol. Kingsley placed a few rocks on the cairn at the summit of Mount Cameroon and threw her card unceremoniously amongst them, 'merely as a civility to Mungo [the mountain], a civility his Majesty will soon turn into pulp. Not that it matters – what is done is done.'[76] For many women travellers the important element of their journey was the discovery not

[73] Gaunt, *A Broken Journey*, p. 93.
[74] Bell to Hugh Bell 4 Feb. 1914, quoted in Bell, *Letters*, p. 335.
[75] Kingsley, *Travels in West Africa*, p. 8.
[76] Ibid., p. 594.

of a foreign land but of themselves, the exploration not of an unmapped river but of the avenues to forging new horizons for their own personal experience and self-fulfillment.

Essential to this experience was the aloneness, meaning separation from European companions, which they celebrated. Women travellers emphasized their privileged position as travellers unencumbered with the trappings, baggage and entourage of male explorers, often contrasting these expeditions to their own more modest journeys. Tibet, said David-Neel, who always travelled with a folding bath tub, is not really a difficult country for 'people who can travel according to the native fashion, as I have done on all my journeys. If one needs large tents, tables, chairs, tinned Western food, an oven to bake the bread, and a gramophone which some explorers carried in their luggage, then perhaps he will get into trouble with the rustic Thibetan paths, and also, perhaps, with the sturdy hillmen who have made them.'[77] Kingsley proudly claimed to have earnt the nickname 'Only Me' from answering 'It's only me' on arriving at each new village, and made cruel comparisons between her own unaided rough travel and that of other Europeans: 'The Fang took my conduct as a matter of course, never having travelled with white men before, or learnt the way some of them require carrying over swamps and rivers and so on,' she wrote. Her experiences would have been very different, she continued, if instead of travelling in remote Fang country, she had stuck to the Coast 'where the inhabitants are used to find the white man incapable of personal exertion, requiring to be carried in a hammock, or wheeled in a go-cart or a Bath chair about the streets of their coast towns, depending for the defence of their settlement on a body of black soldiers.'[78] A commentator on the pioneer missionary Mary Slessor explained,

> Alone among savages she would seem at a greater disadvantage than a man. But, strangely enough, their very defencelessness often appears a safeguard to women, and they are able to penetrate into unexplored lands without opposition, where men could only go at grave risk of their lives . . . the inhabitants of those dark countries should look with suspicion on a white man appearing among them. He would probably carry a gun, in itself

[77] David-Neel, *My Journey to Lhasa*, p. 233.
[78] Kingsley, *Travels in West Africa*, pp. 276–7.

a sign of danger; he may be the precursor of an army, he may have sinister designs on their liberties; but a woman would certainly not have come to fight, and though they cannot understand why she should wish to visit them, they are inclined to regard her as harmless, though probably mad and an interesting phenomenon.[79]

'A woman's strongest protection is the fact that she is unprotected,' colluded Bisland on her round-the-world trip.[80] Durham noted how her modest appearance and one-man retinue diffused her apparent threat as a representative of the British government to a village and its leader. 'My appearance,' she notes, 'justified them in believing my statement that I was of low degree . . . . If he thought I was really the King's sister, he would cut off my head at once. He asked if I were afraid. I, entering into his pleasantry, replied that if some one would lend me a revolver I should be very pleased to shoot him. This is the sort of joke they like.'[81]

While women shared in the benefits of power and influence accruing to them on the grounds of their race, they still felt a limitation on the wielding of this newfound authority, especially when exercised through physical force. 'What they wanted of course was a master to beat them, and as they did not get it, they took advantage of me,' worried Gaunt, frightened of losing hold of her tenuous and temporary exercise of power.[82] Hall experienced similar feelings towards her carriers: 'merely telling them to do a thing, when they know the order is not likely to be backed up by a good thrashing if not obeyed, has very little effect sometimes,' she wrote. 'However, I felt I must maintain my authority somehow, so I kicked over their fire, and they had to go supperless to bed. It taught them a lesson.'[83] When her caravan made a noisy and slow start in the morning she 'harboured the humiliating idea that it arose from want of respect for the authority of my sex.'[84] Bell also wrote, 'there are moments when being a woman increases ones difficulties. What my servants needed last night was a

---

[79] Tabor, *Pioneer Women*, vol. 1, p. 99.
[80] Bisland, *A Flying Trip Around the World*, p. 31.
[81] Durham, *High Albania*, p. 315.
[82] Gaunt, *Alone in West Africa*, p. 12.
[83] Hall, *A Woman's Trek from the Cape to Cairo*, p. 367.
[84] Ibid., p. 344.

good beating and that's what they would have got if I had been a man
– I seldom remember being in such a state of suppressed rage! – But as
it is I have to hold my tongue and get round them.'[85] French-Sheldon,
however, had no such inhibitions; she flogged her porters with her
kibosh. When Christie found it difficult to get a boat from Kabul to
Srinigar, she presumed 'with a woman they try it on more.'[86]

Women travellers felt they had to act the part of male explorers, a
part which did not necessarily come easily to them. Although
French-Sheldon did not shirk from using physical force, if a porter
wished to speak to her he had to provide a box for the traveller to
stand upon. While Gaunt's tiny frame encouraged Africans to think
she was a child, she repeated over to herself 'I must rule this caravan'
to prepare her for a role unrehearsed at home. 'Why they obeyed me I
don't know,' she admitted.[87] As she raised a small hand mirror to her
sunburnt face a stern glare stared back at her, lips set in a straight firm
line, and she wondered whether they would ever soften again into the
woman she knew herself as in Britain. To exert her authority,
Kingsley also consciously assumed a part:

> I noticed that the surface of the mud before us had a sort of
> quiver running through it, and here and there exhibited
> swellings on its surface . . . and feeling it was a situation more
> suited to Mr Stanley than myself, I attempted to emulate his
> methods and addressed my men. 'Boys', said I, 'this beastly hole
> is tidal, and the tide is coming in. As it took us two hours to get
> to this sainted swamp, it's time we started out, one time, and the
> nearest way . . . '. The boys took the hint.[88]

Even French-Sheldon had doubts. 'I looked with amazement over all
these strange black and every shade of brown faces, with much
brutality imprinted thereupon, and marvelled if I should always be
able to control them and make them subservient to my commands,'
she wrote in a rare moment of weakness.[89]

Alongside the practical discrepancies between male and female

[85] Bell to Florence Bell 17 Apr. 1905, Payas, quoted in Bell, *Letters*, pp. 212–13.
[86] Diary entry 17 Oct. 1904, Kabul.
[87] Gaunt, *Alone in West Africa*, p. 137.
[88] Kingsley, *Travels in West Africa*, pp. 298–9.
[89] French-Sheldon, *Sultan to Sultan*, p. 105.

travellers, there were also elements of the male explorer image and the land he conquered which could not be easily applied to women. The Orient, Africa and Asia – the Savage Lands – were portrayed as the female, a sexual entity to be wooed, conquered and penetrated. An African or Asian experience was the acid test of character, the ultimate, encapsulated challenge of masculinity. The wild, the tropics was the stage upon which true manhood was forged – the imperial drama of the untamed and alluring female continent and the lone white man she embraced. The Unknown and Savage Lands simply made a man of you.

A woman traveller could only conquer and penetrate by ignoring the fact of her sex, aligning herself entirely with the white male explorer. Swaying along the West African coast Gaunt recorded,

> There was growing up in me a feeling of satisfaction with myself . . . because I was getting on. I was doing the thing so many men had said I could not possibly do, and I was doing it fairly easily . . . here with my carriers I was on my own, and I began to regard them as the captives of my bow and spear, and therefore I at least could not find the country uninteresting. Who ever found the land he had conquered dull?[90]

But the contradictions of being a woman in a male-defined activity were constantly present, and the fact of gender would always threaten to undermine the women travellers' complete identification with and absorption amongst white male travellers. 'Lady' and 'explorer' was an uneasy combination, and as such women travellers' experiences would differ greatly from those of their male counterparts who fell comfortably within the 'explorer' mould.

All women travellers were aware of this dichotomy of being a woman with a temporary male status, and the resulting tensions were manifested in many ways. A contemporary commentator observed of Alexine Tinne's journals of her Nile journey that they 'preserve many curious details in unconscious illusion of the mixed character of this expedition . . . the handsome woman, mindful of her toilette appliances, as well as the courageous explorer, athirst for knowledge.'[91] At the same time as 'emulating Stanley', both in actions

---

[90] Gaunt, *Alone in West Africa*, p. 163.
[91] Adams, *Celebrated Women Travellers*, p. 188.

and language, Kingsley could call upon traditional feminine attributes. She was, she found, 'a Father and Mother' to her 'men', and 'a very stern though kind set of parents I have been.'[92] French-Sheldon, despite visibly displaying her authority in many ways, was called Bébé Bwana – literally meaning Madame Sir.

The burden of conformity to two contradictory ideals – femininity and male exploration – haunted many of the women travellers even when remote from European settlements. Their more personal and private female identity conflicted with their public identity as a white male traveller. When the road ahead of Kingsley's party is blocked, '"How are we going to get through that way?" says I, with natural feminine alarm. "We are not, sir," says Gray Shirt,' back to her.[93] In charge of a West Coast steamer, Kingsley exhausts herself in 'my dual capacity of skipper and stewardess', ordering the 'men' and taking care of a sick woman passenger.[94] Although David-Neel says she is pretending to be a poor female pilgrim, she wonders 'after all, was it really a disguise?'[95]

How far were attempts to diffuse the tensions between being a woman and an explorer also hoping to define a female tradition of exploration? The women travellers referred back to the experiences of male travellers, and reverted to naming themselves in the masculine, as there was no apparent female tradition of travel to be included in and defined by. But although the number of women travellers was small, it was not this which prevented the formation of female rolemodels. The gallery of male explorers was a select and nameable group – Stanley, Livingstone, Burton, and Du Chaillu, the heroes of popular culture. If women travellers were presented with evidence of other women's travelling experiences, they were often quick to belittle them and distance their own experience and travel. Christie commented that the road west from Islamabad was 'quite good in spite of the description I have been reading in *Afoot through Kashmir Valleys* by Marion Doughty. She tells a heap of lies and talks of "being in the wilds" when she was never further than the Sinde Valley.'[96] North was

[92] Kingsley, *Travels in West Africa*, p. 604.
[93] Ibid., p. 238.
[94] Ibid., p. 416.
[95] David-Neel, *My Journey to Lhasa*, p. 18.
[96] Diary entry 15 Oct. 1904, Vernay.

determined in her attempts to distance her own extensive, if not adventurous, travels from any other woman's journeys. At Smyrna she found a great deal of excitement aroused by,

> a German Fraulein of 'a certain age' who had suddenly come amongst them, and who was ambitious of becoming a second Ida Pfeiffer. She wished to begin her adventures by a journey overland to Constantinople – a road infested by all kinds of robbers and wild tribes. She thought she could ride it all alone with a dragoman and a Turkish dictionary! I made friends with her, and found she drew tolerably, and was a nice modest little woman, but had little idea of the difference between the two semi-civilised ends of the expedition, – and the long wide waste between them. Her ideas of teaching herself deprivations were amusing. She was staying in a rich luxurious family in Smyrna, and insisted on washing her own cuffs and collars (only) herself – scraping them with a penknife – and living on bread and onions. She would carry a big portfolio in one hand, and a bag in the other, and walk through the streeets and bazaars at the rate of a Turkish express train. Of course they thought her mad, and respected her accordingly.[97]

North found herself continually having to fight off other women travellers' intrusion into her own sphere. In Ceylon, she was constantly confronted by people making comparisons between herself and Gordon Cumming; rather than welcoming a fellow female traveller, she persistently rejected their being linked. 'I got quite tired of her name, and heard far more about her than that beautiful country with its orchids and elephants,' she recorded.[98] She was no more flattering of Bird. 'I cannot entirely believe in her,' she wrote when the two travellers met for tea in the gallery of North's paintings at Kew. 'I felt I was entertaining a kind of clever puritanical actress.'[99] Although these comments were intended for publication, a wise editor removed them from the final draft. Durham was equally critical of a fellow woman traveller, Rebecca West, at the publication of *Black Lamb and Grey Falcon* describing her journey to Yugoslavia. 'The

[97] North, *Further Recollections of a Happy Life*, p. 93.
[98] North, *Recollections of a Happy Life*, vol. 1, p. 303.
[99] Manuscript of autobiography, pp. 1028–9.

novelist Miss West has written an immense book on the strength of one pleasure trip to Yugoslavia, but with no previous knowledge of land or people,' she wrote to an influential historian.[100] West's brief references to Durham in her tome were equally uncomplimentary: she is 'the sort of person devoted to good works and austerities, who is traditionally supposed to keep a cat and a parrot.' The novelist was forced to withdraw Durham's name under threat of libel.[101]

Nor did the women travellers encourage others to follow in their footsteps. Gaunt's simple advice to any adventurous woman who expressed an interest in taking to travel was 'Don't'.[102] 'Upon my soul I almost wish there weren't a desert route,' wrote Bell to her father. 'It brings silly females, all with introductions to me.'[103] In her 'Nameless region' in the Rocky Mountains, Bird as forcefully and straightfor-wardly warns 'this is no region for tourists and women', thereby reinforcing the image of a terrain in which she can assume the role and power of a male explorer.[104] When Edwards feels she has reached the edge of civilization at the Second Cataract, she tells other travellers to turn back – then sails on over it herself.[105]

In claiming a place in the gallery of white male travellers, the women were claiming more than a mere explorer accolade. They were claiming a freedom from the gender restrictions of their home societies, found in the white male status they could assume in the Dark Continent, the Orient, the Savage Lands. This freedom and power was dependent upon their exaggeration and exploitation of differences of race over differences of gender. Adopting this male persona was one way, ironically, of deflecting criticism. For although they broke many of the accepted limits of feminine behaviour, they did not confront and challenge any of these restrictions: everything they achieved outside the traditionally feminine they achieved as 'white men'. Only when they assumed the status of 'a Person', 'Bébé Bwana' and 'Sir', which negated their sex, did they also begin to assume masculine power. It was as 'white men' that they canoed up rapids, ascended mountain passes, made pioneering journeys through

---

[100] Durham to G. P. Gooch 4 Mar. 1942, quoted in Hodgson, 'Edith Durham', p. 30.
[101] Ibid., p. 30.
[102] Gaunt, *Alone in West Africa*, p. 217.
[103] Bell to Hugh Bell, 1925, quoted in Bell, *Letters*, p. 725.
[104] Bird, *A Lady's Life in the Rocky Mountains*, p. 61.
[105] Edwards, *A Thousand Miles Up the Nile*, p. 319.

the bush; as women, within the colonial compound, they conformed to all that was demanded of them. This conservatism and exploitation of difference would later be the forming pattern behind their political commitment.

Yet however much they benefitted from their ability to exploit their racial and colonial status, the underlying tensions between being defined at once as racial superiors and sexual subordinates could not be eradicated. They would seek to resolve these by moulding a new image for themselves offered in previously unexplored areas of expertise, where as travellers they could be both professional and feminine.

5

Virgin Territory

As the women travellers rose early with the dawn, packed up their folding furniture, gathered together their cumbersome photographic equipment and ordered the bearers to lift them gently into the litter, they began another long day of an uncomfortable and uneasy journey in the footsteps of male exploration. As they reached their destinations, tables taken down from the tired backs of the pack animals and unfolded, the nightly ritual of recording their experiences in copious diaries and journal-letters to a distant landlocked sister began once again. In these closely written pages, sometimes with lines crisscrossed vertically and horizontally over each other to economize on paper, their turbulent inner lives and perceptions of the outer world were jumbled inextricably together. Awkward participators in the tradition of white male exploration, they moulded an image of these distant lands from their own particular, feminine perspective within it.

As latecomers to the exploration endeavour, women travellers were imbued with the images of the earlier exploits and adventures of the travellers of their childhood reading. Looking back to the great era of discovery of the mid-nineteenth century, they pictured themselves as adventurers in untamed lands, not representatives of colonialism in subjected societies. As they modelled themselves on heroes of a fading world, they also filtered the peoples and cultures who hosted them through this same antiquated light.

On Isabella Bird's first voyage out in 1873, it was the hard-drinking trapper Rocky Mountain Jim who attracted her, 'a man for whom there is now no room,' she wrote, 'for the time of blows and blood in this part of Colorado is past.' It was an attraction for which she later felt obliged to apologize to her British audience: 'I write . . . only as he appeared to me. His life, without doubt, was deeply stained with crimes and vices, and his reputation for ruffianism was a deserved one . . . . It was not until after I left Colorado . . . that I heard of the worst points of his character,' she footnoted.[1] This living relic of the pioneer past, shacked up in a trapper's hut far away from the parlours now dotting the American West, stirred forty-two-year-old Isabella Bird as none of the men of the Edinburgh drawing rooms had done; that she even entertained the thought of marrying him is apparent from her all too frequent, unprovoked denials of any romantic attachment.

From her first journey to West Africa in 1893, Mary Kingsley was also drawn to men rooted in tales of bygone days – the 'palm oil ruffians' lambasted by the press for their emotional and sexual relationships with West African women and open disdain for missionaries. Deserting the missionary compounds, she stayed with the trader R. E. Dennett at his post in Kabinda for two weeks, a considerable time for the constantly shifting traveller. Here she joined the traders' mess for seven o'clock supper each night, arguing over the price of tobacco or the new Colonial Secretary, or admiring Dennett's child by his African wife.[2]

These pioneers and palm oil ruffians were the first characters on whom the women travellers focused their dated visions. From these initial impressions, they built up larger vistas which always looked back to former, golden, imaginary ages. From Albania, Edith Durham wrote to her sister, 'I have in fact had an extraordinary glimpse (for it is only a glimspe) of the life of by-gone centuries. I feel as if I must have dreamt it, or be hundreds of years old.'[3] Being carried under the archways at Yung-ning, Mary Gaunt felt as if she was travelling back through the gateway into the days of the Bible.[4] The physical landscapes of some distant lands provided richer material for such imaginative comparisons than others. While sub-saharan Africa preserved few monuments of antiquity, the palaces of the Indian subcontinent, the forts of the Biblical Lands and the shrines and

---

[1] Bird, *A Lady's Life in the Rocky Mountains*, pp. 92–3.

[2] 'Miss M. H. Kingsley's Visit to Cabinda 1893' by R. E. Dennett, African Trader, unpublished manuscript.

[3] Durham to her sister Nelly, 13 June 1908, quoted in Hodgson, 'Edith Durham', p. 17.

[4] Gaunt, *A Broken Journey*, p. 110.

temples of Egypt stirred visions of ancient but still living worlds. At Thebes, Amelia Edwards seemed 'to be admitted to a glimpse of those original shrines upon which Moses – learned in the sacred lore of the Egyptians – modelled, with but little alteration, his Ark of the Covenant.'[5] The very ground upon which she walked showed evidence of the past. 'It has been aptly said,' she wrote, 'that all Egypt is but the facade of an immense sepulchre. This is literally true; for the terraced cliffs that hem in the Nile to East and West, and the rocky bed of the desert beneath our feet, are everywhere honey-combed with tombs . . . The mummied generations are everywhere – in the bowels of the mountains, in the faces of the cliffs, in the rock-cut labyrinths which underlie the surface of the desert.'[6]

Lack of physical remnants did not deter the creation of a past in the present, however; if there was no ruin or monument to embellish, women travellers constructed romantic landscapes across continents, mingling images and histories indiscriminately in their quest for that perfect era of long ago. Climbing into her sampan at Pao-ting, Mary Gaunt imagined, 'on the banks of the Euphrates or the Tigris in the days before the dawn of history men went backwards and forwards in boats like these we embarked in.'[7] In Mongolia, Beatrix Bulstrode, found 'at last the opportunity of meeting with medievalism untouched.'[8] In Edith Durham's 'Land of the Living Past', 'the wanderer from the West stands awestruck . . . filled with vague memories of the cradle of his race, saying, "This did I some thousands of years ago; thus did I lie in wait for mine enemy; so thought I and so acted I in the beginning of Time."'[9] To emphasize her own participation in this ancient world, she translates her Albanian conversation into antiquated English: 'Art thou wild too?' she asks a tribesman.[10]

This was not a naive, uncalculated recreation of a utopian ancient world, but a conscious search for a landscape in which women travellers believed they could discover their buried selves. Their travelling was undertaken not only to gather information on other peoples, but also as a means to the knowledge and realization of their

---

[5] Edwards, *A Thousand Miles Up the Nile*, p. 423.
[6] Edwards, *Pharoahs, Fellahs and Explorers*, pp. 5 and 12.
[7] Gaunt, *A Broken Journey*, p. 142.
[8] Bulstrode, *A Tour in Mongolia*, p. 1.
[9] Durham, *High Albania*, p. 1.
[10] Ibid., p. 45.

own needs and ambitions. The record of their perceptions became as much a portrait of themselves as of the people and culture about them.

Ancient history was seen as a time of the spirit, not merely of physical existence, a time when primal humanity was allowed to flourish and the essence of human identity emerged. 'I think no place where human beings live has given me such an impression of majestic isolation from all the world,' wrote Edith Durham from the plain of Thethi. 'It is a spot were centuries shrivel; the river might be the world's well-spring, its banks the fit home of elemental instincts – passions that are red and rapid.'[11] Beatrix Bulstrode explained how the medievalism she unearthed in Mongolia met her 'inherent desire to revert awhile to the primitive.'[12] In the Syrian desert, Gertrude Bell wrote, 'while I wonder and rejoice to look upon this primeval existence, it does not seem to be a new thing; it is familiar, it is a part of inherited memory.'[13] Amelia Edwards sat by herself after a day's sketching in the heat, and wondered at the excavations going on about her. 'It is a wonderful place to be alone in,' she recorded, 'a place in which the very darkness and silence are old, and in which Time himself seems to have fallen asleep. Wandering to and fro among these sculptured halls, like a shade among shadows, one seems to have left the world behind; to have done with the teachings of the present; to belong one's self to the past.'[14] Here, in this world unfettered by proprieties, niceties, genteel behaviour, in the brutal stark face of the unbounded force of unchristian Gods, women hoped they might find the self for which they were hunting.

Although images of the 'noble savage' had passed out of popular parlance and been replaced by weak and passive portraits of African and Asian peoples ripe for Christianity and colonization, women travellers persisted in recording savages, cannibals and ferocious tribesmen in countries where the wilderness had long been tamed. To make this image more visual, they dressed the people who were their daily companions in the manner of ancient tribes. Elizabeth Bisland found 'medieval folk' in Japan in the way they wore their jerkins;[15] Edith Durham nicknamed her youthful companion in Dushami 'The

[11] Ibid., p. 119.
[12] Bulstrode, A Tour in Mongolia, p. 1.
[13] Bell to Florence Bell 15 Feb. 1911, quoted in Bell, Letters, p. 273.
[14] Edwards, A Thousand Miles Up the Nile, p. 207.
[15] Bisland, A Flying Trip Around the World, p. 56.

Primaeval'. He bubbled over, she wrote excitedly, 'with animal spirits . . . was wildly jealous of his honour, and had an almost tigerish thirst for blood. His instincts were primaeval, and he rejoiced in his exploits so whole-heartedly that I could not but sympathise with even the bloodiest.'[16]

Aware of their creation and peopling of a legendary past, if not always conscious of the reasoning behind it, women travellers did not flinch from recording jarring instances of disparity between the myth of the primaeval and the reality of the foreign lands which surrounded them. At the ruins of Philae, Amelia Edwards 'forgets for the moment that anything has changed' – but only forgets, for she knows that many things have altered since the Egypt of the Pharoahs.[17] At Ta'i Yuan Fu, Mary Gaunt found herself shocked at the contrast between the walled city and the macadamized road leading up to it. 'I don't know why I should feel that way, for they certainly had paved roads even in the days before history,' she reluctantly admitted.[18] When Marianne North asked the dyaks who paddled her canoe to rub two sticks together to make a fire, 'they laughed at my old fashioned notions and produced lucifer matches from the folds of their turbans.'[19] Gertrude Bell was most perceptive in seeing that she herself was testimony to the fact that the frail image of the past was broken. From the edge of her camp, she watched neighbouring villagers haggling over their purchases: 'But for my incongruous presence and the lapse of a few thousand years, they might have been the sons of Jacob come down into Egypt to bicker over the weight of the sacks with their brother Joseph.'[20]

Although aware of the intrusion of the present, their romantic attachment to and recreation of a landscape of the past made women travellers resistant to and combative of change. Leaving the ancient city of Salt, Gertrude Bell,

> journeyed through wide valleys, treeless, uninhabited, and almost uncultivated . . . I would have nothing changed in the delicious land cast of Jordan. A generation or two hence it will

[16] Durham, *High Albania*, p. 167.
[17] Edwards, *A Thousand Miles Up the Nile*, p. 304.
[18] Gaunt, *A Broken Journey*, p. 23.
[19] North, *Recollections of a Happy Life*, vol. 2, p. 97.
[20] Bell, *The Desert and the Sown*, p. 40.

be deep in corn and scattered over with villages, the water of the Wady Sir will turn mill-wheels, and perhaps there will even be roads: praise be to God! I shall not be there to see. In my time the uplands will still continue to be that delectable region of which Omar Khayyam sings: 'The strip of herbage strown that just divides the desert from the sown'.[21]

The Desert and the Sown became the title of her travelogue in memory of this image.

Neither the construction of an ancient and primitive culture, nor the self-awareness of this creation, was peculiar to women travellers, but was shared by both male and female intruders into exotic societies throughout the nineteenth and earlier twentieth centuries. The quest for the lost self in the sands of the desert, the undergrowth of the jungle, the inland waterways of a tropical swamp, was a common motif in their accounts. Burton, Stanley and Du Chaillu – the models for many of the women travellers – are all obtrusive narrators in the tales of their journeys. How female eyes did differ, however, was in the development of this myth of a primitive society and the uses to which they put it. Women saw, confronted and then put enormous energy into trying to prevent any further intrusion on their outdated visions by European influence, an effort which threw them against the combined and eventually insurmountable forces of expanding colonization, cultural assimilation, proselytization and the demands and ambitions of the exotic peoples themselves.

Acutely aware of the racial status on which their own ability to travel was precedented, 'the primaeval' to whom women travellers were attracted was the 'pure Arab', the 'unadulterated African', which easily implied and translated into a racial distinction based on biological difference. Gertrude Bell was not interested in 'the only Arabs the tourist ever comes to know, a base-born stock, half bred with negro slaves' but the 'Oriental at heart' untainted by non-Arab blood.[22] Amelia Edwards admired two brothers from Khartoum with 'proud heads and delicate aristocratic features . . . their complexions, free from any taint of Abyssinian blue or Nubian bronze, were intensely, lustrously, magnificently black . . . unembittered by the

---

[21] Ibid, p. 23.
[22] Ibid., p. 10 and 26.

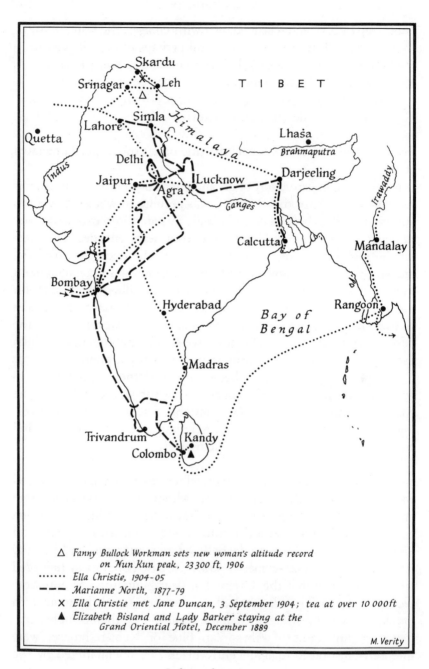

△ Fanny Bullock Workman sets new woman's altitude record
   on Nun Kun peak, 23 300 ft, 1906
...... Ella Christie, 1904-05
--- Marianne North, 1877-79
✕ Ella Christie met Jane Duncan, 3 September 1904; tea at over 10 000 ft
▲ Elizabeth Bisland and Lady Barker staying at the
   Grand Oriental Hotel, December 1889

M. Verity

Indian subcontinent.

world, unsicklied by the pale cast of thought, and glowing with the life of the warm South.'[23] Mary Gaunt contrasted the two guides she hired for her journey to Central Asia; her interpreter, Wang Hsien was a man of the world, educated and artistic but 'little and slight . . . a fool in any language.'[24] Her manservant, Tsai Chih Fu, was of an entirely different mould. Tall and strong, his long pigtail hung heavily down his straight back in defiance of the modern short-cropped fashion. A man not of mental learning but of physical powers, unable to read or write, a mason by trade, yet 'a fine-looking man, dignified and courteous, and I had and have the greatest respect for him,' she wrote. 'He belonged to another era and another civilisation.'[25] Gertrude Bell admired Ibn Sa'ud, Hakin of Najd, 'a man of splendid physique, standing well over six feet, and carrying himself with the air of one accustomed to command . . . he has the characteristics of the well-bred Arab . . . . Politician, ruler and raider, Ibn Saud illustrates a historic type.'[26] That this description is included in a political bulletin indicates the wider importance she felt physical appearance and 'purity' had outside its romantic appeal. Edith Durham would also later use her belief that the Albanians were a 'pure race' to support arguments for their political autonomy.

While women travellers moulded images of the local populations to inhabit the ancient landscapes, those people who conflicted with them were presented with disdain and disrespect. At Alwar, Marianne North spoke of the Raharajah, educated at the new school for sons of the Indian nobility, as 'a spoilt boy'. According to the traveller, he 'had some most objectionable habits. He thought he had a right to everything he fancied, and no-one could refuse him anything. His Highness was the first full-blown specimen of modern "higher education" amongst the Rajahs, and had been "finished" at Mayo College. I cannot say I was deeply impressed by the result.'[27] In the Far East, Ella Christie yearned for the 'old Japan' and found 'the process of "Europeanizing" is most grating.'[28] In Accra, Mary Gaunt wrote, 'you

---

[23] Edwards, *A Thousand Miles Up the Nile*, p. 185.

[24] Gaunt, *A Broken Journey*, p. 8.

[25] Ibid, p. 7.

[26] Bell's report of visit to Basra in *Arab Bulletin*, 12 Jan. 1917, quoted in Winstone, *Gertrude Bell*, pp. 189–90.

[27] North, *Recollections of a Happy Life*, vol. 2, p. 48.

[28] Christie to Alice Stewart 4 May 1907, Imperial Hotel and Villa, Tokyo, quoted in Stewart, *Alicella*, pp. 204–5.

get the half-civilised negro in all his glory, blatant, self-satisfied, loquacious, deadly slow, and very inefficient.'[29]

Again, clothes took on enormous significance and the appearance of non-Europeans in European dress was tut-tutted by the women travellers for its inappropriateness. When a Masai chief appeared before May French-Sheldon in an awkward mix of European and African clothing, she typically made a regal declaration: 'Mireali, why do you wear these clothes? They make you look like a goat. I want to see you in your native cloth, and see you as Mireali, the great African sultan that you are.' The following day Mireali acquiesced to May French-Sheldon's charade; while the traveller dressed up in her white sequinned gown, he donned traditional dress. 'He looked truly majestic,' the White Queen pronounced.[30] Rosita Forbes, who collected together observations on women all over the world in a popular magazine series, captioned a photograph of a Liberian woman dressed in European clothes admiring herself in the mirror with, 'how much more beautiful she would look in her own natural garb of beads and loincloth! . . . silks and cottons are as unbecoming to this girl as nose-rings would be to the American beauty.'[31] Mary Gaunt remarked:

In their own clothes, the Africans always show good taste. However gaudy the colours chosen, never it seems do natives make a mistake – they blend into the picture, they suit the garish sunshine, the bright-blue sky, the yellow beach, the cobalt sea, or the white foam of the surf breaking ceaselessly on the shore; only when the men and women put on European clothes do they look grotesque. There is something in the tight-fitting clothes of civilisation that is utterly unsuited to these sons and daughters of the Tropics, and the man who is a splendid specimen of mankind when he is stark but for a loin cloth, who is dignified in his flowing robe, sinks into commonplaceness when he puts on a shirt and trousers, becomes a caricature when he parts his wool and comes out in a coat and high white collar.[32]

[29] Gaunt, *Alone in West Africa*, p. 178.
[30] French-Sheldon, *Sultan to Sultan*, p. 359.
[31] Rosita Forbes, *Women of All Lands. Their Charm, Culture and Characteristics*, (London 1938), p. 25.
[32] Gaunt, *Alone in West Africa*, p. 188.

Mary Gaunt's boatmen, 1912.
Reproduced by kind permission of Yvonne Fox.

Gaunt held the same notion of appropriateness to interior furnishings, complementing the Jollof pilot's wife on her sanded, earthen floor which the traveller 'infinitely preferred . . . to the black Brussels-carpet on the drawing-room floor of the wife of the President of the Liberian republic.'[33] The educated coastal African, Mary Kingsley explained, was immersed in a superficial 'secondhand rubbishy white culture – a culture far lower and less dignified than that of either the stately Mandingo or the bush chief.'[34] Attempting to analyse her feelings, Mary Gaunt wrote that 'looking on those men in the balconies in only a pair of trousers, or a woman in a skirt pure and simple, among surroundings that to a certain extent spoke of civilisation, there was a wrong note struck. They were not so much barbaric as indecent.'[35] 'East is East and West is West', she chanted, a dictum she even believed was shared by her dog and closest

---

[33] Ibid, p. 68.
[34] Kingsley, *Travels in West Africa*, p. 660.
[35] Gaunt, *Alone in West Africa*, p. 70.

companion on her China journey when he shunned the company of a
flirtatious Pekinese puppy.[36]

Conversely, women travellers themselves insisted on maintaining
strict codes of European dress throughout their travels, rarely adapting
to local climatic and cultural conditions. When Mary Gaunt came
across missionaries dressed in Chinese style, she thought it 'a foolish
fashion . . . for a European in unadulterated Chinese dress looks as
ugly and out of place as a Chinese in a stiff collar and bowler.'[37]
Gertrude Bell's advice to the traveller to the Middle East was, 'he will
be the wiser if he does not seek to ingratiate himself with Orientals by
trying to ape their habits . . . . Let him treat the law of others
respectfully, but he himself will meet with a far greater respect if he
adheres strictly to his own. For a woman this rule is of the first
importance, since a woman can never disguise herself effectually.'[38]

One practical consequence of women travellers' disdain for and
distrust of the europeanization of native peoples was a general feeling
against missionary influence and aims. While missionary activity was
expanding throughout Africa and Asia in the late nineteenth century,
and single women had been incorporated into the missionary
endeavour with special responsibility for administering to the needs of
women and children, women travellers did not in general share the
popular support given to this work. This was not only the result of a
lack of any sense of deep religious conviction themselves; such belief,
which had often been a forming part of their childhood education,
had been abandoned along with their role of dutiful daughter and
maiden aunt. Ella Christie jotted down at Shigar her opinion of a
Swedish missionary couple who had given her a present of a bible in
hope of a conversion. 'They came out totally ignorant of what the
people are, or believe, and seem not to care to know, but try to thrust
their own little narrow views upon them, and wonder that they wont
give up their own religion.'[39] While Constance Gordon Cumming
wrote to Marianne North urging her to restore her belief in a Christian
God, Marianne North recorded in her journal at Cochin, 'Christianity seemed to take all originality out of orientals.'[40] The thrust of

[36] Gaunt, *A Broken Journey*, p. 15.
[37] Ibid, p. 46.
[38] Bell, *The Desert and the Sown*, preface.
[39] Diary entry 15 Sep. 1904, Shigar.
[40] Manuscript of autobiography, p. 750.

women travellers' attacks on the missionary enterprise was on attempts made to convert Asians and Africans not to Christianity but to 'Civilisation'. 'Nothing strikes one so much, in studying the degradation of these native tribes,' wrote Mary Kingsley, 'as the direct effect that civilisation and reformation has in hastening it.'[41] The products of this 'Civilisation' were not objects to be admired. 'The missionary-made man,' she wrote strongly, 'is the curse of the Coast. The pagans despise him, the whites hate him, still he thinks enough of himself to keep comfortable.'[42] She was fond of quoting examples of failures meaningfully to convert Africans to anything but the seeming outer show of Christian behaviour. Shortly after the Brass rising against the Royal Niger Company in 1895 she wrote:

> The outbreak of rank savagery among the Brass men is instructive; for they have been under missionary and civilising influence for years. Now this man Roberts who gaily danced and sang upon the beach with a human fresh foot tied to each ankle, and a human fresh hand to each wrist and another human foot held by the great toe between his teeth, was a man who had been brought up in the Isle of Man and for years regarded as a triumphant example of what you could do with an African brother.[43]

It was all, Mary Gaunt lamented, so *inappropriate* – the key criticism of many travellers' accounts. Why did the technical school have to be housed in massive buildings? What was wrong with a simple tin roof and cement floor, reminiscent of the sanded earth on which she sat in the Jollof pilot's wife's hut?[44]

The women travellers' creation of Lands of the Living Past led them to support and propound theories of racial and sexual difference which were, by the time of their travels, as outmoded as the ancient Egyptians and 'primaeval men' with whom they peopled their Savage Lands. While missionary bodies were preaching a common humanity, backed by the academic sciences' arguments of racial divergence built upon evolutionary stages rather than absolute differences, women

[41] Kingsley, *Travels in West Africa*, p. 403.
[42] Ibid, p. 660.
[43] Kingsley to Hatty Johnson 'July or August' 1895, Consulate, Old Calabar.
[44] Gaunt, *Alone in West Africa*, p. 191.

travellers flew in the face of contemporary theoretical developments. Not all formed a theoretical framework for their frequently and vehemently expressed views, but Mary Kingsley became one of the most forceful exponents of a non-evolutionary approach, and was continually forced to defend herself:

> May I not ask you if I am not justified in saying there is a factor . . . which must be acknowledged, and that that factor is the difference of race? . . . I have *never* said I believe the African to be a low form of human being . . . when I say the African is different from the European and Asiatic forms of humanity, I mean *different* . . . I have to guard myself brutally and plainly because people nowadays are hasty . . . nor will they give time to understanding old-fashioned people like myself.[45]

The African and the Asian could not and would not be saved, raised and cultured into a European, she argued. He – and the exotic was always for Mary Kingsley masculine – was a different form of human being from the European, as different as the male was to the female. 'I feel certain that a black man is no more an undeveloped white man than a rabbit is an undeveloped hare,' she wrote, 'and the mental difference between the two races is very similar to that between men and women among ourselves.'[46] This was an essential and insurmountable difference on which, coincidentally and tellingly, the women travellers' power in foreign lands rested.

Throughout women's travel accounts, ferocious attacks are made on Asians and Africans who are influenced by or partake in Western or colonial culture, especially when this directly, and paradoxically, implied a degree of freedom from European control. Mary Gaunt was horrified by the Liberians, who had celebrated over sixty years of independence, 'an effete race, blatant and arrogant of speech, an arrogance that is only equalled by their appalling ignorance, a race that compares shockingly with the Mandingo or Jollof of the Gambia, the stately Ashanti, a warrior with reserve power, or the busy agricultural Yoruba.' While all the latter lived under British colonial rule, they were, according to Mary Gaunt, 'gentlemen in their own

[45] Mary Kingsley, 'West Africa from an Ethnologist's Point of View', *Transactions of the Liverpool Geographical Society*, 1897, p. 66.
[46] Kingsley, *Travels in West Africa*, p. 659.

simple, untutored way, courteous and dignified'. In contrast, the self-governing Liberian was, 'only a travesty of the European, arrogant without proper dignity, boastful with absolutely nothing in the world to boast about unless it be the amazing wealth of the country he mismanages so shamefully.'[47]

Women travellers celebrated their freedom, in particular freedom from sexual harassment, when travelling among 'unadulterated' peoples. They felt most at ease where they felt most different from the local populations – where they were European and colonials, in contrast to the black, conquered Africans and Asians surrounding them. Here their gender was of the least importance, their racial difference of the most. Conversely they felt most threatened among those they felt to be closest to them in culture, language and manner. At Safita, 'Your Excellency' Gertrude Bell found most of the town's inhabitants were Christian, spoke English with an American accent through emigration, and 'had acquired a familiarity of address that did not please me, and lost some of the good manners to which they had been born.'[48] As a travelling companion she preferred 'a Sheikh from Nejd to a dragoman from Jerusalem.'[49] After years of African and Chinese travel, on arriving at Moscow – a white land, free of British control – Mary Gaunt felt 'for the first time in my life, I was in a country where my nationality did not count, and it was not a pleasant feeling.'[50] 'It seems to me that the farther you get from civilisation the more courteous the population,' she commented.[51] She was afraid of the 'half-civilised' African Preventive Force stationed along the edge of the Volta river as she canoed up it. 'Again and again they made me remember, as the ordinary peasants never did, that I was woman alone and very very helpless.'[52] While she felt vulnerable walking through the streets of Monrovia as the trousered Liberians leant over their balconies – symbol of the colonial lifestyle – she had 'been only moved to friendliness when the fetish man of an Ashanti village, with greasy curls flying, with all his wierd ornaments jingling, tom-toms beating, and excited people shouting, came dancing towards me and pranced

---

[47] Gaunt, *Alone in West Africa*, pp. 77–8.
[48] Bell, *The Desert and the Sown*, p. 211.
[49] Bell to her family 23 May 1900, Ain el Baida, quoted in Bell, *Letters*, p. 110.
[50] Gaunt, *A Woman in China*, p. 5.
[51] Gaunt, *Alone in West Africa*, p. 106.
[52] Ibid, p. 216.

round me with pointing fingers that I hope and believe meant a blessing. Can anyone tell me why this was?'[53]

For women who relied on their racial status and the trappings of colonial costume to endow them with the ability and authority to travel freely around Asian and African lands, the maintenance of distance between African, Asian and European was crucial. The women travellers had themselves adopted a colonial culture and temperament that was essentially unfitting for them – essentially male – and placed it shakily on their feminine shoulders. It was a guise of the white man allowed by the fact of the colour of their skin. If Africans and Asians too were to take upon themselves the outward show of European culture – trousers, blouses, and balconies, presented in shorthand as 'Civilisation' – the gap between the women travellers and indigenous populations would be dangerously narrowed. When the gulf threatened to be bridged between black and white, their femininity would once again become an important factor with which they would have to contend. On what grounds, if their symbols of white masculine power were shared, could they maintain the unprecendented freedom and authority these trappings allowed?

The most threatening of all breaking down of racial barriers and appropriate forms of behaviour for the women travellers was marriage between white women and black men. The vehemence with which the women travellers all, without exception, spoke out against these personal relationships reveals the inadequacy of explaining their attraction to the 'unadulterated' and 'primitive' as simply a romantic yearning for a basic humanity smothered by rigid Victorian society. The freedom the women travellers found was not in the seeming abandon, anarchy and open sexuality of the foreign lands, but in their racial status as 'white men' within them.

In the marriage of a white woman to a black man the fact of gender was highlighted with brutal force, and the very inverse of the relationship which the women travellers sought was established. Marriage was a blatant example of how differences in gender could once again outweigh those of race, and control be reasserted over the travellers as women – control by the very same men over whom they had so enjoyed asserting their newfound authority.

[53] Ibid, p. 70.

Gertrude Bell was considered an Arabophile, a supporter of Arabic culture and fluent in many Middle Eastern languages. Yet when it came to close relationships between European women and Arab men, she flinched. Despite, or maybe because of, regarding Muhammad Ali Pasha of Aleppo as a close friend, a perfect gentleman, and happily married, she was disturbed by his having as a wife 'a pleasant little lady from Brixton'. 'I could not as a general rule recommend Turkish pashas as husbands to the maidens of Brixton,' she wrote simply.[54] Amelia Edwards accepted the common belief that racially mixed marriages were likely to be infertile and any offspring have a slim chance of living long and healthy lives. She supplied eye-witness accounts of the high mortality rate of the children of such unions. 'The sun and soil of Egypt demand one special breed of man, and will tolerate no other,' she explains.[55] Mary Kingsley was accused of being a 'negrophile' by contemporary critics and was regarded as the leading authority on African culture, yet when she heard of a white woman marrying a prominent Sierra Leonean lawyer she felt 'mentally sick'.[56]

Mary Gaunt, who inherited Mary Kingsley's mantle of concern in West African affairs, followed and expanded upon her in this subject as in so many others. Before travelling to West Africa, she had chosen to write a novel based around the theme of an interracial marriage. In *The Arm of the Leopard*, Margaret Rivers, an Englishwoman, sails out to Liberia to marry an 'educated nigger', Cambridge-trained Dr James Craven of Accra. They had met and fallen in love in Britain, and Miss Rivers had agreed to travel out to Liberia to be the doctor's wife. (Mary Gaunt was herself a doctor's widow.) It is here, in the West African context, and not in the Cambridge parlours, that Miss Rivers notices the vast gulf between herself and her husband-to-be, for it is in this setting that her authority, like Mary Gaunt's, depended above all on the colour of her skin. On first sighting the handsome Dr Craven as the ship came into port, Miss Rivers felt 'a repulsion such as one feels for snakes, and it seemed to her she understood why the Coast had set its face against mixed marriages . . . "Don't touch me!" she said; "don't touch me!" And he knew that the feeling of race antipathy was upon her.'[57] The gallant Lindsay, fellow voyager to West Africa and,

[54] Bell, *The Desert and the Sown*, p. 268.

[55] Edwards, *A Thousand Miles Up the Nile*, p. 104.

[56] Kingsley to Violet Roy 26 Aug. 1893, SS Lagos, Bonny River.

[57] Mary Gaunt and J. Ridgewell Essex, *The Arm of the Leopard. A West African Story*, (London 1904), p. 32.

interestingly, of lower educational background than the doctor, woos and finally wins Miss Rivers from her African fiance, and proper social relations are restored.

When Mary Gaunt herself steps down on African shore only four years later, she is anxious to explain to her readers, before imparting any other impressions of the new world about her, the distance of race between her and the African people, making absolutely explicit the interdependence of racial purity and dominance:

> It is no good trying to hide the fact: between the white man and the black lies not only the culture and knowledge of the West – that gulf might, and sometimes is bridged – but that other great barrier, the barrier of sex. Tall, stalwart, handsome as is many a negro, no white woman may take a black man for her husband and be respected by her own people . . . . Even the missionaries who preach that the black man is a brother decline emphatically to receive him as a brother-in-law. And so we get, beginning here in the little colony of the Gambia, the handful of the ruling race set among a subject people; so the white man has always ruled the black; so, I think, he must always rule.[58]

Her first novel published on return from her West African journey, *The Silent Ones* (1909), tackles this same subject. *The Uncounted Cost*, published the following year, was banned from lending libraries because of its incidental dealing with the subject of free love. It was set on the West African coast. Throughout her writing career Mary Gaunt would harp back to this theme. When confronted five years later with an English wife of a Chinese man, she is quick to highlight the marriage's weaknesses and problems. 'This woman had committed the unpardonable sin of the East, the sin against her race, the sin for which there is no atoning,' she writes in uncharacteristically devout language. 'She has committed the one error that outclasses her, and she is going to pay for it in bitterness all the days of her life.' 'East is East and West is West', repeats Mary Gaunt like a religious litany, 'and never,' she hopes, 'the twain shall meet.'[59]

While women travellers emphasized racial difference and were

---

[58] Gaunt, *Alone in West Africa*, p. 16.
[59] Gaunt, *A Broken Journey*, p. 18.

attracted to the primaeval, they appealed to a cultural relativism which those who perceived Asians and Africans as less mature Europeans did not share. The missionaries and their supporters held European culture as the shining pinnacle to which their converts must climb; the women travellers, however, saw a whole mountain range of cultures spread out before them, each with its own summit from which, across the vast chasms, it was impossible to leap to the next. This fierce belief in absolute and essential differences – whether based on biological, social, or cultural factors, or a combination of all three – at once produced a deeply conservative adherence to racial purity and encouraged a defence of indigenous cultures from encroaching European administrative, political and religious interference.

Alongside the women travellers' attacks on European attempts to crush native authorities and culture there arose, therefore, an appeal for the understanding of non-European cultures as valuable, deserving of respect, and, most importantly, appropriate in their native settings. From India on her first journey out in 1868, committed Christian Constance Gordon Cumming confided,

> I frankly confess that there is something startling in the rapidity with which one gets quite at home amongst all this paraphernalia of heathenism, and how very soon idolatory ceases to shock the mind. Six months previously the sight of a veritable temple with its hideous idols and devout worshippers was a thing from which I shrunk in shuddering pity. Now . . . it was all perfectly natural, and seemed so entirely in being with the tastes of the people.[60]

In the preface of her most poignant travelogue, Gertrude Bell begs the reader to see the Arab from his point of view: 'Their wisdom is that of men whose channels of information and standards for comparison are different from ours, and who bring a different set of preconceptions to bear upon the problems laid before them,' she wrote. 'His action is guided by traditions of conduct and morality that go back to the beginnings of civilisation.'[61] Similarly, Edith Durham warned her audience that 'the perspective of everything, life and modern politics

---

[60] Constance Gordon Cumming, *From the Hebrides to the Himalayas. A Sketch of Eighteen Months Wanderings in Western Isles and Eastern Highlands*, (London 1876), vol. 2, pp. 313–4.

[61] Bell, *The Desert and the Sown*, preface.

included, depends entirely upon the point from which it is viewed.'[62] In China, Isabella Bird, who of all women travellers was most in sympathy with missionary aims, nevertheless warns,

> it is essential for us to see quite clearly that our Western ideas find themselves confronted, not with barbarism or with debased theories of morals, but with an elaborate and antique civilisation . . . which has many claims to our respect and even admiration. They meet with a perfectly organized social order, a system of government theoretically admirably suited to the country . . . under which . . . the governed enjoy a large measure of peace and prosperity.[63]

The appropriateness of these systems of law to the societies in which they operated meant they flourished just as well if not better than British society at home, women travellers argued. 'As regards uprightness, charity, justice, and mercy,' wrote Amelia Edwards of her 'savages', the ancient Egyptians, 'they would not, I think, have much to learn from us, if they were living to this day beside the pleasant waters of the Nile.'[64] 'It is the fashion among journalists and others to talk of the "lawless Albanians,"' wrote Edith Durham. 'But there is perhaps no other people in Europe so much under the tyranny of laws . . . . And lest you that read this book should cry out at the "customs of savages", I would remind you that we play the game on a much larger scale and call it war.'[65] Similarly, Mary Kingsley measured British against West African morality: 'I have no hesitation in saying that in the whole of West Africa, in one week, there is not one-quarter the amount of drunkenness you can see any Saturday night you choose in a couple of hours in the Vauxhall Road,' she wrote. 'And you will not find in a whole year's investigation on the Coast, one seventieth part of the evil, degradation, and premature decay you can see any afternoon you choose to walk in the more densely-populated parts of any of our own towns.'[66] Fifteen years later Mary Gaunt echoed her thoughts:

[62] Durham, *High Albania*, p. 20.
[63] Bird, *The Yangtze Valley and Beyond*. p. 11.
[64] Edwards, *Pharoahs, Fellahs and Explorers*, p. 233.
[65] Durham, *High Albania*, pp. 40–1.
[66] Kingsley, *Travels in West Africa*, pp. 663–4.

Now there is not in all the length and breadth of Africa, I will
venture to swear, one quarter of the unutterable misery and vice
you may see any day in the streets of London or any great city of
the British Isles. There is not a tribe that has not its own system
of morals and sees that they are carried out; there is not the
possibility of a man, woman, or child dying of starvation in all
West Africa while there is any food among the community. Can
we say that of any town in England?[67]

To counter the apparent absurdity, lawlessness and savagery – to
British eyes – of distant societies, women travellers asked their
audience to imagine how Britain looked to the Savage eye. The Druze
scribe who rode with Gertrude Bell on her journey to Salkhad
questioned her on the laws of marriage and divorce in Britain. 'He was
vastly entertained at the English rule that the father should pay a man
for marrying his daughter (so he interpreted the habit of giving her a
marriage portion), and we laughed together over the absurdity of the
arrangement.'[68] Edith Durham was particularly anxious to stress that
her view of Albanian society could only be that of an outsider, and 'of
outsiders' views on Balkan problems we are, most of us, tired.'[69] Yet in
realizing the peculiarity of her own cultural perspective, she also
pleaded for the recognition of that of others, and, although often
portraying brutal and violent scenes, managed to report without
condemning at a time when such an attitude was rare. At Berisha, the
traveller was taken to a rock where the magical imprint of a man's
hand – (to Edith Durham it appeared as no more than a scratch) – was
supposed to divine hidden gold:

> As we returned to the humble huts and partook of sheep-cheese
> and *rakia*, I remembered that many of the tribes of my own land
> believe in planchette and tableturning – consult palmists and
> globe-gazers, are 'Christian Scientists' and 'Higher Thoughters' –
> and reflected that all the training of all the schools had but little
> removed a large mass of the British public from the intellectual

[67] Gaunt, *Alone in West Africa*, p. 393.
[68] Bell, *The Desert and the Sown*, p. 83.
[69] Durham, *High Albania*, preface.

Edith Durham and the Bariaktar of Kopliku at Scutari, 1913.
Royal Anthropological Institute.

standpoint of High Albania, whereas for open-handed generosity and hospitality the Albanian ranks incomparably higher.[70]

Mary Kingsley took her ethnologist's eye to the miscellaneous chapels in which she found herself lecturing on her return to Britain. 'I think I ought to give lectures in Africa on the juju of the North Sea Islands,' she told her publisher. 'I am getting up Baptists thoroughly, and know a general from a particular and a sprinkler from an immersionist at sight.'[71] Sitting sketching at Devich, a crowd gathered around Edith Durham and she had the anthropological tables turned on her:

> For months I had been incessantly questioning about manners and customs, now I was myself the victim. I was asked all about all that I did, and then 'why?' The thing that bothered everyone was my straw hat; they had never seen one before; 'Why do you wear wheat on your head?' Every one broke a little bit off the brim to make sure it really was 'wheat.'
> 'Do you wear it in the house?' 'Do you sleep in it?' 'Do you wear it to show you are married?' 'Did you make it?' 'Are all the women in your vilayet (province) obliged to wear wheat on their heads?' 'Is there a law about it?' . . .
> 'I wear it because of the sun,' I said desperately . . .
> It occurred to me that if there was a Devich Anthropological Society it might report that it had found traces of sun-worship in the English, and mysterious rites connected with it that no questioning could elicit.[72]

Amelia Edwards took the travel writer's convention of nicknaming non-European companions with simple titles which highlighted particular physical or occupational characteristics and subverted it, naming her European companions on the *dahabeeyah* the Little Lady, the Painter, the Idle Man and the Happy Couple. Amelia herself was the Writer.

Like Marianne North and, to a lesser extent, Ella Christie, Amelia Edwards displayed remarkably little interest in the people about her,

[70] Ibid, p. 192.
[71] Kingsley to George Macmillan 20 Oct. 1897, Addison Road, London.
[72] Durham, *High Albania*, p. 258.

focusing her attention and energies on the monuments of the past. As a result, she did not stereotype the Egyptians with whom she came into contact, unusually calling all the staff of her *dahabeeyah* by their real names. Those who did people her imaginary landscape, however, were the ancient Egyptians, and these she called 'savages', as Marianne North called the plants and flowers on which she focused 'tribes'. Amelia Edwards' emotional commitment and imaginary powers were spent on describing her savages from the past as displayed through the monuments they left behind. In her reaction to Rameses the Great, represented on a colossus at Abou Simbel, is all the sensual experience that other women travellers expressed towards still living subjects.

> [He] must have been one of the handsomest men, not only of his own day, but of all history . . . . The face is oval; the eyes are long, prominent, and heavy-lidded; the nose is slightly aquiline and characteristically depressed at the tip; the nostrils are open and sensitive . . . . A godlike serenity, an almost superhuman pride, an immutable will, breathe from the sculptured stone. He had learned to believe his prowess irrestible, and himself almost divine. If he now raised his arm to slay, it would be with the stern placidity of a destroying angel.[73]

Those few turn-of-the-century women travellers who did not, wittingly or unwittingly, advocate an ideology of essential difference – which often translated itself within them British context to differences between the sexes and led them to be active opponents of women's suffrage – were often, ironically, the least sympathetic portrayers of foreign peoples. Ardent American suffragist May French-Sheldon exercised a callousness towards her African employees which rivalled the most brutal of male explorers. She neither displayed nor argued for any of the cultural relativism present in other women's perceptions, and continually employed evaluative terms when describing African peoples – 'debased', 'wretched' and 'degenerated' being the most common among them. The African therefore became, to her late Victorian eyes, an inferior Englishman who could be cajoled and bullied into betterment.

[73] Edwards, *A Thousand Miles Up the Nile*, pp. 285–8.

When women travellers emphasized essential difference between peoples they were both supporting racial assumptions which claimed the Savage and the Oriental could never be a European and, at the same time, challenging them through their associated appeal to judge the exotic societies on their own terms. Ironically, women who exaggerated and relied upon constructions of racial difference therefore also became defenders of the foreign peoples and their culture.

It was a small step for many women travellers from an appeal to see the African and the Asian from his own particular standpoint to their own identification with the people they were portraying. For while Mary Kingsley strove to 'think in black' and 'penetrate the African mind forest', she was imaginatively placing herself in the footprints of her subjects' bare feet. Soon she was calling herself a 'savage', as Mary Gaunt and Marianne North both began to refer to themselves as 'heathen'. Gertrude Bell began to dot her letters with '*inshallah*' (Allah willing), as Mary Kingsley restricted her swearing not to the Christian God but to 'Allah!', much to her missionary correspondent's horror. 'You will find me savage,' wrote Gertrude Bell to her close friend Valentine Chirol, 'for I have seen and heard strange things, and they colour the mind.'[74]

It was nearly always with the African and Asian man that the women travellers drew their intimate comparisons, for while they were travelling they both were perceived and saw themselves as masculine. In contrast, women missionaries in the field, employed in the feminine sphere of administering to women and children, portrayed foreign societies with a specially keen eye on and sympathy for women's place within it. When Mrs Pringle travelled to East Africa with her missionary husband in 1880, she openly identified not just with African women but, in particular, with mothers.[75] Women who travelled with male relatives, when their gender determined their relationships with their travelling companions, also focused on the details of female lives. Jane Moir, who accompanied her husband on a journey through East Africa for the African Lakes Company in 1890, made frequent references to the lives of the African women she saw *en*

savage

---

[74] Bell to Valentine Chirol 5 Apr. 1914, Baghdad, quoted in Burgoyne, *Gertrude Bell, 1889–1914*, p. 304.
[75] M. A. Pringle, *Towards the Mountains of the Moon*, (Edinburgh 1884).

route.[76] When Mary Hall journeyed alone through the same area fifteen years later she paid scant attention to female life.

During the early development of anthropological fieldwork, an appropriate role for women was found within it. Mrs Amaury Talbot was assigned a woman's sphere of study in team with her husband; while he wrote more general ethnological studies, she produced one of the earliest anthropological works on West African women, *Women's Mysteries of a Primitive People. The Ibibios of Southern Nigeria.* Amaury Talbot herself wrote,

> that all this came into our lives . . . is due to the fact that, unlike Mary Kingsley and the small band of women travellers who followed in her footsteps, my sister and I were not alone. A never-failing watchful care always surrounded us, smoothing each difficulty, and, as far as humanly possible, providing against every discomfort and danger . . .
>
> During this time we were naturally anxious to do something in return for all that was done for us, and soon discovered that the chief way in which we could be of use was by making clear copies of rough notes jotted down in spare moments by my husband . . .
>
> When, therefore, a kind request came from England for a paper embodying 'the women's point of view' . . . the idea of separate authorship seemed to one who, up till then, had only acted as an unofficial secretary, almost as startling as if a pen from the inkstand had been asked to start writing of its own account.[77]

Soon, in very different spirit from the solo women travellers without a husband's watchful and caring eye, she began writing of the 'women's mysteries' and 'information denied [her husband] by ancient law' with 'no intervening male influence'.[78] In the epilogue, she declares that it is necessary to find out why women have become subservient through studying African women at an earlier stage of development. As the missionary women and travelling wives, Amaury

---

[76] Jane F. Moir, *A Lady's Letters from Central Africa. A Journey from Mandala, Shire Highlands, to Ujiji, Lake Tanganyika and Back*, (Glasgow 1891).

[77] D. Amaury Talbot, *Women's Mysteries of a Primitive People*, pp. 1–2.

[78] Ibid, p. 7.

Talbot was herself female within the context of her African experience, her gender contrasted with that of her accompanying professional husband.

Independent solo women travellers, however, assumed masculine power, authority and freedom and, therefore, saw the foreign worlds through white masculine eyes. It is marked how rarely they mention women of foreign societies, and how little attention they pay to female culture and family life. For Mary Kingsley, the African with whom she so strongly identified was always 'he'. 'She conversed with [the women] but little and that in a language which few of them understood,' wrote Dennett of her stay at Kabinda.[79] Women travellers displayed little understanding of or sympathy for indigenous forms of female organization and expression of power and influence, lacking in this one respect the very cultural relativism of which they were such strong advocates. Even Edith Durham, who cast a remarkably sympathetic, unwestern eye on Albanian society, found 'gentlemen of all nations are consumed with curiosity about the secrets of the harem', so she divulged the inside information to her readers: 'being kept mainly for breeding purposes, [the women's] conversation was much like what that of a cow might be, could it talk.'[80]

Women travellers continually compared African and Asian women's depressed and limited circumstances to the elevated status of women in British society, portraying an image of life for the middle-class British woman which contrasted sharply with their personal experience – the very experience which had so often propelled them into travelling. Although Amelia Edwards admitted she 'had little opportunity of observing domestic life in Egypt', she nevertheless pitied the women of the harem, 'living after the usual dreary way of Eastern women, with apparently no kind of occupation and not even a garden to walk in . . . . A little embroidery, a few musical toys of Geneva manufacture, a daily drive on the Shubra road, pipes, cigarettes, sweetmeats, jewellery, and gossip, fill up the aimless days of most Egyptian ladies of rank,' which, with the exception perhaps of smoking, seems to differ but slightly from the experiences of

[79] Dennett, 'A Visit to Cabinda', pp. 26–7.
[80] Durham, *High Albania*, pp. 290–1.

a middle-class woman in Britain.[81] Gertrude Bell portrayed Eastern women as imprisoned and victims:

> 'Allah!' said one, 'you go forth to travel through the whole world, and we have never been to Hamah!'
>
> I saw them in the gateway when I turned again to wave them a farewell. Tall and straight they were, and full of supple grace, clothed in narrow blue robes, their brows bound with gold, their eyes following the road they might not tread.[82]

In China, women travellers were particularly shocked by bound feet. While they themselves were rejoicing in a newfound physical strength, they were both disturbed by and sought to distance themselves from this obvious manifestation of the destruction of women's bodily wellbeing. 'The women at Hong Kong were a horrid sight,' Ella Christie wrote unsympathetically to her sister. 'One would think they had wooden sticks for legs as they totter along leaning on an umbrella or someone's arm.'[83] 'But the evil does not stop at the foot,' warned Mary Gaunt. 'It seemed to me every woman's face was marked with the marks of suffering. Travelling I often got a glimpse of one peering out of a cart or litter at the foreigner, and that face invariably was patient, pallid and worn, for foot-binding brings no end of evils in its train.'[84] The only hint of admiration for women of another culture in many of the women travellers' accounts was for working-class women who exhibited the same physical strength after which they themselves hankered. 'The happiest women in Egypt,' wrote Amelia Edwards, are those 'who work hard and are bitterly poor; but they have the free use of their limbs, and they at least know the fresh air, the sunshine, and the open fields.'[85] Only in West Africa did Mary Gaunt find women she admired – the traders in the Tarkwa market:

> In all my travels I never saw such gorgeously arrayed mammies as here . . . . Many of them are rich, and in this comfortable

[81] Edwards, *A Thousand Miles Up the Nile*, p. 479.

[82] Bell, *The Desert and the Sown*, pp. 237–8.

[83] Christie to Alice Stewart 4 Mar. 1907, SS Prinz Ludwig, on voyage from Hong Kong to Shanghai, quoted in Stewart, *Alicella*, p. 193.

[84] Gaunt, *A Broken Journey*, p. 81.

[85] Edwards, *A Thousand Miles Up the Nile*, p. 480.

country they are all of them self-supporting wives. They sell their
wares, or march about the streets, happy, contented, important
people, very sure of themselves. Let no-one run away with the
impression that these women are in any way down-trodden.
They look very much the reverse . . . curiously enough whenever I think of thoroughly contented, thoroughly independent,
well-to-do women, I think of those women in the goldmining
centre of West Africa.[86]

What were women travellers to do with the perceptions of foreign
societies they were accumulating? While some had found the role of
white male explorer a temporary shelter, the awkward ambiguities it
forced upon them could never allow it to be a permanent home. They
searched for an area of expertise where they could at once be feminine
and professional; they sought for their own peculiar contribution to
the study and portrayal of foreign peoples.

As the late nineteenth century saw the growth of the two new
professions of anthropology and archaeology, a forum for the
expression of their newfound knowledge and special insight began to
emerge. Both disciplines had developed out of local clubs and informal
collecting activities – areas in which women were active contributors.
But the founding practitioners in both areas of study had been the very
'armchair travellers' whose work the women travellers were at pains to
criticize and contrast with their own on-the-spot expertise. E. B.
Tylor, James Frazer, A. C. Haddon and Andrew Lang – all later
correspondents and enquirers of the women travellers – based their
scholarly work on theory rather than first-hand experience. Working
within a university environment, the studies of these eminent men
differed radically from the non-academic, personal knowledge the
women travellers brought to their subjects. The contrasting
approaches were made explicit by the reviewer of *The Thousand and
One Churches*, a scholarly book jointly researched and authored by the
leading archaeologist Sir William Ramsay and Gertrude Bell, in the
Archaeological Journal. Although the *Journal* only indexed the book
under Ramsay's name, the reviewer admitted it was 'mostly the work
of his collaborator'. Here, however, his praise ended, for while
recognizing the thoroughness of Gertrude Bell's method and research,

---

[86] Gaunt, *Alone in West Africa*, p. 324.

Gertrude Bell taking measurements at Ukheidir, 1909.
University of Newcastle Upon Tyne.

he was displeased by the strict empiricist approach she applied to her evidence. The book was too narrow, he complained, and concentrated too exclusively on simple facts; he advised Gertrude Bell to make 'recognition of a wider principle' from the outset of the work.[87] Here was a clear example of the conflict between the academic, theorized approach and the specialist, personal experience being claimed by many of the women travellers. Here, in the fluid boundaries of the new professions and the development of fieldwork, women forced an area for their peculiar contribution.

Women travellers' claims to be active in fieldwork were first made cautiously. 'I desired to write not so much a book of travel as an account of the people whom I met or who accompanied me on my way, and to show what the world is like in which they live and how it appears to them,' wrote Gertrude Bell on her 1905 journey through the Middle East.[88] Although Edith Durham set out for Serbia in 1902 with the express purpose of collecting material for a book, she disclaimed any serious intent. 'I explained that I wished only to note things characteristically Servian, such as the costumes of the peasants, the houses, and so forth. "In short," said a gentleman, "you are making geo-ethnographical studies." This struck me as a remarkably luminous idea; I should never have thought of it myself.'[89] Scepticism over women's claims to professional status led even university-educated Gertrude Bell, a future Director of Archaeology at Baghdad's museum who spent days supervising digs, making casts of inscriptions too worn for rubbings and drawing meticulously detailed and measured plans of sights in pencil in her small notebooks, wrote to her mother, 'I have had the most delightful day today playing at being an archaeologist.'[90] Mary Kingsley faced continual deprecation of her knowledge and skills in the field. She wrote to her friend Alice Stopford Green concerning one of her many lectures on West African law and customs: 'Men are fools. One of them has been handbilling me all over Tunbridge Wells as an entomologist and then writes to say "it will be so interesting to the farmers". Here I am in for a nice thing? I said Ethnologist and now I suppose I must discourse on wire worms and turnip fly.'[91] When Margaret Fountaine's investments suffered

[87] Review by Theodore Fyfe in *Archaeological Journal*, vol. 67, (1910), pp. 204–7.
[88] Bell, *The Desert and the Sown*, preface.
[89] Durham, *Through the Lands of the Serb*, p. 186.
[90] Bell to Florence Bell 31 Mar. 1905, Kalaat Simian, quoted in Bell, *Letters*, p. 208.
[91] Kingsley to Alice Stopford Green 22 Nov. 1897, Addison Road, London.

from the Great War, she was forced into making some sort of living from her butterfly collecting. She was amused when Ward's Natural Science Establishment replied to her queries as 'Mr Fountaine'.

Alongside these couched and cautious claims, however, which doused threats to their femininity, women travellers began to make more strident assertions of professional status. They wanted to celebrate the specialist knowledge they were acquiring, and began to insist upon its importance in understanding and conveying all they saw. 'The traveller is ill equipped who goes through Egypt without something more than a mere guide-book knowledge,' wrote Amelia Edwards. 'In the desolation of Memphis, in the shattered splendour of Thebes, he sees only the ordinary pathos of ordinary ruins. As for Abou Simbel, the most stupendous historical record ever transmitted from the past to the present, it tells him a but half-intelligible story. Holding to the merest thread of explanation, he wanders from hall to hall, lacking altogether that potent charm of foregone association which no Murray can furnish.'[92]

The authority of fieldwork, unlike that of other forms of scientific knowledge, was anchored in subjective experience. Women could, therefore, claim that their independent perspective gave valuable insight into foreign cultures which sponsored, officially-backed, encumbered male practitioners could not provide. Lack of resources became something to be celebrated; Alexandra David-Neel, who disguised herself as a poor pilgrim, claimed, 'no other traveller than one who was really believed by them to belong to the same peasant stock could have gathered the same observations that I collected.'[93] While in-depth knowledge was important, first-hand experience was even more so, argued the women travellers, many of whom had been denied access to academic training. 'Unless you live among the natives,' stated Mary Kingsley categorically, 'you never get to know them.'[94] 'One must live the life of the people,' echoed Edith Durham with her one guide.[95] 'Seton-Watson for example,' she later explained of the editor of the *Slavonic Review*, a writer on Balkan history with degrees from Berlin, Paris and Vienna universities as well as Oxford,

---

[92] Edwards, *A Thousand Miles Up the Nile*, p. 263.
[93] David-Neel, *My Journey to Lhasa*, p. 95.
[94] Kingsley, *Travels in West Africa*, p. 103.
[95] Durham, *High Albania*, p. 20.

took all his information presumably from ambitious politicians and lived himself in comfortable hotels. He had and has no idea what the peoples are like. He wrote the article on Montenegro in the *Encyclopaedia Britannica*, which infuriated the Montenegrins, after staying for a fortnight (so far as I have learnt) at the Grand Hotel, Cetinje. I never heard of him up country.'[96]

Gertrude Bell, although herself highly educated, claimed special insight beyond that of academic Arabists:

Often when one sets out on a journey one travels by all the roads according to the latest maps, one reaches all the places of which the history books speak. Duly one rises early and turns one's face towards new countries, carefully looks and laboriously one tries to understand, and for all one's trouble one might as well have stayed behind and read a few big archaeology books. But I would have you know that is not the way that I have done it . . . . Here is a world of history that one sees with the eye and that enters into the mind as no book can relate it.[97]

She also boasted, 'I do know these people, the Arabs; I have been in contact with them in a way which is possible for no official, and it is that intimacy and friendship which makes me useful.'[98] Although she worked with the renowned archaeologist William Ramsay at Daile, she wrote in confidence to a friend, 'I can do things and see things that Ramsay and his learned like could scarcely do and see.'[99] Mary Kingsley similarly claimed that without the weight of learning behind her she could gain a truer, more vivid picture of the societies she encountered. 'These white men who make a theory first and then go hunting travellers' tales for facts to support the same may say what they please of the pleasure of the process,' she wrote. 'Give me the pleasure of getting a mass of facts and watching them. It is just like seeing a crystal build itself up. But it *is* slower I own.'[100]

[96] Durham to G. P. Gooch 13 Dec. 1943, quoted in Hodgson, 'Edith Durham', p. 15.

[97] Bell to Florence Bell 12 Apr. 1907, Miletus, quoted in Bell, *Letters*, pp. 228–9.

[98] Bell to Hugh Bell 14 May 1916, GHQ Basrah, quoted in Bell, *Letters*, p. 375.

[99] Bell to Valentine Chirol 12 May 1907, Konia, quoted in Burgoyne, *Gertrude Bell, 1889–1914*, p. 245.

[100] Kingsley to Alice Stopford Green 27 Mar. 1897.

May French-Sheldon was again most forthright in making claims to being an anthropologist before even arriving in East Africa. On the voyage out she spent free hours arranging and rearranging her luggage and equipment for her porters and 'jotting down points for anthropological and ethnological observation in order to lose no opportunity, when once in the field, of probing every topic to the heart and thrashing out the subjects thoroughly.'[101] She was almost unique in claiming a special feminine eye to worlds shut to the wandering white male. She delivered a lecture on East Africa to the Anthropological Institute 'with special reference to women and children.'[102]

Fieldwork also appealed by containing many of the ambivalences experienced by women on their travels, thereby complementing their own fractured and often contradictory lives. In fieldwork, the archaeologist or anthropologist strove to describe her subject before Western intrusion – the very ancient landscape and 'pure', 'unadulterated' African and Asian to whom the women travellers had been drawn. But the anthropologist herself was often a forerunner and even integral part of that very same intervention – an indissoluble reminder that the untouched tribe, the unadulterated native is no longer so.

This strange blend of preserver and destroyer of indigenous culture was reflected in the attitudes and perceptions of the women travellers. For while many mistrusted and spoke out against europeanization, they were also fervent imperialists. The contradictions inherent in this position are made apparent by Gertrude Bell's dislike of the europeanized Arab yet support for British intervention in the Middle East. She described her meeting with the Vali of Aleppo:

> [He] spoke French, and spoke it very well. He received me in an offhand manner . . . 'How old do you think I am?' said the pasha.
>
> I replied tactfully that I should give him thirty-five years.
>
> 'Thirty-six!' he said triumphantly . . . 'A man like me needs the society of educated Europeans.'
>
> (Mistrust the second: an Oriental official, who declares that he prefers the company of Europeans.)
>
> 'I am very Anglophil,' said he.

---

[101] French-Sheldon, *Sultan to Sultan*, p. 31.
[102] *Journal of the Anthropological Institute*, vol. 21, (1891–2), p. 358.

I expressed the gratitude of my country in suitable terms.

'But what are you doing in Yemen?' he added quickly.

'Excellency,' said I, 'we English are a maritime people, and there are but two places that concern us in all Arabia.'

'I know,' he interpolated. 'Mecca and Medina.'

'No,' said I. 'Aden and Kweit.'

'And you hold them both,' he returned angrily.[103]

While defending the 'pure Arab' and the fighting mountain Druzes, Gertrude Bell also gave unquestioning support to British imperialist ambitions in the area. 'All over Syria and even in the desert,' she wrote, 'whenever a man is ground down by injustice or mastered by his own incompetence, he wishes that he were under the rule that has given wealth to Egypt.'[104] At first against the surrender of the British mandate in Iraq to self-government, she later became a supporter of Faisal's claim to the throne. In her attitudes towards this royal family her conflicting ambitions and emotions were clearly expressed. For while she was attracted to the 'pure Arab' – of which she believed Faisal to be a fine representative – she also equated rule and government with European culture. So when she first thought Faisal's brother, Abdullah, would be elected Amir, she expressed her approval, for he 'is a gentleman who likes a copy of the *Figaro* every morning at breakfast time. I haven't any doubt we should get on with him famously.'[105] And when Faisal eventually suceeded to the throne with Gertrude Bell's complicity, she wrote to her father asking him to send out catalogues from the best British furnishing shops to help the new king decide how to decorate his palace. His eventual choice, guided by the Oriental Secretary Bell, was ordered from Waring and Gillow.[106] The defender of African legal systems, Mary Kingsley advocated that 'what we want at present in West Africa [is] . . . to extend our possessions northwards, eastwards, and south-eastwards, until they command the interior trade routes.'[107] And while Mary Gaunt despised the europeanized West Coaster, she was a constant advocate

[103] Bell, *The Desert and the Sown*, p. 265.

[104] Ibid., p. 58.

[105] Bell to Florence Bell 14 June 1920, Baghdad, quoted in Burgoyne, *Gertrude Bell, 1914–1926*, p. 140.

[106] Bell to Hugh Bell 1 Mar. 1923, Baghdad, quoted in Bell, *Letters*, p. 663.

[107] Kingsley, *Travels in West Africa*, p. 640.

of the extension and consolidation of British rule in the West African region.

A fieldworker also had to be part of yet apart from the society she studied. She must possess enough sympathy to see the societies from the inside, yet her authority and ability to travel rested upon maintaining distance from that same society. 'Going native' or 'bush' was frowned upon – a literal *bête noire*. The understanding of an insider, combined with the detachment and objectivity of an outsider, was considered the most professional and illuminative relationship. Women travellers continually juggled their identities in the foreign lands to meet these turbulent emotions of sympathy yet distance, and found comfort in a role which did not necessitate the resolution of these seemingly insurmountable conflicts of interest. The guise of a fieldworker allowed them to both be of and not of, be rebels against European authority yet exploiters and even agents of it. Attempts to establish consistency in how they presented themselves, both in their private letters and journals and on the public platform, are therefore misguided. They could be and were at the same time 'savage' and 'white men', defenders of indigenous culture and destroyers of it, imperialists yet against the europeanization of non-European peoples. It is this complexity in the experience of fieldwork which made it a natural home for women travellers.

Many accommodated the fracturing of their lives between the sympathetic woman traveller and the detached professional scientist by publishing parallel accounts of the same journey under these two different guises. While it was initially the restricted circumstances under which they laboured which encouraged women travellers to claim a special contribution to knowledge, they soon learnt to remove the 'I' from their work and thereby claim an objectivity which consolidated their position within the scientific profession. Reviewers noted how their later travel books lacked the 'careless rapture' of their first ventures into print, as they sought to include more scientific data not necessarily based upon their own first-hand experience.[108] Although Mary Kingsley originally intended to write one weighty tome on her two West African journeys, she found the dovetailing of her anthropological evidence and personal narrative increasingly more cumbersome; her information was, she warned her publisher, 'facts,

---

[108] David Hogarth on Gertrude Bell's *Amurath to Amurath*, comparing to *The Desert and the Sown*, *Geographical Journal*, vol. 68, (1926), p. 366.

good healthy facts as they are, all hopelessly adrift and mixed up pretty nearly as much as cargo in a palm oil trader – missionary intelligence entangled in the Lippoums Genera of beetles – trade statistics with the habits of fish.'[109] She eventually published the popular *Travels in West Africa* separately from the larger volume of 'fetish' which became *West African Studies*. Agnes Smith Lewis spent one summer writing a popular account of her visits to the Middle East, *In the Shadow of Sinai*, and also co-authoring with Rendel Harris *The Story of Ahikar*, a scholarly work from the Arabian Nights which contained translations in seven languages. Gertrude Bell's poetic *The Desert and the Sown* was matched by considered scholarly articles in the *Revue Archéologique*. Like many women travellers, the segmentation of her life was as thorough as the constant recording of her experiences in photographs, diagrams and the written word. She kept two diaries while digging – one outlining her professional work for her family, and another her emotional life for her married lover Dick Doughty-Wylie. In the first, she was the male professional, in the second she lamented the limits put upon her as a woman in Arabia. Mary Gaunt expressed her splintered interests by writing a factual travelogue and a novel on each of her journeys. While *Woman in China* gave a detailed account of the people and culture she encountered, *A Wind from the Wilderness* was a work of fiction, a collection of short stories about China seen through the first person eyes of 'Rosalie Grahame'. Amelia Edwards' *A Thousand Miles Up the Nile* followed the same popular style of travel narrative as had her earlier *Untrodden Peaks and Unfrequented Valleys*, both portraying the narrator as an amateur yet interested wandering woman. In *Pharoahs, Fellahs, and Explorers*, however, a collection of essays on Egyptology, there is very little of Amelia Edwards and a great deal of information about Egyptian history, culture and archaeology. The traveller of this account is always referred to in the masculine gender; in this way any contradictions between being a female traveller and a professional archaeologist or anthropologist were lessened.

Women travellers had found in the pursuit of fieldwork an area which could incorporate their many and often conflicting interests and ambitions – both professional and personal. But before them loomed a

---

[109] Kingsley to George Macmillan 18 Dec. 1894, Addison Road, London.

new and obstacle-ridden terrain to conquer. While they saw themselves as specialists, professionals and fieldworkers, the public awaited them with open arms but very different visions. The intrepid ladies of the jungle, the female globetrottresses of the deserts, began their painful journeys home.

Part III

A lady an explorer? a traveller in skirts?
The notion's just a trifle to seraphic.
Let them stay and mind the babies, or hem our
ragged shirts:
But they mustn't, can't and shan't be geographic.
Punch 1839

6

A Heroine's Welcome

The Liverpool Landing Stage was shrouded in mist as the small landing craft pulled into dock. In the biting first hours of daylight, the stevedores moved slowly out from behind the warehouses, ready to unload cargo. The ring of the carthorses' hooves and the creak of the slow wheels were dampened in the wet and heavy morning air.

It was still too early for the onlookers and idlers who spent lazy afternoons strolling too and fro along the floating piers, attracted to the spectacle of the onloading and offloading of exotic goods and peoples, and the finery of the first class passengers. Marianne North, her face cracked and bronzed by the Caribbean sun, stepped gingerly on to the almost empty timber quay. There was no welcoming party; there were no flags flitting in the coast breeze, their colours vibrant in the harsh glare of the punishing sun as had greeted Mary Gaunt on her West African landing; there were no schoolchildren lining the streets from the harbour as had heralded Mary Kingsley in Calabar. Marianne wrapped her shawl still tighter about her and made her way to the telegraph office to send a cable to the flat in Victoria Street – Is there room? The answer came back – No, there's not. Mr and Mrs Campbell, family friends, had moved in during her absence.[1] Feeling the intrusive nip of the morning air, a hunched Marianne made her way towards the hotel where she would spend her first hours back after a year's wandering around North America and the island of Jamaica. Did the forty-two-year-old spinster perhaps whisper sarcastically to herself, 'Welcome home'?

On landing back in the grey worlds of their childhood, the women

[1]Manuscript of autobiography, p. 461.

travellers were not greeted with flags and parades, nor with the welcoming arms of close family or friends, but with incessant requests from newspapers and societies to write, talk and be interviewed about their journeys. While they had been on the move, short notices in the press had merely recorded for the more observant reader that Miss Kingsley was at present in the Belgian Congo, Miss North was crossing by ferry from Ceylon to the Indian mainland, or Miss Macleod was feared murdered by savages in Central Africa. But on their return to British shores, the in-the-flesh lady travellers were in constant demand to reveal their stories to a broader public. This was a popularity, however, in which the travellers themselves were initially unwilling to collude. 'No! it was not a pleasant surprise to me to find my portrait in the paper and my doings talked about,' Mary Kingsley told a woman reporter. 'I thoroughly dislike all this publicity.' But the persistent interviewer retorted, 'Will you not make allowance for a hero-worshipping public who like to hear a little about those who have *done* something?'[2] Miss Kingsley was not convinced; when approached by J. Saxon Mills of the *Daily News*, she refused to meet him, instead asking the persistent pressman to submit a list of questions for her written answer. 'Please, please don't supply information about me or photos of me to newspaper correspondents,' pleaded Gertrude Bell to her stepmother. 'I've said this so often before that I thought you understood how much I hate the whole advertisement business. I always throw all letters . . . asking for interview or a photo straight into the waste paper basket and I beg you do the same on my behalf.'[3]

However difficult for journalists to track them down, the lone journeys of a single woman through hostile and distant terrain were far too good copy to be dropped. Where hard facts were in short supply, hyberbole, the poetry of the hacks, took over. 'Miss North . . . may be said to have put a garland about the earth, if not a girdle . . . . She has climbed mountains, been rowed down strange rivers or floated down, supported by inflated skins and been driven through wild plains in small wagons, guarded by an escort of natives,' wrote the local *Daily Tribune* as her ship docked at New York.[4] Only a week after the

---

[2] Isabel S. Robson, 'A Lady Explorer's Adventures in West Africa', *Osborne Magazine*, Apr. 1897, p. 258.

[3] Bell to Florence Bell 6 Sep. 1917, Baghdad, quoted in Bell, *Letters*, p. 424.

[4] *New York Daily Tribune*, 28 May 1881.

Bakana landed at Liverpool, a brief note in the *Illustrated London News* informed readers that 'Miss Kingsley has returned from West Africa with an interesting account of her experiences in the Gaboon country. The expedition was rather venturesome, for the natives were inclined to cannibalism; and Miss Kingsley occasionally lighted upon a larder in which cold human joint was only too conspicuous.'[5]

While the women travellers had been botanists, anthropologists and archaeologists in foreign lands, at home the guise of a professional could not be so easily maintained. In Britain, the importance of their femininity came once again to the fore. If their travels in the Orient and Dark Continent were predicated on the fact that their sex was subsumed in their role as 'white men', on returning to the land of their birth they were portrayed as *lady* travellers. While they had tried so very hard to distance themselves from female counterparts, their journeys were celebrated by the British public and in popular culture as those of *female* travellers. *Good Words* ran a series on 'Celebrated Women Travellers' in 1901. Magazines and periodicals could do joint reviews of up to a dozen women's travelogues at the same time. Anthologies of *Pioneer Women*, *Adventurous Women*, *Celebrated Women Travellers* and *Heroines of Travel* evoked a tradition of travelling women spanning back over five hundred years.[6] These female globetrottresses were formed in an image separate from that of missionary women. For although the collections of potted biographies and reviews of their work occasionally included the story of a single woman missionary who had served long and alone in a remote station – Mary Slessor, Christina Forsyth – or those who had undertaken independent journeys under the guise of evangelism – Annie Taylor, Mildred Cable and Francesca French – these stories were by and large kept apart from the atheistic journeys of the lady travellers. Mary Slessor could appear in *Pioneer Women* next to Isabella Bird, but *Heroines of the Cross*, *Heroines of the Faith*, *Women of Worth*, *Four Noble Women* and *Three Brave Women* did not include any travellers.[7] Nor was a female traveller ever included in such titles as *Stories of*

[5] *Illustrated London News*, 7 Dec. 1895 p. 694.

[6] Margaret E. Tabor, *Pioneer Women*, (London 1925); Eleanor Scott, *Adventurous Women*, (London 1935); Frank Mundell, *Heroines of Travel*, (London 1897); W. H. Davenport Adams, *Celebrated Women Travellers of the Nineteenth Century*, (London 1897).

[7] Frank Mundell, *Heroines of the Cross*, (London 1897), *Heroines of the Faith*, (London 1898); Jennie Chappell, *Four Noble Women*, (London 1898), *Women of Worth*, (London 1908) and *Three Brave Women*, (London 1920).

Travel Adventure, Pathclearers of Central Africa, and *Heroes of Discovery,* which exclusively highlighted male achievement.[8]

As the proliferation of anthologies suggests, commentators and critics were continually tempted to draw parallels between women travellers who differed enormously both in the time and place to which they journeyed, and in their public and private achievement and commitment. Do not forget Lady Hester Stanhope and Lady Ellenborough (Jane Digby) when reading Anne Blunt's *Bedouins of the Euphrates,* advised one reviewer.[9] Isabella Bird's hagiographer opens the biography of her heroine by drawing attention to four women who had established themselves as famed travellers – Mrs Bishop (Isabella Bird), Miss North, Miss Kingsley, and Miss Gordon Cumming.[10] In reviewing Olive Macleod's account of her journey to Lake Chad in 1910, a critic manages to refer to Mrs Mary Livingstone, Mary Kingsley and May French-Sheldon.[11] Edith Durham, it was claimed, had 'the same strong prejudice and frankness in revealing life . . . the same innate sympathy . . . the same interest in tribal affinities and tribal customs, the same inability to express herself according to the laws of grammar and syntax' and 'a similar sense of humour' to Mary Kingsley.[12]

Yet at the same time as connecting women's travels over fifty years apart, there was also a seemingly contradictory stress on the new and recent nature of the phenomenon of the female traveller. A magazine in 1854 noted with regret the new species of 'British Spinsterhood Abroad'.[13] 'Since Isabella Bird first crossed the Rockies [1873] the age of the Lady Adventurer has set in. Girls in the Carpathians were suceeded by wives in Arabia and spinsters in West Africa,' declared one newspaper.[14] Ten years later the author of *Celebrated Women Travellers* noted 'the great and rapid increase in the number of female travellers.'[15] In 1912 the *Times Literary Supplement* was still claiming that 'until comparatively recently women took part in the exploration

---

[8] Frank Mundell, *Stories of Travel Adventure,* (London 1899); James J. Ellis, *Pathclearers of Central Africa,* (London 1928); Samuel Mossman, *Heroes of Discovery,* (Edinburgh 1868).

[9] 'The Romance of Modern Travel', *Quarterly Review,* vol. 149, (1880), p. 221.

[10] Anna Stoddart, *The Life of Isabella Bird (Mrs Bishop),* (London 1906), p. v.

[11] 'Across Lake Chad', *TLS,* 9 May 1912, p. 193.

[12] 'Darkest Europe, *TLS,* 16 Dec. 1909, p. 500.

[13] 'British Spinsterhood Abroad', *Dublin University Magazine,* vol. 43, (1854), pp. 267–74.

[14] 'The Desert and the Sown', *TLS,* 25 Jan. 1907, p. 28.

[15] Adams, *Celebrated Women Travellers,* p. 383.

of Africa only when they happened to be the wives or daughters of men who had devoted themselves to that fascinating pastime.'[16]

Although including many German, Austrian, French and Scandinavian travellers in their overviews, the particularity of the English lady traveller would also be highlighted. Other countries, said one reviewer, 'have not the same well-read, solid looking, – early rising – sketch-loving – light-footed – trim-waisted – straw-hatted specimen of woman.'[17] He continued: 'Sometimes one is tempted to fancy that they had quitted home and all its comforts for the express purpose of bonding the British Government in relations of closer amity with those of the rest of Europe, and, as we have said, of some parts of Africa, than the mere official modes of intercourse had been able to effect.'[18] In reviewing Edith Durham's first travel book, a critic noted, 'The author belongs to that type of enterprising and unconventional woman which seems to be almost a monopoly of Anglo-Saxon countries, and of which the late Miss Mary Kingsley was a typical representative.'[19]

As the evidence of many years of women travelling alone to distant and unknown lands was an indisputable if unpalatable fact, press reports sought to soften the threat such a tradition might pose to perceived appropriate activities for women in two ways: first, by manipulating the women travellers' experiences to fit a pattern which more closely resembled that deemed fit for women; and secondly, by stressing their uniqueness, which sought to establish them as exceptions to rather than representatives of a trend. This latter path also necessitated a stress on women travellers' unique attributes – whether unmatched and unmatchable courage, extreme physical endurance, or language abilities, which made their journeys possible in a way they would not have been for the ordinary woman.

So while limitless parallels were drawn and connections made between contemporary women travellers and those of history, commentators at the same time underlined the one-off nature of the women's experiences. 'Miss Kingsley is unique,' wrote the *Young Woman*, while Edith Durham's experiences were, it was claimed, 'not

---

[16] 'Across Lake Chad', *TLS*, 9 May 1912, p. 193.
[17] 'Lady Travellers', *Quarterly Review*, vol. 76, (1845), p. 102.
[18] Ibid., p. 128.
[19] 'In the Balkans', *TLS*, 8 Apr. 1904, p. 107.

in the least like those of the ordinary lady-globetrotter.'[20] These
accounts colluded in claims made by the travellers themselves that
they were the first white women to enter a certain region, ascend a
certain river, climb a certain mountain. And while many anthologies
of biographical essays on women travellers and articles on their travels
were aimed at a young and adolescent audience, if any young woman
thought she might join in the tradition thus presented she was advised
against so doing. 'A visit to Lake Chad is not one which can be
recommended to ladies in search of diversion,' warned a critic.[21]
Another wrote he would be 'far from recommending solitary travel in
Africa, or similarly barbarous regions, to any woman . . . for a white
female to go alone among wild races and hideous solitudes appears a
risk to something more than life [and] . . . ought not to be imitated.'[22]
'I don't recommend you do just what [Mary Kingsley] did,' wrote a
woman journalist, and 'in fact, you couldn't, and there's an end of
it.'[23]

How are these two apparently contradictory trends explained – the
argument for and establishment of a tradition of women travellers and
an equally strong claim that each woman traveller was unique? There
are, perhaps, other feminine traditions which have been approached
from the same confused standpoint – that of the female soldier, from
Joan of Arc onwards, and those of female missionaries and saints. But
in the collections of stories on these exemplary lives, the feminine
models evoked are those displaying the virtues of self-sacrifice –
whether for country, religion or loved one. In the lives and
experiences of the women travellers, however, commentators were
faced with a feminine tradition which seemed to display none of these
traditionally feminine virtues. It was not for Queen and country that
Mary Kingsley sailed to West Africa, it was not for missionary zeal that
Marianne North painted the tropics, it was not for a spurned love that
Ella Christie climbed to over 10,000 feet in Ladakh. And it was
difficult for the media to portray the motives behind the women
travellers' wanderings as anything more than they were – essentially,
gloriously selfish.

[20] 'From a Woman's Point of View' by Deas Cromarty, *Young Woman*, Nov. 1897, p. 74;
'Darkest Europe', *TLS*, 16 Dec. 1909, p. 499.
[21] 'Across Lake Chad', *TLS*, 9 May 1912, p. 193.
[22] *Daily Telegraph*, 3 Dec. 1895, p. 4.
[23] Cromarty, 'From a Woman's Point of View', (1897), p. 73.

Women travellers' biographies were therefore massaged to conform more closely to ideals of feminine duty. 'In no case has their travelling enthusiasm involved the sacrifice of obvious domestic duty; nor has it brought out any qualities inconsistent with the modesty, the grace, and the gentleness that must always be regarded as the fitting ornaments of the sex,' reassuringly concluded one reviewer.[24] But merely stating that they had not abandoned the obligations of femininity was not enough: women's travel experiences had to be reinterpreted to make them assume the guise of service and duty. A personal friend of Gertrude Bell's from her Oxford days noted this transformation: 'It was startling to those who had known her intimately, who remembered her free, glancing thought, her brilliant talk, her gay laughter, all her bright, un-self-conscious, unforgettable personality, to find her figuring as the "Lesson for the Day" in the handbook of a semi-religious fellowship . . . her service had in a sense been pure accident.'[25] Mary Kingsley, it was reported, knew,

> everything that a good housewife should know . . . . Her father, curious to tell, had little leaning towards scholarly women and refused to allow his daughter to learn German until she had thoroughly mastered ironing and starching. That her father, in the end, fully believed in her domestic capabilities is evident, since he allowed her to help him in his Oriental and Semitic researches; and after his death she went to West Africa to continue his work.[26]

Although this was written at the time of her death, there had been no evidence in her travelogues that she had in fact undertaken such studies; but it was an image of feminine sacrifice and a supportive, secondary role which echoed throughout posthumous accounts of her work. Olive Macleod, it was also claimed, went to West Africa in 1910 on a 'self-sacrificing tribute' to investigate the exact circumstances of the sudden death in Central Africa of her lover, Boyd Alexander.[27] Although this was the indisputable spur behind her journey – she left Britain only a few weeks after the news of Boyd's

[24] 'Lady Travellers', *Blackwood's Edinburgh Magazine*, vol. 160 (1896), p. 66.
[25] Janet E. Courtney, *The Women of My Time*, (London 1934), pp. 77–8.
[26] 'Cosy Corner Chat', *The Gentlewoman*, 16 June 1900, p. 771.
[27] *Boyd Alexander's Last Journey* with a Memoir by Herbert Alexander, (London 1912), p. 41.

murder reached Britain – in her own account she only fleetingly refers to her fiance. 'I am told that it is expected of the writer of a book of travels to set forth clearly and concisely the objects with which his or her journey was undertaken and the results achieved,' she wrote. 'I must beg leave to be excused from so business-like a proceeding, and further ask my critics not to read on if they expect more than a simple unexaggerated narrative of travel through little-known regions.'[28] Although she reportedly visited Fort Lamy to speak to the French officers with whom Alexander Boyd had spent the last months of his life, she simply records the African housing conditions, crafts and European inhabitants.

Lady Jane Franklin, wife to the leader of the fated Franklin Arctic expedition, was also presented as a woman who was spurred by duty to a ghost. Although she had travelled extensively by herself before a late marriage, she achieved fame for organizing and financing an expedition in search of an explanation for the disappearance of her husband and his crew. She became the first woman to be awarded the Patron's Gold Medal of the Royal Geographical Society in 1860 for this vicarious contribution to travel. But it was to this determined woman's position as the widow of Sir John Franklin that the award was made, and not to Jane Franklin herself. 'The list of such worthies cannot be more appropriately enriched than by offering the Patron's Medal of the year to the consecration of the deeds of Franklin,' declared the President. Lady Jane was praised for 'her noble and self-sacrificing perserverance in sending out, at her own cost, several searching expeditions, until at length the fate of her husband has been finally ascertained.'[29] As women were not admitted to the Society, Sir Roderick Murchison accepted the medal on her behalf. Her apparent unquestionably selfless motives also allowed her, unlike other women travellers, to be included in anthologies of devout and pious women; in suffragist Ellen Clayton's *Celebrated Women. Stories of Their Lives and Example* she appeared as 'The Indefatigable Wife'.[30]

In addition to serving the memory of a loved one, religion could be evoked as an acceptable motive for women's travels. The first voyage

---

[28] Macleod, *Chiefs and Cities of Central Africa*, p. v.

[29] Address by Earl de Grey at Anniversary Meeting of the Royal Geographical Society 28 May 1860, *Proceedings of the Royal Geographical Society*, vol. 4, (1861), pp. 111–12.

[30] Ellen Clayton, *Celebrated Women. Stories of Their Lives and Example Literary, Social and Historical. A Book for Young Ladies*, (London 1875).

undertaken by round-the-world Austrian traveller Ida Pfeiffer was a nine month trip to North Africa and the Middle East in 1842. Her book of this journey, carefully entitled *Travels of a Viennese Woman to the Holy Land*, was received with great acclaim. For although Ida Pfeiffer had waited until her two sons were grown before embarking on her journeys, and was motivated into travel by an unhappy and unrewarding marriage, a trip to the Lands of the Bible was assumed to be religiously rather than personally inspired. Isabella Bird's and Constance Gordon Cumming's interest in and reporting of missionary activities on their journeys was also overemphasized in media accounts. Despite the fact that Alexandrine Tinne never spoke out or wrote about what she saw on her Nile journey, her popular biography states, 'all her remarkable labours seemed to be performed solely out of love to the cause that she espoused so early in life; namely, that of exploring Africa, and carrying intelligence to the poor negro, and doing what lay in her power to abolish that most terrible scourge of Africa, the internal slave-trade.'[31] The suggestion of religious motivation was often bolstered by the inclusion in anthologies of women travellers of one or two of the more adventurous single women missionaries. The personal declarations of agnosticism, atheism or pantheism, and frequent criticism of the missionary endeavour expressed by many of the women travellers in their writings were conveniently overlooked.

In conjunction with the rewriting of the motives which induced women to take to travelling came an equal stress on their femininity. The unabating insistence on their womanly appearance and virtues is an indication of how much travelling was presumed to threaten them. In Britain, as on their journeys, physical attributes, dress and manner assumed enormous importance. As young women, they had been acutely aware that they lacked many of the finer physical qualities deemed necessary for their feminine charm. But on returning from distant lands they found themselves lauded for the possession of these very same attributes. And while they laid claim to exploits of considerable courage and an awakened sense of power in their own bodies, their physical vulnerability was exaggerated. 'One is apt to think that a woman who accomplished such really remarkable feats of

[31] Professor William Wells, *The Heroine of the White Nile, or What a Woman Did and Dared. A Sketch of the Remarkable Travels and Experiences of Miss Alexandrine Tinne*, (New York 1871), pp. 9–10.

endurance and energy must have been endowed with great physical strength and robust proportions,' wrote an author on Ida Pffeifer. 'But such was by no means the case. Her stature did not exceed – nay, was below – the average, and there was nothing masculine in her face or figure.'[32] 'There was nothing of the Amazon about her,' confirmed another journalist. 'She was, too, a devoted mother, a warm friend, and a true Christian.'[33]

The language used to describe the women travellers' physical appearance was both excessive and repetitive. Isabella Bird, like Ida Pfeiffer, possessed 'nothing of the Amazon. She is small and fair, with a gentle yet penetrating voice.'[34] Although Mary Kingsley constantly contrasted her own looks with those of the missionary wives she met in West Africa, *The Gentlewoman* wrote of the 'intense femininity about her,' with 'her calm grey eyes' and 'her musical voice [which] gained your ear and held it.'[35] Another magazine noted her 'madonna-like face', implying the very missionary associations the traveller herself was so anxious to avoid.[36]

Many commentators were anxious to share their astonishment at finding, upon personal acquaintance, women very different from those they had imagined at a distance, which at once acknowledged popular images and at the same time confronted them. 'I was asked often,' wrote a personal friend of Ménie Muriel Dowie, author of *A Girl in the Karpathians*, '"What is she like? Very strong, I suppose and sturdy," and the picture I drew of her, used to leave a blank and rather incredulous surprise.'[37] 'Knowing all about her African adventures,' wrote the seafarer and author Frank Bullen of Mary Kingsley, 'I expected to see a masculine creature with a harsh voice and an air of command. Instead, I saw a graceful willowly figure, most womanly, the large eyes alight . . . a woman manifestly nervous.'[38] A member of staff at the British Museum remembered Margaret Fountaine's first

---

[32] Adams, *Celebrated Women Travellers*, p. 239.

[33] Hobson, 'Celebrated Women Travellers. IV Ida Pfeiffer', p. 485.

[34] Archibald R. Coloquhoun, 'Celebrated Lady Travellers. III Isabella Bishop, née Bird', *Good Words*, vol. 42, (1901), p. 243.

[35] 'Cosy Corner Chat', *The Gentlewoman*, 16 June 1900, p. 771.

[36] Ethel F. Heddle, 'Celebrated Lady Travellers. I Ménie Muriel Dowie (Mrs Henry Norman)', *Good Words*, vol. 42, (1901), p. 17.

[37] Ibid., pp. 16–17.

[38] Frank T. Bullen, 'Some Memories of Mary Kingsley', *Mainly About People*, 16 June 1900, p. 570.

visit. 'Having heard something of Miss Fountaine's exploits the announcement conjured up visions of a well-worn battleaxe,' Norman Riley wrote. 'Instead I met a tall, attractive, rather frail-looking, diffident, but determined middle-aged woman. The strongest impression she gave me was of great sadness.'[39]

Complementing the gentle manners with which these pretty vapid women wafted around jungles, canoed through mangrove swamps and climbed mountains, were the soft feminine eyes, like a muslin veil, through which they were attributed with perceiving the foreign worlds. In their anthropological and archaeological work they had been criticized for the narrowness of their vision in contrast to the grand, broad theories of armchair academics. But the popular press complemented the women travellers for bringing a meticulous woman's eye to foreign societies and peoples, and with this a special role:

> There are peculiar powers inherent in ladies' eyes . . . we mean that power of observation which, so long as it remains at home counting canvas stitches by the fireside, we are apt to consider no shrewder than our own, but which once removed from the familiar scene, and returned to us in the shape of letters or books, seldom fails to prove its superiority . . .
>
> Every country with any pretensions to civilisation has a twofold aspect, addressed to two different modes of perception, and seldom visible simultaneously to both. Every country has a home life as well as a public life . . . . Every country therefore, to be fairly understood, requires reporters from both sexes.[40]

Women are 'unquestionably more observant of details and quicker to receive impressions,' wrote one reviewer. 'Their sympathies are more alert, and they get in touch with strangers more readily.'[41] 'In her powers of observation and her ability to gather and weave infinitesimal details into a compact web lies the essential difference of the woman-traveller and the male-traveller,' wrote another. 'He may get the big, broad impression, but he often fails in those intimate

---

[39] Quoted in Fountaine, *Butterflies and Late Loves*, p. 166.

[40] 'Lady Travellers', *Quarterly Review*, vol. 76, (1845), pp. 98–9.

[41] 'The Desert and the Sown', *TLS*, 25 Jan. 1907, p. 28.

details which in the life of every country are its essence. Miss Christie misses none of them.'[42] Etta Close remained 'feminine in her delicacy of perception' while ordering nine porters through East Africa.[43] So while the women's published as well as private accounts of their journeys in fact display very little 'feminine eye' and attention to domestic detail, in the attempts to feminize their achievements they were credited with this peculiar perspective.

Traits in their character or experience could also be reinterpreted or explained away by describing them as male attributes, thereby divorcing their achievements from the women themselves and attributing them instead to an amorphous masculine culture. Here again the language and imagery offered by other traditions of female heroines could be drawn upon. 'If one were to select the two qualities which have accomplished most in the world of adventure,' wrote a reviewer, 'they would almost certainly be courage and self-assurance. They are qualities which would most naturally be called masculine.'[44] Isabella Bird, like Queen Elizabeth, 'carried in her bosom a man's heart, and was never wanting in courage or resolution.'[45] Mary Kingsley was congratulated on her 'manly strength'.[46] Gertrude Bell possessed a 'masculine vigour' tempered, thankfully, by 'feminine charms and a most romantic spirit.'[47] This method of robbing women travellers of their achievements was not without its own problems, however, as a verse in *Punch* noted:

> Mrs. Sheldon is back from her travels abroad
> Were she only a man, we should hail her as manly;
> As it is, there are some who, in wishing to laud,
> Are accustomed to call her the feminine Stanley.
> But now this adventurous, much-daring she
> Through such perils has gone, and so gallantly held on,
> In times that's to come Mr. Stanley may be
> Merely known to us all as the male Mrs. Sheldon![48]

[42] Annie S. Swan, 'A Fine Travel Book', *British Weekly*, 10 Dec. 1925.

[43] 'A Woman in Kenya', *TLS*, 7 Aug. 1924, p. 488.

[44] 'A Woman in West Africa', *TLS*, 8 Feb. 1912, p. 50.

[45] Adams, *Celebrated Women Travellers*, p. 433.

[46] 'Cosy Corner Chat', *The Gentlewoman*, 16 June 1900, p. 771.

[47] David Hogarth in *Geographical Journal*, vol. 68, (1926), p. 363.

[48] *Punch*, 3 May 1890, quoted in Dorothy Middleton, 'Some Victorian Lady Travellers', *Geographical Journal*, (1973), p. 73.

It was only when in the Savage Lands that these masculine qualities could be safely displayed. 'She dies at last a woman's death in the centre of civilisation,' wrote a women's magazine on Mary Kingsley nursing Boer prisoners-of-war, 'but perhaps that will only strengthen people's memories to recall that she had lived like a man in strange countries where civilisation had not gained a mastery.'[49] 'While playing a man's part in the world,' wrote a friend and biographical essayist of Isabella Bird, 'she has retained the qualities essential to refined womanhood.'[50] 'She had all the charm of a woman combined with very many of the qualities that we associate with men,' said the President of the Royal Geographical Society of Gertrude Bell. 'She was known in the East for these manly qualities.'[51]

While the women travellers could act as men in the Orient and Savage Lands, the evaluation of their achievements by the popular press in Britain was nevertheless designed to ensure that they did not receive male accolades, contrasting their claims with those of men in an attempt to establish a separate, non-threatening tradition of female travel. 'Although it is true that Mrs Gaunt took journeys which no white woman has yet taken,' confirmed a commentator, 'and deserves a high tribute for her physical endurance and courage, it is also true that these journeys involved no extraordinary danger or difficulty. They were not those of a pioneer in an unknown and unsubdued country.' He rounds off by summing her up with one insulting word – 'tourist'.[52] While the women travellers had consciously imitated earlier explorers, on returning to Britain their experiences and achievements were continually contrasted to those of their male counterparts. Although Davenport Adams gathered together in one volume more than twenty globetrotting females, it was felt necessary to point out that 'generally speaking, [travellers] constitute two great classes: those who discover . . . and those who simply follow in the track of their bolder and more fortunate predecessors . . . . To the latter class, as this volume shows, belong our female travellers, among whom we find no companion or rival to such pioneers as a Livingstone, a Barth, a Franklin, or a Stewart.'[53] In reviewing Isabella Bird, Arabist Anne

[49] 'Far and Near', *The Lady*, 21 June 1900, p. 976.
[50] Colquhoun, 'Celebrated Lady Travellers. III Isabella Bishop, née Bird', p. 243.
[51] David Hogarth at RGS, *Geographical Journal*, vol. 70, (1927), p. 21.
[52] 'A Woman in West Africa', *TLS*, 8 Feb. 1912, p. 50.
[53] Adams, *Celebrated Women Travellers*, p. 215.

Blunt, and round-the-world yachtswoman Anna Brassey, the *Quarterly Review* said 'in the present article we have not noticed a single work by those who are our great explorers *par excellence*.'[54] Even by 1912 it could be written that 'it cannot be said that any piece of actual exploration of the first importance has yet been accomplished by a woman.'[55]

Not only the generic female traveller but the achievements of individual women were given this cavalier treatment. After listing all Ida Pfeiffer's considerable travels, *Blackwood's* concluded, 'Madame Pfeiffer cannot be classed with those travellers who have explored and brought to light unknown regions, or added substantially to our knowledge of the globe.'[56] The same reviewer insisted that Olive Macleod's journey to Lake Chad would not have been possible without the cooperation of the veteran anthropologists Mr and Mrs Amaury Talbot. This opinion was echoed by Boyd Alexander's brother: 'Without the help of these experienced travellers it would have been well-nigh impossible for Miss Macleod to have accomplished her purpose.'[57] Similarly, although Ménie Dowie had travelled extensively before her marriage, and subsequently often broke from her husband's path to find her own way back, her ability to travel was attributed to her husband's skills.

Another, minority view expressed of the women travellers in the late nineteenth century was that they were 'New Women', responding to recent political and social openings for women. On the Tuesday following Mary Kingsley's landing at Liverpool on her return from her second journey to West Africa, the *Daily Telegraph* was writing at length of her 'surprising and courageous adventures'. But not only did this paper break with other press portrayals by comparing her journeys to those of the male explorers Speke, Grant, Burton, Stanley, and Selous – it also called her a 'New Woman'.[58] Other, more subtle descriptions of the female traveller as a manifestation of emergent demands and aspirations of the late-nineteenth-century woman were made without the use of such explicit language. The 'great and rapid increase in the number of female travellers' was at least partly due, said one 1880s writer, 'to the greater freedom which women of late years

---

[54] 'The Romance of Modern Travel', *Quarterly Review*, vol. 149, (1880), p. 229.
[55] 'Across Lake Chad', *TLS*, 9 May 1912, p. 193.
[56] 'Lady Travellers', *Blackwood's*, (1896), p. 51.
[57] *Boyd Alexander's Last Journey*, pp. 41–2.
[58] *Daily Telegraph*, 3 Dec. 1895, p. 3.

have successfully claimed, and to the consequent development of powers and faculties, their possession of which was long ignored or denied.'[59] And while the *Young Woman* shunned the language of progressive women's demands, emphatically declaring 'you must not think of [Mary Kingsley] as a specimen of the New Woman, wildly, incoherently bent on astonishing the world and "breaking the record" in some direction – any direction', it nonetheless reported that 'whether there are any notions left of what is proper and becoming for women may be doubted. They are not things to mind about if you have a good object in view. Nurses are absolved from them, and doctors, and missionaries' wives; Mrs Bishop [Isabella Bird] absolved herself, and Miss Kingsley has proved her own right to freedom.'[60]

The surprise many commentators recorded on meeting delicate, petite and even attractive women in contrast to the viragos their names conjured up suggests that not everyone believed women travellers could remain essentially feminine, and still be explorers. The Resident at Bauchi in West Africa was pleasantly surprised to find the traveller and mountaineer Miss Benham 'violently "antisuffrage"; altogether quite different to what I expected.'[61] When Mary Kingsley was confronted with a colonial official at a dinner party she soon learnt about one side of her popular image. She recorded their conversation: 'Not knowing who I was, a pretty thing, he said "Do you know Miss Mary Kingsley?" "I never met her," said I. "Oh!" he said after a few words, "you know *we* say she smells of the palm oil tub." Of course I never let on.'[62]

It was partly in response to the threat of this particular public image that emphasis on feminine appearance, manner and training appeared so frequently in press reports. When accusations of being New Women arose, these too had to be countered. Complimentary remarks on the travellers' reluctance to engage in political debate surrounding women's issues began to appear. Looking back on the life of Mary Kingsley 'hope revives in the breasts of those who have been dismayed by the attitude taken up by the women-workers of this end of the century,' wrote a women's magazine, 'and the belief is strengthened

[59] Adams, *Celebrated Women Travellers*, pp. 383–4.

[60] Cromarty, 'From a Woman's Point of View', (1897), p. 73.

[61] Selwyn Macgregor Grier to mother [Grace Grier] 16 Dec. 1912, Bauchi, Council of World Mission archive.

[62] Kingsley to John Holt 24 Feb. 1900, St Mary Abbot's Terrace, London.

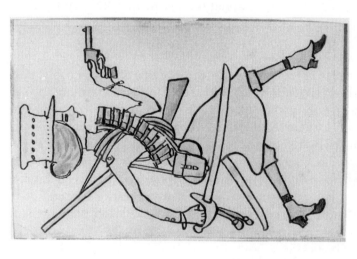

Cartoons of Mary Kingsley by students in an audience at a Cambridge University debating society at which she argued the motion 'That it is better for us to understand Alien Races than for Alien Races to understand us', 1899. Reproduced by kind permission of the Master and Fellows of Trinity College Cambridge.

that it is those women who never suffered one to forget their sex, and are never desirous of aping the other, being secure in their own strength, who really make progress and advance the interests of Woman.'[63] Over twenty years later, a commentator on Gertrude Bell was grateful 'she escaped, thanks to a lifelong indifference to what are called Feminist Movements, that advertisement by others which some distinguished members of her sex have suffered.'[64]

There was no uniform response to the women travellers; they were an awkward set of female figures to fit into prevailing feminine imagery, and because of this they might be portrayed in different ways by and for different audiences. Their popular interpretation would, inevitably, affect the women's own portrayals, tinged by hindsight, of their journeys. After their initial shyness, many began to court the publicity they soon realized could be exploited to their own personal and political ends. But which of the many portraits offered did they support, and why?

Of all the images offered to them in the British press and popular culture, it was that of a challenging New Woman against which the women travellers most vehemently fought. Rather than opting for portraits as strong and ground-breaking women, they reinforced, in a few instances to the point of caricature, their feminine attributes and the unthreatening nature of their claims. While they had imitated the male explorers and acted as 'white men' in the Savage Lands, in Britain the women travellers felt they had to be 100 per cent feminine. With the acute consciousness of this dilemma in mind, they set out to defend and bolster their feminine reputations against all those who dared to question them.

When the *Times* reported that Isabella Bird had 'donned masculine habiliments for greater convenience' while traversing the Rockies, the infuriated traveller responded immediately. She inserted a prefaratory note to the second edition of *A Lady's Life in the Rocky Mountains*, together with a pen and ink sketch of the Hawaiian riding dress which had been so described. Her costume was 'the "American Lady's Mountain Dress"', she explained, 'a half-fitting jacket, a skirt reaching to the ankles, and full Turkish trousers gathered into frills

[63] 'Mary Kingsley', *The Lady's Pictorial*, 16 June 1900.
[64] David Hogarth, *Geographical Journal*, vol. 68, (1926), p. 363.

which fall over the boots – a thoroughly serviceable and feminine costume for mountaineering and other rough travelling in any part of the world.'[65] Mary Kingsley's first venture into print was not, as generally supposed, in defence of the 'unadulterated African' and her much-maligned friends the West African traders, but in reply to the *Daily Telegraph* report which identified her as a 'New Woman'. She was no such thing, she declared in her swift letter of reply, and had not undertaken any activities on her travels 'without the assistance of the superior sex' – publicly denying the very independence she had in private so desperately and determinedly sought.[66] She was adamant in conforming to the most conservative of social manners and dress, always wearing (in public at least) an old-fashioned high-necked blouse, black skirt and small sealskin bonnet. She wrote to her friend the political hostess Alice Stopford Green, 'I implore you if you hear it said in Society that I appear on platforms in African native costume and a smock or a trade shirt to contradict it – honour bright I had got my best frock on.'[67] She always adopted when lecturing, the voice and mannerisms of a middle-aged, middle-class lady, neither of which she strictly was. No longer was she the 'white man' in Africa, but would rhetorically ask her audience if she didn't remind them of their 'maiden aunt'.[68] This straightened asexual image stood in stark contrast to the sensual awakening so many women travellers had felt in the distant lands.

Agnes Smith Lewis was also accused of acting in a manner unfit for British womanhood abroad. When the scholar and traveller read an account of her professional relationship with the Prior of the monastery where she studied in Sinai, she was horrified. On reaching the monastery the aged monk had greeted Agnes Smith Lewis in a manner entirely different from that of the rest of the party, claimed the writer. 'He patted her affectionately, he felt her garments, he made her sit by his side with his arm around her shoulders . . . . Several young monks watched this unecclesiastical mode of reception with unmoved faces. We tried to do the same . . . we did not relish the thought that we might have to submit, in our turn, to similar

---

[65] 'Note to Second Edition', *A Lady's Life in the Rocky Mountains*.

[66] *Daily Telegraph*, 5 Dec. 1895, p. 8.

[67] Kingsley to Alice Stopford Green 30 Apr. 1898, Addison Road, London.

[68] E. Muriel Joy to Dorothy Middleton 7 Feb. 1965. Miss Joy was a pupil at Cheltenham Ladies College when Mary Kingsley delivered a lecture.

familiarities.' Agnes Smith Lewis immediately wrote a 2,600 word disclaimer to the editor of the *Cambridge Chronicle*, hoping to reach the eyes of the circle of Middle Eastern academics who would read such a book. Any other editor who dared to review *Our Journey to Sinai* and quote from the offending passage was similarly answered.[69]

Women travellers were open to innuendos not only of improper behaviour but also of inappropriate and unwomanly motives, striking to the very heart of the legitimacy of their travels. While critics had been kind about Ida Pfeiffer's first lone journey, they were not so lenient or accepting of the reasons for her second voyage to Iceland. A journey to the Holy Land could be shrouded under religious motives, but to Iceland – why would a woman undertake such a journey alone? At the publication of her account, *A Visit to Iceland*, Ida Pfeiffer felt obliged to answer these critical queries. 'I am surely simple and harmless enough,' she pleaded, 'and should have fancied anything in the world rather than it would ever be my fate to draw upon myself in any degree the notice of the public. I will merely indicate, as briefly as may be, my character and circumstances, and then I have no doubt my conduct will lose its appearance of eccentricity, and seem perfectly natural.' She elaborates, in language which evokes religious imagery and metaphors, a disingenuous explanation: she undertook this second journey with the same unfailing religious inspiration as the first, she claims, for she wanted to witness all God's natural phenomena in their full glory – and where better to do this than in Iceland?[70] Mindful, like Agnes Smith Lewis, of the need to counter any notions of sexual impropriety, she reminds the reader that she was in any case born in the previous century and is therefore quite old. And although she always travelled armed, she at the same time denied being the sort of woman who carried a 'pistol in my belt'.

The women's fervent and frequent denials that they exhibited improper or challenging behaviour often broadened into active opposition to women's rights and suffrage. The essentially selfish nature of their journeys, undertaken for highly personal and private reasons, did not encourage them to judge their experiences in any collective sense. So although their lives may appear exemplarily feminist, their voices contradict this image and make it impossible to

[69] Whigham Price, *The Ladies of Castlebrae*. pp. 157–8, who quotes Agnes D. Bensly, *Our Journey to Sinai – A Visit to the Convent of St Caterina*, (London 1896).

[70] Ida Pfeiffer, *A Visit to Iceland and the Scandinavian North*, (1846; 1852 translation), p. viii.

portray them so. A pattern also emerges of an inverse relationship between the depth and breadth of experience of a woman traveller and her support for women's demands in the political and social arena in Britain. Paradoxically, the more strident the woman traveller's actual personal achievements, the more vehemently she opposed the extension of these opportunities to other women on her return to Britain. So while Amelia Edwards', Ella Christie's and Mary Gaunt's journeys do not compare to those of Gertrude Bell, Marianne North and Mary Kingsley in the extent of their lone travel, scientific data accumulated, and physical challenges and threats encountered, it was the former and not the latter group that supported women's suffrage. Mary Kingsley, Marianne North and Gertrude Bell were, among other women travellers, active opponents of women's political movements, often openly speaking against women's involvement in political and professional circles. Gertrude Bell was a founding member of the Anti-Suffrage League and devoted the little time she spent in Britain to organizing fund-raising and meetings for the organization. 'The strongminded women are getting too rampageous here,' wrote Marianne North to a friend. 'They want now to start an agricultural college for women! . . . It is a pity clever women make themselves laughed at.'[71]

A major concern of the more adventurous women travellers such as Marianne North was to distance themselves from the 'laughed at' suffragists and agitators, an open alliance with whom, they feared, would belittle their own reputations as travellers and professionals, and detract from the uniqueness of their achievements. Although Marianne North intended to make this explicit in her autobiography, her sister Catherine, entrusted with its editing after Marianne's death, chose to omit all references to her anti-suffragism. Catherine, herself a wife and mother, felt no need for the display of and stress on her femininity which her more controversial elder sister did. So while Marianne wrote, 'I should be terribly bored by the possession of a vote and those sensible women would certainly not use it if they had one, and thus give a dangerous majority to the wild women in the world of petticoat government – and another thing struck me how ugly all those strongminded females and their pet parsons were! They ought always to be kept down' – this was edited out of the *Recollections*.[72]

---

[71] North to Arthur Burnell 17 Jan. 1880, Victoria Street, London.

[72] Manuscript of autobiography, p. 382.

Mary Kingsley equally opposed the advancement of opportunities for women within her own professional sphere. When she was approached by a petitioner for women's admission to the learned societies, she wrote to warn the Secretary of the Royal Geographical Society of the impending danger. 'I am just as fond of women as you are – it is unnecessary to say more,' she told him, 'but these androgines I have no use for.'[73] Her personal descriptions of women's rights advocates colluded with the unflattering popular portrayals. 'I was at the writers' club yesterday,' she wrote to a female friend, 'and was an utter failure – because I was frightened by a little woman about four feet six high who had been to Kimberley. It wasn't that that terrified me but her shirt and fixings, real shirt, starched, studs, waistcoat and coat and hat on side of head, talked of how women should let people see they could *boss* it. I shrunk into a corner with a little lady who had really been to the Faroe Islands and who could have whipped up the other one, shirt and all in fact the whole room full only she did not know it, and told me lots of things.'[74] Mary Kingsley's separatist philosophy as applied to differences between the races was equally vehemently and rigorously applied to differences between the sexes, and even supplemented with the hierarchical, evaluative judgements she so carefully avoided when contrasting African and European. 'A great woman,' she wrote, 'either mentally or physically, will excel an indifferent man, but no woman equals a really great man.'[75] Interviewed for *Good Words* women travellers' series, Ménie Dowie, who had travelled about Central Europe dressed as a boy, said she 'should like something said to show that I am not a woman's rights woman, in the aggressive sense; that I do not rejoice in ugly clothes . . . and that I am not desirous of reforming the world, or doing anything subversive.'[76]

In contrast, Amelia Edwards, whose one major journey was made in the company of other Europeans and to an area relatively well traversed, was Vice President of the Society for Promoting Women's Suffrage. Ella Christie, who also made no claims as a pioneer traveller, was a member of the Scottish Women's Suffrage Society, and attended

---

[73] Kingsley to John Scott Keltie 1 Dec. 1899, St Mary Abbot's Terrace, London.

[74] Kingsley to Hatty Johnson 25 Jan. 1896, Addison Road, London.

[75] Kingsley, *Travels in West Africa*, p. 659.

[76] Heddle, 'Celebrated Lady Travellers. I Ménie Muriel Dowie (Mrs Henry Norman)', (1901), p. 18.

meetings of the Women Writers' Suffrage League. Although she was supported in this opinion by her younger sister, Alice's husband forbade her to take any part.

The more adventurous women travellers' repeated denials of any allegiance to or sympathy with women's demands must, however, be seen in the light of their attempts to gain social and later political respect and even power. Many quickly learnt how to give an easily swayed public the tales they wanted to hear. A disparity between the public image they sought to project and the private reality of their lives can often be traced.

The first action of many when thrust, initially unwillingly, on to the public platform was to deny any claims to achievement. While they themselves had undergone immense emotional challenges, they sought to lessen the impact of these upon their public audience, insisting that they remained the same duty-bound spinsters as when they had left British shores. Their first books begin not with claims to credit and acclaim, but with self-abnegation. 'What this book wants is not a simple Preface but an apology, and a very brilliant and convincing one at that,' wrote Mary Kingsley at the very start of *Travels in West Africa*. Georgina Mackenzie and Adelina Irby began their jointly written travel books on Central Europe with apologies for their limitations. 'This book has no pretensions to be either historical, scientific, or political,' wrote Ella Sykes of her account of her travels through Persia with her brother 'being merely the record of a very happy period of my existence, which I have, in a way, re-lived by writing about it.'[77] Isobel Gill denied any pretensions to being a traveller in the title of her book – *Six Months in Ascension. An Unscientific Account of a Scientific Expedition*. Yet these disclaimers were often matched by gross exaggerations of the extent and unaided nature of their journeys. While Amelia Edwards painted a picture of the explorer with 'perhaps a dozen half-naked Arabs and some fifteen or twenty children' to help in the archaeological work, in fact she was aided by over one hundred adults.[78] Mary Kingsley reported several conversations with Africans whom she happened to bump into on remote forest paths – although, as she only spoke English and a smattering of pidgin, they could not possibly have held any language in common.

[77] Ella Sykes, *Through Persia on a Side-Saddle*, (London 1898), preface.
[78] Edwards, *Pharoahs, Fellahs and Explorers*, p. 13.

Women travellers' ventures into print and on to the public platform
were often directed towards particular, calculated ends. Missionary,
local philosophical and university debating societies, working men's
clubs, YMCAs, women's meetings all hosted them, and talks
accompanied by lantern slides could attract audiences in the
thousands. Women travellers found themselves in constant demand,
often having to turn down a lecture from overbooking. Mary Kingsley,
like many other women travellers, quickly realized that she had
'caught the public eye' and soon began to direct that powerful glare
towards the specific area she wanted it to light upon.[79] As she began to
identify her area of commitment as support for trader interests in West
Africa and non-interventionist systems of imperial control, this
political goal was presented in a more palatable form to her popular
audience. 'Cornhill will have some [18]93 stories in this month,' she
wrote, referring to light-hearted tales of life in West Africa she had
collected on her first journey. 'Let's hope it will be good for trade.'[80]
Throughout her first year back in Britain she contributed a large
number of short articles to magazines designed to educate and inform.
The image of an interpid lady explorer in the jungle which had intially
so angered her could draw large crowds who then received political
statements sugared with tales of African adventure. This, she had
learnt, was what the public wanted; this was the most effective way to
put her controversial views across. 'These literary and scientific
institutions amuse me much,' she wrote. 'They always write and
inform you they don't want science – literature presumably they don't
expect. What they want is "something bright and amusing and magic
lantern slides." I have moments of grave doubt as to whether the
Times and the Spectator are right when they say the British Public
insists on being taken seriously.'[81]

Amelia Edwards also sought to disguise her message in addressing
the broad audience she attracted. While committing herself to the
discovery and preservation of archaeological remains since her return
from Egypt in 1874, focusing her energy on the formation of the Egypt
Exploration Fund with this object in mind, her popular work
contained little of the detailed academic expertise she sought to
promote. Nor did her one-woman propoganda machine stop at British

[79] Kingsley to John Scott Keltie 14 Dec. 1895, Addison Road, London.
[80] Kingsley to George Macmillan 19 Jan. 1897, Addison Road, London.
[81] Kingsley to E. Sydney Hartland 25 Mar. 1897, Addison Road, London.

12 10

WOMEN'S EMERGENCY CORPS

LECTURE on KHIVA

BY

MISS ELLA R. CHRISTIE, F.R.G.S.

WILL BE DELIVERED IN THE

FREEMASONS' HALL, George Street,

TUESDAY, 2nd MARCH 1915, AT 8 P.M.

DOORS OPEN AT 7.30.

A Scotchwoman's journey through the Dominions of our Russian Allies in Central Asia.

Limelight Illustrations from her own Photographs.

Chairman: Sir W. M. RAMSAY, D.C.L., LL.D., etc.

IN AID OF

WOMEN'S EMERGENCY CORPS and BRITISH RED CROSS SOCIETY

TICKETS, 3s., 2s., 1s. Some Free Seats for Men in Uniform.

From Messrs Paterson & Sons, 27 George Street; Messrs R. W. Pentland, 24 Frederick Street; and at Women's Emergency Corps, 29 Drumsheugh Gardens.

Ella Christie's lecture Notice.
The Trustees of the National Library of Scotland.

shores, for in 1889 she went on an extensive lecture tour of the United States and, on her return, published her talks in book form as *Pharoahs, Fellahs and Explorers* to reach an even wider audience. Even apolitical Isabella Bird 'strove by conversation, by lectures, by articles, to arouse public attention' in defence of the alleged persecution of Armenian Christians by the Kurds.[82] All her best-selling travelogues, based on letters to Britain, were prefaced with hard data and statistics on the regions they covered, adding weight to her popular accounts.

Women travellers devoted themselves to these commitments as fiercely as they had earlier devoted themselves to their families. Mary Kingsley wrote to a Cambridge friend from Yorkshire, 'I came here last night leaving London at ten, arriving at 4.45, and lecturing at 5.30. Tomorrow I drive twelve miles to Richmond, lecture again and on Tuesday go to Newcastle to lecture some more, and on Friday go to Liverpool, home on Saturday, therefore my reliable address is Addison Road.'[83] Her brother disparagingly nicknamed his hall-hopping sister 'the lecturer'. 'It seems a Sisyphus, for the more I do the more I have got to do,' she complained.[84] Even Gertrude Bell, who had shown such reluctance to answer press enquiries and requests, wrote that she would like to deliver some lectures on 'my province', the political situation in the Middle East, on her projected return to Britain.[85] Soon she became even more ambitious. 'I wish we could reach a far larger public,' she wrote. 'What we want is cinematographic films. I feel certain we would get something, with Faisal a central figure.'[86] Mary Gaunt was also a dedicated self-publicist. On publication of her historical novel, *As The Whirlwind Passeth*, she wrote to the *Times*, *Truth*, *Observer* and the *Daily Mirror*. She also sent a copy of the book to Gaumont Pictures in the hope they might make it into a film.[87]

It was Marianne North, however, the most retiring and seemingly proper of the women travellers, who played her popular appeal to the fullest. In the summer of 1879 she hired a small fashionable gallery for an exhibition of her Indian sketches and approached Dr Burnell with

[82] 'Lady Travellers', *Blackwood's*, (1896), p. 62.

[83] Kingsley to Hatty Johnson 7 Mar. 1897, 'Yorkshire at large'.

[84] Kingsley to Alice Stopford Green 22 Nov. 1897, Addison Road, London.

[85] Bell to Florence Bell 31 Jan. 1919, Baghdad, quoted in Bell, *Letters*, p. 467.

[86] Bell to G. E. Shickburgh at Colonial Office, Aug. 1921, Baghdad, quoted in Winstone, *Gertrude Bell*, p. 241.

[87] Gaunt to John Murray 6 July 1936, Bordighera, Italy.

publicity ideas. Could you write to the *Academy*, she asked him? Do you think the India Club would put up a notice? If I send you a pack of printed cards can you distribute them to your Indian friends?[88] The success of the show led her to lay the ground for even greater plans. After missing a train at Shrewsbury station a month later, she wrote from the platform to Joseph Hooker, Director of the Gardens at Kew, concerning a scheme she had been turning over in her mind for some time. In a calculated letter, she played on her image as a feeble spinster and drew attention to her critical appeal:

> Often when I have wondered over Kew and got beyond all its houses and into the beautiful park I have felt quite dead, and longing for a rest house for my feet and poor old bones – especially in rainy weather, not uncommon in this dear old English climate – and it came into my head the other day after reading that bit in the *Pall Mall* about my flower paintings, that I should like very much to place them near their live neighbours and if a piece of spare ground could be found in or close to the pleasure grounds at Kew I would build a suitable gallery for them which might be a rest house for the tired visitors.[89]

Marianne North offered two thousand pounds towards the cost of the building, asked that a live-in caretaker and his wife might provide refreshments to attract an even broader public, and suggested architect James Fergusson work with her on the gallery's design.

Marianne North's offer of time, energy and finance for the project was a proposition even the cautious Board of the Royal Botanic Gardens was, after much considered and drawn-out deliberation, unable to refuse. But the refreshments were vetoed. For Marianne North, who saw the establishment of this monument to her work as the one way in which she could attract public attention, this was a critical issue. While many of the less scientifically minded general public (the 'GP' as Mary Kingsley personified them) might not be attracted to a gallery of botanical paintings they might be tempted by tea and cakes, and it was this mass audience North wanted to entice.

Not only, however, did she receive slow permission from the Board for her self-financed publicity stunt, but the architect she had chosen

[88] North to Arthur Burnell June 1879, Victoria Street, London.
[89] North to Joseph Hooker 11 Aug. 1879, Shrewsbury Railway Station.

was privately regretting accepting the commission. There was little professional prestige, he obviously felt, in designing a small building to house the paintings of a wandering woman. 'I *felt* but did *not* say, what an infernal fool I had been to meddle in a matter for which I could obtain neither credit nor profit, and which promised to be a source of infinite annoyance and heart burning to the end,' he wrote to Hooker.[90]

Progress on the construction of the mock-Greek gallery and the arrangement of the paintings was slow; Kew prevaricated and North, angered and frustrated by the time it was taking to make the simplest arrangements, with characteristic impatience left on another journey. In Borneo, Australia, New Zealand and returning via the West Coast of the United States, she added further to her already enormous collection of oil colours. While in Britain, she dedicated, to the point of physical and nervous exhaustion, her time to the setting up of the exhibition and opening of the gallery. By the spring of 1882 the project was almost complete, and Marianne North was spending long days hanging her paintings from all around the world in geographical divisions. She chose to display only her later oils, and almost exclusively those paintings with botanical interest, although she had executed a number of landscapes and pictures of monuments and market scenes. By concentrating on her work on plants and flowers, however, she was discreetly presenting herself before the public not merely as a painter, a female dabbler in artistic pursuits, but as a professional in the scientific field of botany. William Botting Hemsley was asked to produce, from a rough draft prepared by North, a catalogue to accompany the paintings containing further details of botanical interest and drawing attention to the extraordinary nature and scope of the collection.

At the back of the gallery Marianne North had insisted on a studio where she could paint, and where visiting artists could be entertained and work. She designed the gallery, in fact, to cater to a number of different publics: the general, non-specialist audience for whom she hoped teas would be provided; the scientific establishment, who could see accurate and detailed representations of plants not seen before in Britain; and the artistic community, who could be hosted among over 600 paintings. But although she courted publicity and approval at

---

[90] Fergusson to Joseph Hooker 3 Jun. 1880.

The Marianne North Gallery, Royal Botanic Gardens, Kew.
Photograph by D. Birkett.

these three different levels, it was the public eye which was drawn to the garish, highly-coloured portrayals of exotic plants at the opening of the Marianne North Gallery in June 1882. The *Daily News* noted how, following the pictures, 'one proceeds as it were upon a botanical expedition literally all round the world.' The reporter drew attention to the carniverous plants of North America, the sacred lotus of India, the cotton tree of Jamaica which is held in 'superstitious veneration'.[91] The *Times* was attracted to the chameleon-like qualities of many of the plants depicted, 'leaves like red limpids or squatting toads, and creepers like serpents, while flowers assume *aliases* of the most fantastic kind.'[92] And in case any paper might miss the opening, North sent out cards and drew on those personal contacts she had acquired to guarantee full coverage. Seven thousand copies of the catalogue were sold in the first year.

But although consciously wooing public attention, Marianne North's relationship with the press and general public was as ambiguous as that of other women travellers. At first happy to be able to fracture and direct different aspects of themselves to different public and private audiences, women travellers soon felt broken by the often conflicting personalities they projected and relationships they engendered with the British world. When the gallery was completed after a three-year struggle, Marianne North felt it an anticlimax. 'I have had enough of all this and am tired of it,' she told Hooker frankly, less than a month after the opening, 'and altogether rather out of humour, as you see at this moment, and shall be glad of a good rest at sea again, away from all troubles and letters.'[93] As many other travellers felt, heightened press and public interest was not complemented by personal satisfaction. Many began to feel they were increasingly looking at themselves in a distorted mirror and were unable to recognize the portrait reflected back at them. Who was 'the Mystery Woman of the East, the uncrowned Queen, the Diana of the Desert' Gertrude Bell saw herself described as in the press?[94] How did Mary Kingsley, the publicly self-declared 'immediate English successor, in the way of travellers, to Mr Winwood Reade' reconcile privately writing to the Secretary of the Royal Geographical denying any such

[91] 'A Botancial Picture Gallery', *Daily News*, 8 June 1882.
[92] 'Miss North's Exhibition', *Times*, 7 Aug. 1882, p. 7.
[93] North to Joseph Hooker 18 July 1882, Victoria Street, London.
[94] Bell, *Letters*, p. 776.

connection: 'This morning a friend has sent me a Brighton paper with a thrilling story full of native chiefs and arrows. Possibly a gem from some boys' book of adventures. I don't remember it in Winwood Reade or Du Chaillu, the authorities I find usually supply my experiences in the newspapers. Still I wish they would not say I told them the yarns.'[95] Confused and frustrated by the colourful images awaiting them on their arrival back in Britain, some began to seek a new audience based not in the public arena but in private, small but influential circles. Turning from the pages of the press and popular platforms to dinner parties and clubrooms, the women travellers began their most difficult journeys – into the dark interior of British political society.

[95] Kingsley, *Travels in West Africa*, p. 347; Kingsley to John Scott Keltie 13 Jan. 1897, Addison Road, London.

7

Exploring the Interior

Mary Kingsley sat motionless on the small platform. Dressed, as always, in nothing but black, her long inexpressive face registered no reaction as the Deputy Chairman of the Liverpool Geographical Society read out a vivid account of canoeing down rapids, being upset by a hippopotamus, attacked by crocodiles, sucked by leeches and ascending a 13,000 foot mountain in 'a hurricane raging in a fog'. It was a familiar story to the silent listener, for it was her story, the story of her nine month lone journey through West Africa in 1895. In the guise of a 'white man', she had undertaken this solo journey through the distant lands; as a woman, she had to sit on the platform while her experiences were read out on her behalf in her home country. She waited for the sting in the sugared tale; for in this talk, delivered in the port-city of West African interests in Britain, Miss Kingsley publicly articulated her economic imperialism for the first time. 'The most important thing in West Africa is the trade,' she heard her own words pronounced:

England is the great manufacturing country of the world, and as such requires markets, and requires now markets far more than colonies. A colony drains from the mother country, yearly, thousands of the most able and energetic of her children, leaving behind them their aged and incapable relations. Whereas the holding of the West African markets drains a few hundred men only – only too often for ever; but the trade they carry on and develop enables thousands of men, women, and children to remain safe in England in comfort and pleasure, owing to the wages and profits arising from the manufacture and export of articles used in that trade. So I trust those at home in England will give all honour to men who are still working out there, or lying buried in the weed-grown, snake-infested cemeteries and the pathless swamps of the coast; and may England never again dream of forfeiting or playing with the conquests won for her by those heroes of commerce, whose battles have been fought out on lonely beaches, far away from home or friends.[1]

The audience of traders, teachers, businessmen, shippers, missionaries and colonial administrators clapped politely as the speaker James Irvine returned to his chair. They had laughed at the stories of 'plenty too much' gorillas, been astonished by the conquering of Mount Cameroon by a new path, and been flattered by the heroic portrayal of the trading community from which the majority of them came. Mary Kingsley had watched these moving faces intently from the platform. But what, she undoubtedly wondered, did they think of a woman daring to make proclamations on economic and imperial policy?

The spotlight welcoming the women travellers on their return to Britain had filtered through into more specialist circles, and the scientific establishment became eager to cull information from their travels. Books were often slow to appear, so following quickly upon the incessant requests from newspapers and magazines for interviews came invitations to talk from the geographical and professional societies. When the Secretary of the Royal Geographical Society (RGS) learnt from a letter in the *Times* that Gertrude Bell had returned to Britain from Baghdad in the summer of 1914, he wrote immediately: 'I congratulate you on your escape. One heard very unpleasant rumours about what had happened to you somewhere or another' – and would Miss Bell honour the RGS with a paper?[2] Zélie Colvile was asked to deliver a talk on Madagascar to the Liverpool Geographical Society, 'being the only white woman lucky enough to cross that isle', a lecture she toured around the local geographical societies.[3] The Royal Society asked Marianne North to lend paintings

---

[1] Miss M. H. Kingsley, 'The Ascent of Cameroons Peak and Travels in French Congo', *Transactions of the Liverpool Geographical Society*, 1896, pp. 49 and 52.

[2] Secretary of RGS to Gertrude Bell 13 June 1914.

[3] *Transactions of the Liverpool Geographical Society*, 1898, p. 17.

for a meeting.[4] The RGS requested Isabella Bird to give a lecture after her return from Persia in 1891.[5] But as Mary Kingsley's silent vigil as she listened to her paper suggests, women's incorporation into the work of geographical and professional societies was awkward and tenuous. Although Mary Kingsley had been interviewed and written about by the popular press since her return from West Africa three months earlier, her talk to the Liverpool Geographic was only her second appearance on the platform of a select society.

The degree of women's inclusion into the geographical and professional societies was important both for their acceptance and definition as travellers, and for their access to informal, influental political circles. For the geographical and related learned societies, including the Royal Society, Botanical Society, Royal Asiatic Society, Linnaen Society, Geological Society, Royal Anthropological Institute and British Association for the Advancement of Science, were forums which attracted men involved in travel and its political counterpart – the development of British imperialism. In the second half of the nineteenth century it was common for a traveller to be slowly incorporated into the administrative machine abroad, through first unofficial and then eventually official positions attached to the Colonial and Foreign Offices. The careers of both Frederick Lugard, a political opponent of Mary Kingsley whose career culminated in the Governorship of Northern Nigeria, and the consul-trader John Petherick followed this path from traveller to government official. The integration of these societies into official colonial circles was also reflected in their membership, and multi-membership was common. Prominent Fellows were often involved in colonial affairs; Frederick Curzon, arch-opponent of women's admission to the societies, was Viceroy of India before becoming President of the Royal Geographical Society. The informal networks created by membership of many different societies provided an alternative forum for discussion, formation and dissemination of colonial ideology and policy. Recognition as integral and valuable members was therefore crucial to the women travellers' professional acceptance and the furtherance of their particular political goals.

Women had been active in the geographical and professional societies for decades. Marianne North and Anna Brassey had

[4] North to William Thistleton-Dyer 1 June 1886.
[5] Bird to John Murray 14 Jan. 1891, Regents Park, London.

contributed ethnological specimens for exhibition at the Royal Anthropological Institute. Isabella Bird borrowed books from the RGS library under her publisher's name. Later, Gertrude Bell received instruction from Mr Reeves in the RGS Map Room on surveying and astronomical matters before leaving for archaeological work in Asia Minor in 1907. All these manifestations of women's participation did not, however, challenge exclusive control by the male membership. Precisely because women's involvement had been unrecorded, there was no necessity to recognize their contribution or incorporate it into official practice. The hidden nature of women's work also guaranteed that institutionalized positions of authority within the societies were closed to them.

As long as women's involvement was invisible and undocumented it did not threaten male hegemony or require the inclusion of women amongst the gallery of travellers whom the societies embraced. But as pressures and demands to include women in their structure were put upon older societies in general, and the RGS in particular, fierce debates ensued. As the oldest society of travellers, the Royal Geographical was almost self-defining in its membership. A Fellow who could boast the prestigious initials of FRGS in articles and books was guaranteed to the reader to be a traveller. If women were allowed to use these coveted initials after their published work, it would be demonstrated often and openly that they had been recognized as travellers.

Attempts earlier in the century to endow women with the accredited status of RGS Fellowship had reflected the popular portrayals of women travellers as unique and exceptional. In 1868, Honorary Fellowship was requested by the explorer Speke for Alexandrine Tinné and her two female companions for their journeys along the Nile. In this way a woman traveller could be seen as an aberration, rather than as the first sign of a growing trend. By the early 1890s, however, with immense popular interest in the increasing number of adventurous women, this position was becoming more and more untenable. The unpalatable fact that the female traveller constituted not one of a few, isolated and individual cases but a more extreme representative of the numerous women increasingly interested and knowledgeable in geographical matters, challenged the very core of male hegemony in the field of travel. A more far-reaching implication – that they were simply one manifestation of female involvement in professional, scientific activities in a much broader arena – was even more difficult for opponents of women's admission to swallow.

Isabella Bird's chequered involvement with the Royal Geographical Society reflected the ambivalent and unformulated attitude towards the inclusion of women in societies where their presence might suggest they were professionals and travellers. On her return from the Gulf in 1891, she was asked to give the prestigious Anniversary Address to the Scottish Geographical Society. But while the four foot eleven inch traveller was addressing an enormous audience gathered to hear her account of 'The Upper Karun Region and the Bakhtiari Lurs', 400 miles away in the rooms of the RGS, debates were raging as to the propriety of admitting women as Fellows. While the new, less prestigious and more educationally-based local geographical societies had admitted women since their foundings in the 1880s, the parent society had, despite attempts since the 1870s, staunchly held out against such a seemingly drastic and disruptive step.

The Scottish Geographical Society, aware of the debates seething at the RGS and with an astute eye for a publicity coup, opened a London branch in the spring of 1892. It hoped to upstage the RGS and draw crowds away from the older, learned academic society into their less formal rooms. On the last day of May, Isabella Bird delivered 'A Journey to Lesser Tibet' to a large audience in an act of quiet defiance.

With the Scottish Geographical established just around the corner from the RGS Saville Row headquarters, the debate was pushed to a new head. The RGS Council announced at the 4 July 1892 meeting that they would, 'throw open the Fellowship of the Society on the same terms and conditions to both sexes. The increasing number of ladies, eminent as travellers, and contributors to the stock of geographical knowledge . . . were, in the opinion of the Council, sufficient reason for at once making the proposed extension, which will, it is believed, be to the advantage of the Society.'[6] The Council could no longer argue for the recognition of one woman on exceptional grounds, nor argue that Isabella Bird's contribution to geographical knowledge was an isolated case.

[6] *Proceedings of the RGS*, vol. 14, (1892), p. 553. All the following quotes come from the minutes of meetings surrounding the admission of women as Fellows to the RGS from November 1892 until April 1893, unless otherwise stated.

At the General Meeting following the announcement of the Council's decision in the *Proceedings*, fifteen women, including Isabella Bird, were elected Fellows. But although the Council believed the move 'would meet with general approval among the Fellows', an opposing faction had already formed. Arguments drew out through several meetings, both sides were forced to consult legal opinion, and the decision to admit women as Fellows was first endorsed, then overturned. But the debate still raged on. At the May Annual General Meeting of the following year, immediately after the Chair had been taken, a Fellow rose and said, 'before proceeding to the business of the meeting, I should like to call your attention, Mr Chairman, to the fact that ladies are present, and to ask you whether it is right and proper that they should be here.' His remarks were followed by applause. A vote was taken on the issue and reported in favour of allowing those women already elected to remain Fellows of the Society. Between the November 1892 and April 1893 General Meetings, twenty-two women Fellows had managed to slip through this brief chink in the door.

Throughout the RGS debates, supporters of women's Fellowship had accused their opponents of being old-fashioned; the Fellow is 'behind the period who proposes the exclusion of ladies from any legitimate rights,' it was argued by the orientalist Robert Needham Cust, whose daughter Maria (already a member of the Royal Anthropological Institute of which her father was Vice-President) he proposed for election. 'I need not point to the list of distinguished women who are worthy of admission. I need not point to the support that many noble travellers have had in equatorial Africa and elsewhere from women, the way in which Queen Victoria has always encouraged this Society. When you admit women into public life as doctors where the greatest knowledge and skill has to be manifested it would be most irrational to exclude them here,' argued another. The explorer H. M. Stanley, friend of May French-Sheldon, spoke on behalf of women's admission: 'the time is coming for a great many things to be changed. Fifty years is a long time, to some it appears antediluvian; fifty years ago I was a small boy and the continent of Africa was not so crowded with names . . . who knows but the ladies themselves may be very prominent in giving their aid towards enlightening us in Africa, Asia or America.'

It was exactly this notion that female travellers suggested a growing trend rather than a small and nameable group that the opposition feared. Recognition of individual, exceptional women was not incompatible with the rejection of the incorporation of women as a whole into the circle of travellers. Admiral Montagu Ommanney, soon to raise his voice in opposition to women's Fellowship, supported one woman's application by agreeing to be one of the two FRGS signatories required to support her election.[7] 'The reason I do not wish for the admission of women is that in the past, and I believe it will be in the future, the admission of women into public life and offices has been and will be again most disastrous,' explained one Fellow. If the women travellers were more extreme examples of a much broader development, the mere tip of an ever-growing iceberg, not only would women have to be recognized by the male-dominated scientific establishment, but even more disturbingly – where would this development come to a halt? The argument at the RGS was not simply one of Fellowship, but of women's access to power and influence. The initial objection to women's admission *per se* was soon suceeded by arguments over the restriction of their role and power within the Society. The concern of the opposition at the RGS was the possibility of a woman being elected to Council. This fear was expressed from the first General Meeting discussing women's admission in November 1892, when Admiral Cave pointed out that the Charter allowed every Fellow to stand for Council, and he 'should be very sorry to see this ancient Society governed by ladies.'

To challenge arguments that women were beginning to infiltrate circles of geographers and scientists – previously regarded as a male preserve – opponents to women's Fellowship argued that the trend emerging was not identical to that already existing among their male counterparts. The women who presented themselves as travellers and put themselves forward for FRGS were not, they argued, *bona fide* explorers. The most vehemently offered argument was based on brutal biology – 'lady' and 'explorer' were mutually exclusive terms. Women's physical weakness, the argument went, made them simply unfit for geographical and scientific expeditions. 'We contest *in toto* the general capability of women to contribute to scientific geographical knowledge,' wrote the vociferous opponent Curzon. 'Their sex and training render them equally unfitted for exploration.'[8] The

[7] Emmeline Porcher's Election Certificate to FRGS.
[8] *Times*, 31 May 1893, p. 11.

following year Horace Woodward, President of the Geologists' Association which had admitted women since its founding in 1858, outlined activities he nevertheless felt inappropriate for women: 'If there was one part of Geology that I should have thought unsuitable, it would have been that of geological mapping . . . there may be visits to pits and quarries, to railway-cuttings or mines, where none but men – and not always polite men – are at work . . . . Nor do I personally like the idea of women toiling at such arduous work as that of geological mapping.'[9]

But the chivalrous argument of women's moral and physical weakness was only a minor objection; many female occupations which involved great physical exertion and contact with working-class people – such as philanthropic and nursing work – did not receive such staunch criticism. The real contention was that 'lady' and 'explorer' simply did not go together – they referred to different types of human beings. This was implicit, if not explicit, in most of the opposition's arguments. 'Although the admission of ladies might make the Society more or less enjoyable and pleasant I do not think it would intensify the Geographical character of it,' wrote Admiral McClintock, who had personally benefitted from a woman's interest in exploration when appointed commander of the *Fox* yacht by Lady Jane Franklin, encharged with ascertaining the fate of her husband's Arctic expedition. 'The people we wish to attract are explorers, geographers, men employed in trade and commerce and missionaries who seek for geographical knowledge, and I do not think the admission of a large number of ladies will add to our utility in these respects,' he added.

Not only would the Society's scientific status be threatened if women were admitted, but the opposition believed women could not be feminine and scientific. While journalists were surprised to find 'slight and willowy' women travellers, the learned establishment was astonished that a woman could be knowledgeable on geographical subjects. When Flora Shaw was the first woman to give a talk to the Royal Colonial Institute in 1894, Sir James Garrick, Agent General in London for Queensland, opened the discussion with the compliment that, 'her papers from Australia were so accurate, so profound, and in difficult questions so abstruse, that men friends of [his] expressed incredulity that they had been written by a woman.' His comments

[9] 'The Work of Women', *Proceedings of the Geologists' Association*, vol. 13, (1893–4), p. 265.

were followed by cheers and laughter.[10] A Fellow at the April RGS meeting asked, 'what kind of woman it is proposed to introduce. If they are to be young and beautiful, if they are to be old and scientific.'

The RGS Fellows believed that not only women's femininity, and therefore the perceived differences between the sexes, was threatened, but also class divisions. Women's admission to Fellowship was seen by its opponents as synonymous with lowering the class composition of membership. Organisations with less class-specific membership had not raised such strong objections to women's involvement; the Scottish Geographical Society prided itself in having drawn its large membership from 'all grades of society – noblemen and country gentlemen, men of science and men of letters, professionals and schoolmasters, merchants and shippers, clergymen, lawyers and physicians, and women as well as men.'[11] Derogatory references to school teachers and governesses were made frequently during the RGS debates. The Council was quick to point out that many male Fellows came from the teaching profession, but the opposition feared that female membership would lower the class status of Fellowship in a way which their male counterparts did not. 'The object of a large body of Fellows in introducing ladies is to enable mistresses of Schools, Teachers, and Governesses and all Young Ladies who look upon teaching as a future profession to write FRGS after their names and so receive a certificate of competency,' complained Admiral Cave at the April Special General Meeting. 'We all in this Society know that the FRGS does not really mean that the man may necessarily be able to read a map even. But to the outside public FRGS really means a very clever person. I think the Society should not be a registry office for teachers and Governesses and that kind of thing.'

The belief that women's Fellowship would lower the class make-up of the Society is a reflection of the problems involved in attributing class status to women. Those women who had attended meetings throughout the century were guests of male members, so their class was assured by identification with their host. It was the single woman, without an accompanying male relative to guarantee her class respectability, who was most feared. The frequent references to spinsters and widows in the debates reflects this anxiety. The problem was how to identify a woman's class independently of a man.

---

[10] 'The Australian Outlook' by Flora Shaw, reported in the *Times*, 10 Jan. 1894, p. 11.
[11] 'Scotland and Geographical Work', *Scottish Geographical Magazine*, vol. 1, (1885), p. 18.

Accusations that women were unfit to be travellers did not stop, however, at attacks on their physical and social credentials. Soon the very nature of the their journeys was scrutinized. Were they *really* geographic and scientific? Women may appear to be travellers, went the argument, but closer examination revealed that only one, or maybe two, of them counted as such. When applied to women, the term 'geographical knowledge' was used in its narrowest sense – that of mapping new routes and terrain – rather than the broader meaning of extensive and pioneering travel, which was its interpretion for male Fellowship. 'The genus of professional female globetrotters with which America has lately familiarized us is one of the horrors of the latter end of the nineteenth century,' wrote Curzon in a letter to the *Times*.

> In our teeth are thrown the names of one or two distinguished ladies, such as Mrs Bishop [Isabella Bird], whose additions to geographical knowledge have been valuable and serious. But in the whole of England these ladies can be counted on the fingers of one hand; and in the entire range of modern geography I question if history will preserve the names of half that number . . . I am most unwilling that the initials [FRGS] should sink to an even lower market value, as must inevitably be the case if they are paraded by vagrant womanhood on visiting cards and in books.[12]

'Even if five hundred representative ladies, carefully selected by Mr Freshfield [RGS Secretary], were made Fellows to-morrow,' he wrote less than a week later, 'I venture to assert that not ten of their number would ever have contributed, or ever would contribute, anything – but their guineas – to geography.'[13] 'I hope you will allow me to ask who of the twenty two ladies elected by these gentlemen,' echoed the journalist William Russell, 'with the exception of Mrs Bishop and the lady who was Miss Dowie, were elected for "real services to geography"?'[14]

While the RGS sought to attract prominent women travellers as speakers, this did not prevent them from giving their guests consistently unsympathetic coverage in their publications. The

[12] *Times*, 31 May 1893, p. 11.
[13] *Times*, 5 June 1893, p. 10.
[14] *Times*, 1 June 1893, p. 4.

Geographical Journal, organ of the RGS, was particularly cutting in its criticisms. Mary Gaunt's first travel book, *Alone in West Africa*, 'does not add directly to the sum of geographical knowledge,' the review announced.[15] By her second travelogue on China, the *Journal* was commentating that, 'the present work contains little beyond the average impressions of a cultivated tourist.'[16] And by her third they stated, 'it would be misleading to count it as serious book of travel.'[17] Alexandra David-Neel's account, in which she claimed to be the first white woman to enter the forbidden city of Lhasa, was treated as dismissively: 'The geographical results are very meagre,' wrote the Central Asian explorer Francis Younghusband, who had led the British expeditionary force into Lhasa in 1904 and been awarded the Founders Medal by the RGS for his journeys.[18]

Other professional journals were as persistent in seeking to establish that they included women's words only as a courtesy, and that female travellers had no right to claim professional status. 'Miss North was not a botanist,' wrote the *Journal of Botany* of the woman who had four new species – *Crinum northianum* (Borneo), *Nepenthes northiana* (Borneo), *Northea seychellana* (Seychelles), and *Kniphofia northiae* (South Africa) – named after her. 'She never attempted to master the technicalities of systematic botany. Yet she was a great observer,' the author complimented, placing her firmly within an amateur rather than professional tradition.[19] Other specialist journals were quick to fault her; the *Gardeners' Chronicle* noted that the double rainbow in her painting of Niagara Falls had the tints in the wrong sequence.[20] And while Margaret Fountaine contributed to *The Entomologist* and the *Transactions of the Entomological Society of London*, a member of that scientific establishment wrote that she was not 'a great scientific lepidopterist.'[21]

Obituaries were especially anxious to write the life of the woman traveller as that of a lady amateur tourist rather than of a male

[15] 'Alone in West Africa', *Geographical Journal*, vol. 40, (1912), p. 435.

[16] 'Travels in Northern China', *Geographical Journal*, vol. 45, (1915), pp. 524–5.

[17] 'A Broken Journey' by C. H. H., *Geographical Journal*, vol. 54, (1919), pp. 55–7.

[18] Francis Edward Younghusband, 'My Journey to Lhasa', *Geographical Journal*, vol. 71, (1928), p. 85.

[19] W. Botting Hemsley, 'In Memory of Marianne North', *Journal of Botany*, vol. 28, (1890), p. 329–34.

[20] *Gardeners' Chronicle*, 10 June 1882, p. 764.

[21] Mr Eggeling, former conservator of forests in Uganda, quoted in Fountaine, *Butterflies and Late Loves*, p. 143.

professional explorer. 'It would be unfitting to allow the death of the well-known lady traveller, Miss Constance Gordon Cumming, to pass unnoticed in this *Journal*,' the RGS declared in a short obituary. 'For although her travels led her over no positively new ground they were sufficiently varied and extensive to bring her prominently before the public, at a time when lady-travellers in outlying parts of the world were far less common than they are now.' Although she was made a life Fellow of the RGS in 1914, her fame and accolades, the obituarist underlined, came from the attention her sex had drawn to her and not to her achievements in themselves.[22] 'Her work did not . . . lead her into any entirely unknown countries,' the *Journal* wrote on the death of Mary Kingsley, who had crossed from the Ogooué to Remboué Rivers by a route never before attempted by a European, 'and her contributions to geographical science were but incidental to her more definite labours in other fields. Still, she did much to bring before the public a clear understanding of the nature of the West African countries, for which, in spite of their many drawbacks, she continued to feel a surprising enthusiasm.'[23] The disguise the women travellers had consciously adopted on the public platform was not recognized as such by the more academic establishment, and their primary role was seen as that of propagandists rather than professionals, addressing a popular audience and not a scientific elite.

The frequent letters to the *Times* and cartoons and verses in *Punch* drew the attention of a wider audience than the Fellows themselves to the RGS debate. Among them was Isabella Bird, who followed the arguments closely through the pages of the press and personal contacts. But never once did she or any other woman traveller raise her voice on behalf of the pro-women's Fellowship lobby. Even at the meetings following the admission of twenty-two female Fellows, when women were present, they are not recorded as having entered into the heated debates. But behind this apparent lack of concern lies a private interest in developments in the field of women's incorporation into the circle of travellers.

Although it was generally believed that the debate was triggered off by the lady traveller's refusal to read a paper before a society which did not admit women as Fellows, Isabella Bird herself vehemently denied

[22] *Geographical Journal*, vol. 65, (1925), p. 87.
[23] *Geographical Journal*, vol. 16, (1900), p. 115.

that this was the case. She conscientiously avoided taking any part in the debate, writing to her publisher on receiving a circular from Douglas Freshfield encouraging Fellows to vote in favour of women's Fellowship, 'I don't care to take any steps in the matter as I never took any regarding admission.'[24] But her assumed disinterest is followed by a request to be kept informed. When, however, her name was brought to the fore in the public controversy, she again wrote to John Murray restating that she refused to get involved:

> I am annoyed to see that Mr Freshfield both in a circular and in a letter to Saturday's *Times* had referred to my declining to read a paper for the RGS in an inaccurate way which makes me ridiculous. My health was breaking down at the time, and I could not prepare a paper and I added in declining in a friendly note these words as nearly as possible 'It seems scarcely consistent in a society which does not recognise the work of women to ask women to read a paper.' I never made any claim to be a geographer, and hope that none of my friends have ever made it for me. As a traveller and observer I have done a good deal of hard and honest work and may yet do more but I never put forward any claim to have even that recognised by the RGS. If I had thought any use would be made of my note I should not even have written the above remark.[25]

The woman traveller's struggle for academic recognition was waged clandestinely. Open agitation for women's Fellowship could have damaged her reputation and threatened to make Fellowship itself even more elusive. The fears expressed by the opposition, their vision of the type of woman who would apply for Fellowship, the break that would be made with conventional feminine behaviour, and the effect this would have on the Society's standing proved in practice to be unfounded. Women were quick and eager to counter such arguments and insinuations, as they had been answering the popular press's accusations of agitating for women's rights and suffrage. Publicly assumed humility prolonged acceptance as outspoken militancy would not have done. They had before them many examples of privileges withdrawn which acted as a constant reminder of the tenuous and

[24] Bird to John Murray 27 May 1893, Leamington Gardens, Eastbourne.
[25] Bird to John Murray 6 June 1893, Leamington Gardens, Eastbourne.

fragile nature of their involvement. The RGS was only a more extreme example of such a reversal of policy. There had been brief periods at the Ethnological Society, the Geological Society and the British Association when male Fellows were allowed to bring their wives and daughters along to meetings; within a few years, all these societies had reversed their decisions. Botanist Marian Farquharson's humbly-worded petition to the Linnean Society asking for women to be admitted to the rights and privileges of Fellowship, explicitly excluding eligibility to stand for executive posts, provoked a four-year battle. But of the sixteen women's names put forward for Fellowship for the first time in November 1904, fifteen were elected – all except Marian Farquharson.[26]

The impression of a passive and reactive women's interest must, therefore, be measured against the background within which the women travellers had to operate and articulate their demands. Women's concern neither to challenge accepted gender roles nor to appear ambitious can be read as a tactic for guaranteeing maintenance of their small foothold of power rather than a reluctance to take part in public life. Women's cultivation of a passive and conservate façade was a sophisticated response to a political environment which encouraged short term self-censorship in order to gain long term goals and recognition.

Isabella Bird's story of her admission to Fellowship of the RGS is not the only acocunt of a woman traveller whose public denial of claims to geographical expertise is matched by a private insistence on professionalism. The twenty-two women elected Fellows of the RGS did not attempt publicly to challenge male-defined professionalism in their applications. Only one, the charismatic, highly individualistic and American May French-Sheldon, described herself in anything approaching the language of male exploration; she wrote 'Traveller in Africa' under the heading 'occupation' on her Election Certificate. Kate Marsden, who had journeyed extensively throughout Russia treating lepers and could therefore legitimately claim traveller and medical status, was so unpresumptious as to describe herself simply as 'Spinster'. Others merely recorded themselves as 'Wife of . . .' or 'Widow of . . .'.

Nor were male fears of lower middle-class women clamouring for

[26] A. T. Gage, *A History of the Linnaen Society of London*, (London 1938), p. 87.

membership justified. In practice, women's Fellowship tended to consolidate class interests rather than challenge them. The early mid-century intrusions into male exclusivity were made by established, upper-class women, often related to a prominent male Fellow who acted as a guarantor of their class position. Their economic and social security enabled them to take the risk of making such demands. The first women fellows of the Anthropological Institute, for example, elected in 1876, were all titled – the Honourable Lady Hamilton-Gordon, Lady Maude Parry, and Lady Claude Hamilton. Their class status was considerably higher than that of the contemporary male applicants.

The twenty-two Fellows reflected this respectable, middle to upper-class background, and were often of independent means. At least eight of the female Fellows were elected by a male relative; they may already have been familiar faces as guests at meetings, so their class was not open to any question. Only one woman fellow, Miss Florence Small, was a governess. In other societies a similar pattern developed, and many of the women members were related to prominent officeholders. Tylor's wife Anna and Cust's daughter Maria both joined the Royal Anthropological. When there was no male relative available to guarantee their social standing, references to a woman traveller would frequently begin with a sentence concerning her family background. Mary Kingsley was nearly always indentified as a member of the distinguished literary Kingsley family, and often incorrectly said to be the daughter of its most prominent member, Reverend Charles Kingsley, rather than his younger and less respected brother. Women travellers' continuous and calculated attempts always to dress and speak in a manner considered appropriate for middle-class womanhood also helped counter any doubts concerning their class background they feared might be raised.

Women connived to bolster their unthreatening image. Of the many requests they received to speak at the RGS, most, like Isabella Bird, refused. 'I am vexed to see a paragraph that is going the rounds saying I am going to read a paper before the RGS,' Mary Kingsley wrote to the Secretary. 'I should not if you asked me and you have not asked.'[27] Gertrude Bell wrote to the same man twenty years later, in response to his request for a paper, that she was far too busy with war

---

[27] Kingsley to John Scott Keltie 14 Dec. 1895, Addison Road, London.

work, was in any case about to leave for France, and simply had no time to prepare a lecture.[28] Did these responses, like Isabella Bird's, indicate modesty, self-censorship or a subtle form of protest?

Both Mary Kingsley and Gertrude Bell were eager, publicly, to counter any claims to professional accolades. When the RGS belatedly awarded Gertrude Bell the Gill Memorial for 'her many years' work in exploring the geography and archaeology of Syria, Mesopotamia, and other parts of Asiatic Turkey, and for the excellent works in which the results were recorded,' she wrote to the Secretary, 'The Geographical Society is doing me far too much honour and I feel profoundly that my travels have not deserved the recognition which they are about to make me.'[29] Four years later she repeated her formula reply, saying on the award of the Founders Medal that it was 'far too great an honour'; at the ceremony where he received the award on his daughter's behalf, Hugh Bell echoed her words to reassure the assembled Fellowship that she was making no undue claims to academic status. When she filled out her form for the Red Cross she had simply described herself as 'age 46, height 5 ft 5½ . . . *no profession.*'[30] Mary Kingsley assured a pillar of the anthropological establishment, A. C. Haddon, that she was 'not a member of the Anthropological or for that matter of any society. They are not "woman palaver."'[31]

But while women travellers never openly agitated for admission to all-male societies, they often applied for membership as soon as it was open to them. Within eighteen months of denying she was a member of the Anthropological, Mary Kingsley had taken out her subscription. Marianne North was a Fellow of the Royal Anthropological Institute, as were Anna Brassey and Edith Durham. Ella Christie applied for FRGS, not realizing that women's Fellowship had been rescinded; so she joined the Royal Scottish Geographical Society instead.[32] She was also a member of the Central Asian Society. Lady Anne Blunt, Agnes Smith Lewis and Fanny Bullock Workman joined the Royal Asiatic Society. Mary Gaunt gave as one of her reasons for

[28] Bell to John Scott Keltie 19 Nov. 1914, Clandon Park Hospital, Guildford.

[29] *Geographical Journal*, vol. 41, (1913), p. 359; Bell to John Scott Keltie, Saturday [1913], Sloane Street, London.

[30] Bell to Dick Doughty-Wylie 1914, Boulogne, (my italics), quoted in Winstone, *Gertrude Bell*, p. 150.

[31] Kingsley to Alfred Cort Haddon 8 June 1896, Addison Road, London.

[32] See Ava Stewart to John Murray 8 Apr. 1955.

attempting to journey across China to Central Asia that she wanted to qualify as a Fellow of the RGS.[33] When the RGS finally did admit women in February 1913, Gertrude Bell, Ella Christie, Mary Hall, Olive Macleod and Fanny Bullock Workman were among the influx of female applicants within the first month.

Behind public refutations of ambition and claims to self-importance lay a personal world of women's demands and search for self-fulfilment. While they did not want to be seen publicly to challenge the bastion of the male travellers' establishment at the RGS, they would speak at local geographical societies up and down the country where women had been admitted since their foundations. Lilian Hamilton lectured to the Liverpool Geographical on Afghanistan; Mrs W. R. Rickmers (FRGS and member of the Royal Asiatic Society) spoke on her journey to Bakhava; Annie Taylor addressed the Scottish Geographical in December 1893, and ten years later Mary Gaunt gave them a similar honour with an illustrated talk.[34] May French-Sheldon spoke to the Anthropological Institute on her journeys in East Africa with the aid of lantern slides and her collection of African artefacts.[35] The British Association welcomed women speakers at its meetings throughout Britain; Ménie Dowie spoke on the Karpathians, while Mary Kingsley, May French-Sheldon and Isabella Bird also contributed.

Six years after her refusal to speak to the RGS, Isabella Bird was writing to its Secretary boasting that her talk to the Scottish Geographical had attracted an audience of two thousand. 'I hear myself so continually spoken of as "the distinguished traveller" that I am arriving at the very natural conclusing that I am as well entitled to a medal as Mr Curzon or some others!' she added.[36] (The two travellers had met on board a steamer on the Tigris while both were gathering material for their books.) She wrote vehemently to her publisher once the controversy at the RGS had blown over, asking him to send off a copy of her latest book, *The Yangtze Valley and Beyond* to the Scottish Geographical for recognizing her travels in the award of an Honorary Fellowship. 'Though my work has not been distinctly

[33] Gaunt, A Broken Journey, p. 5.

[34] 'A New View of West Africa' delivered in Aberdeen 3 Dec. 1912 by Mary Gaunt, *Scottish Geographical Magazine*, vol. 29, (1913), pp. 111–33.

[35] *Journal of the Anthropological Institute*, vol. 21, (1891–2), p. 357.

[36] Bird to John Scott Keltie 4 Dec. 1897.

geographical yet I think that I have contributed so much to the sum of general knowledge of different countries that I had been a man I should undoubtedly have received some recognition from the Royal Geographical Society. I consider myself to deserve it at least as much as Mr Warrington Smyth!' she wrote.[37] Mr Warrington Smyth FRGS, author of *Journey on the Upper Me Kong* (1895) and *Five Years in Siam* (1898), had received the Murchison grant from the RGS towards his travels. He had dared to comment upon Isabella Bird's paper on the Mantzu of Western Sze-Chuan given to the Anthropological Section of the British Association the previous winter.[38]

Marianne North was also quietly eager to gain recognition. She was delighted when Joseph Hooker recommended her for the Order of the Cross of Malta in a desperate attempt to gain some official token for her contribution to botanical knowledge. 'The more I think the more I like to have that gift from the Queen,' she wrote.[39] But her wishes were not granted, for Hooker was informed that the only women eligible for this discretionary award were royalty and the wives of Indian Princes and high-ranking colonial officials. In a letter from the sovereign's secretary, Marianne North learnt that 'the Queen regrets to learn from her Minutes that Her Majesty's Government have no power of recommending to the Queen any mode of publicly recognising your liberality.' The Empress of India sent her, as scant recompense, a signed photograph.[40] Rival travelling painter Constance Gordon Cumming also bemoaned her lack of recognition. She would, she said, have made a permanent exhibition of her own paintings – à la Miss North – but she had neither the time nor the money. Instead she lent more than three hundred of her paintings for a few months at a time to different exhibitions – including the Indian and Colonial in London – but 'all this involved a good deal of trouble, especially in re-arranging catalogues, and no advantage whatever, beyond receiving a couple of medals,' she lamented.[41]

In fact, women applicants for FRGS could have claimed qualifications exceeding those of the vast majority of their male predecessors. Lilly Grove wrote to the Secretary shortly after her election informing

[37] Bird to John Murray 17 Nov. 1899, Tobermory.
[38] 'Anthropology at the British Association', *Nature*, 15 Dec. 1898, p. 163.
[39] North to Joseph Hooker 23 Apr. [188?], Victoria Street, London.
[40] Henry F. Ponsonby to Marianne North 28 Aug. 1884, Osborne.
[41] Gordon Cumming, *Memories*, p. 351.

him that she could lecture in four languages, drawing on the experiences of her extensive travels.[42] Nevertheless, the RGS never asked her to speak, although she toured the local societies. Her talks included 'The Deserts of Atacama and Tarapaca' and 'The Islands of Chiloe and the South of Chili' to the Liverpool and the Scottish Geographical. Although Ella Christie confidently wrote in her application for FRGS a month before women's admission was officially approved, that she was 'a well known lecturer on geographical subjects' and had 'visited every country in Europe except Ireland, also India, Leh, Baltistan, Ceylon, Burma, Malay States, China, Japan, Korea, Siberia, Tashkent, Samarkand, Dohazar, Khiva, the Caucasus, Palestine, Egypt, Algeria, Tangiers etc etc' – she never spoke before the Fellowship.[43] At the Anthropological Institute, Marianne North and Lady Brassey were both well-seasoned travellers, and at the Royal Asiatic Lady Anne Blunt had travelled extensively in the Middle East, while Agnes Smith Lewis was a leading Syriac scholar.

The recognition women sought was not as extraordinary and unique women travellers – the image they had exploited to gain broad coverage and mass appeal – but as professionals, regardless of their sex. 'I've just got Mother's letter of December 15th saying there's a fandango about my report,' wrote the Oriental Secretary Gertrude Bell to her family. 'The general line taken by the press seems to be that it's most remarkable that a dog should be able to stand up on its hind legs at all – i.e., a female write a white paper. I hope they'll drop that source of wonder and pay attention to the report itself.'[44] When women travellers described themselves in their professional capacities, they would tellingly revert to the masculine as they had done on their travels. Gertrude Bell wrote to her father explaining her position in the British administration in Baghdad:

I must tell you a curious problem that arose – I hope you'll think I decided rightly. To-morrow Sir Henry [Dobbs] gives an official dinner to the King, Cabinet and Advisors, a male dinner . . . . When I came back I found an invitation to myself and I went to him and asked him, as man to man, whether he wanted me to come. He said "yes of course if you won't feel smothered". I said I

[42] Grove to John Scott Keltie 3 Feb. 1893.
[43] Ella Christie's Election Certificate for FRGS, Jan. 1913.
[44] Bell to Hugh Bell 22 Jan. 1921, Baghdad, quoted in Bell, *Letters*, p. 583–4.

thought as a high official in his office, I was sexless and that I ought to come and would. Sir Percy [Cox], on these occasions (levees and so on) always treated me simply as an official and I don't think there's any other way. So I'm going.[45]

Isabella Bird contacted the RGS in order to correct an error concerning her work in their *Journal*: 'You know better than most people that a traveller's reputation for accuracy is everything to him.'[46] While women travellers' popular talks often stressed in content and presentation that they were alone and female, those to learned societies were always made simply as travellers and their sombre titles never once suggested the lecturer's sex.

Women travellers sought more, however, than recognition from professional circles for their skills and contribution. They sought the influence and access shared by members of the small group of prominent societies interested in colonial affairs. As they had clandestinely laid claims to expertise and knowledge, they would exploit the same unobtrusive, hidden methods to exert their opinion on those close to and even holding the reins of power. The informal nature of this network, with office bearers involved in several societies at the same time, allowed women to come in frequent contact with those close to the centres of power. In this way they could wield in private power and influence denied them in public life.

Throughout her short career as a political agitator, Mary Kingsley sought to alter, challenge and form colonial policy. In the midst of the controversy surrounding the taxation of African housing in Sierra Leone, she wrote to the trader John Holt encouraging him to put pen to paper and enter the fray. 'Don't for goodness sake let the mention of me occur,' she warned. 'Then perhaps I shall be asked if your law is right, indirectly, I think with what genuine enthusiasm I can then endorse your statements and sagely shaking my cap frills say, did I not tell you those men have sound detailed knowledge.'[47] She also fed the young journalist E. D. Morel with information for the press. Her favourite ploy was to stir up an artificial controversy between them, simply to keep her issues in the public eye. Gertrude Bell was equally

[45] Bell to Hugh Bell 31 Dec. 1923, Baghdad, quoted in ibid., p. 678.
[46] Bird to John Scott Keltie 17 Apr. [189?].
[47] Kingsley to John Holt 26 Apr. 1899.

conniving in her schemes. An article in the *Times* riled her into a characteristic response. She wrote to her close friend at the same paper, Valentine Chirol,

> Government offices never seek to take up the cudgels – will you not do something for us from time to time? Get from my Father all the letters I have written to him since Faisal's arrival – the full account. You will realize that they are very private and that much I say can't be used, but they'll give you the atmosphere . . . . Won't you sometimes take up the cudgels for us? No one puts our side. I'm going to write some articles – one for Blackwood is on the stocks – but I can't sign them, and if I did the evil-disposed would say I was prejudiced.[48]

The sphere to which women had so often been relegated – the domestic and social – now became the place where they could exert their own particular form of power. The role of hostess, which as young women they had found emotionally unfulfilling, could be exploited for political and professional ends. At dinner parties, at evening meetings, at soirées and in the course of social entertaining, the more politically ambitious women travellers saw an avenue to realize their own manipulative ends. While they sought recognition as professionals and travellers apart from their sex, the methods they used to gain this position were peculiarly and particularly female. It is the informal, behind-the-scenes nature of women's politicking which has often led to an underestimation of their interest and influence in colonial affairs.

Mary Kingsley was particularly adapt at behind-the-scenes manipulation. From early on in her public career she had utilized her popular appeal as the 'daring and courageous' Miss Kingsley for more political ends. Complementary to her assaults from the public platform on behalf of West African traders and against the missionary-led temperance lobby there soon grew a more private agitation. 'I am going for this mission party with feminine artfulness, not like a bull at a gate,' she wrote to John Holt, the Liverpool-West African trader whom she hoped to recruit to her political causes.[49] While on the

[48] Bell to Valentine Chirol, July 1921, Baghdad, quoted in Burgoyne, *Gertrude Bell, 1914–1926*, pp. 233–4.

[49] Kingsley to John Holt 1 Jan. 1898, Addison Road, London.

popular rostrum her arguments focused on humanitarian issues to arouse sympathy and concern, in private correspondence and meetings she highlighted political and economic considerations.

In her agitation against the imposition of a tax on African housing in Sierra Leone, which she believed was in direct conflict with native law, her two-pronged attack was exploited to the full. At the same time as she wrote to the editor of the *Spectator* she also sent a private letter to 'a person I knew would show it to Chamberlain', the Secretary of State for the Colonies.[50] The response was speedy; on the same day as her letter was published, she wrote to Holt, 'tell *no one in Liverpool*, but I have just had a long talk with Chamberlain over the hut tax affair.'[51] Again, it was her first-hand knowledge of the area in question which she stressed, an expertise which the armchair policy-maker could not challenge. She explained further to Holt the nature of her politicking. 'The truth is Mr Holt every bit of solid good work I have done has been done through a man. I get more and more fond of doing things this way. It leaves me a free hand to fight with.'[52] To another influential contact, St Loe Strachey, editor of the *Spectator* and, Mary Kingsley believed, a 'back stairs to Chamberlain',[53] she wrote: 'In the seclusion of private life, in the gentle course of private friendship I shall do my best in language worse than you have ever heard from me, to weld my men together . . . against the existing system.'[54]

Mary Kingsley also realized that being a woman in this informal sphere held advantages which should be used to their full. Through informal channels she made contact with the Second Secretary at the French Embassy in London, hoping to form an alliance between French and British trading interests in West Africa. She wrote to John Holt, 'If you can let me have a definite list of complaints I will fire them in to him . . . . A Frenchman would not listen to an Englishman talking to him about how to manage his colonies, but he don't mind a woman doing so.'[55] Similarly, although the *Times* refused to review her controversial books, she could arrange to meet the editors at a dinner party and thrash out the issues with them in this

[50] Kingsley to John Holt 13 Mar. 1898, Addison Road, London.
[51] Kingsley to John Holt 19 Mar. 1898, Addison Road, London.
[52] Kingsley to John Holt 26 Apr. 1899, St Mary Abbot's Terrace, London.
[53] Kingsley to John Holt 19 Nov. 1898, St Mary Abbot's Terrace, London.
[54] Kingsley to John St Loe Strachey 5 Feb. 1899, St Mary Abbot's Terrace, London.
[55] Kingsley to John Holt 13 Dec. 1898, St Mary Abbot's Terrace, London.

social forum. In this manner she hoped to exert private influence where public access was denied.

The power Mary Kingsley felt lay in this form of politicking was expressed in one of her final letters to her confidante and ardent anti-suffragist Alice Stopford Green. On board the boat to South Africa, looking back on her brief life as a political activist, she advised her friend:

> Do not dream of in any way sacrificing yourself for any cause – I am not saying causes are not worth it, but merely that they cannot be helped by sacrifice of that kind. Set yourself to gain personal power. Don't grab the reins of power, but they are lying on the horse's neck; quietly get them into your hands and drive. You can do it. Therefore do not lament the lack of leaders – be thankful for it and supply the want yourself.[56]

Women were not past exploiting each other's contacts and Mary Kingsley, who felt no sisterly bonds, was particularly active in this sphere. 'I want to have a chat with you over Chalmers' report,' she wrote to Mrs Im Thurn, hoping to trade off her relationship as sister-in-law to the Special Commissioner sent to investigate the house tax in Sierra Leone.[57] She in turn wrote to warn Holt, 'Just a line to put you . . . on your guard about Chalmer's report. Last night I met a lady who is cousin or something, anyhow an intimate of Sir David [Chalmer's] wife. She says C thinks . . .'[58] She suspected the Commissioner's report, which supported her anti-tax standpoint, would be suppressed by the Colonial Office. 'Now you say how do I know,' she wrote to Holt,

> Well I will just tell you. I went down to tea with Mrs Antrobus [whose husband was Assistant Under Secretary at the Colonial Office] over colonial nursing affairs, and she asked me if I knew Chalmers was ill, and I said I had heard from Isabella, Mrs Bishop, but I hoped it was nothing serious. She looking deeply vexed, said his report was ridiculous, and he must have been got hold of. I said goodness gracious! and no more. Then I go out to

[56] Kingsley to Alice Stopford Green 14 Mar. 1900, RMS *Moor*.
[57] Kingsley to Mrs Im Thurn 23 May 1899, St Mary Abbot's Terrace, London.
[58] Kingsley to John Holt n.d.

see a lot of lantern Sierra Leonides that evening in a private
house . . . . Well there were more officials there . . . . They asked
me if I knew Chalmers. I said only by name. They said he seems
a queer man. Subsequently I went to Isabella and said is
Chalmers a queer man? She deeply vexed said firmly 'Sir David is
the soul of Justice.' So I laughed and she said what amuses you.
Oh, I said, there will be larks then, and she blew me up for my
method of expression.[59]

One way in which Mary Kingsley attempted to make concrete this
hidden power was in the formation of a society concerned with
colonial affairs. But although she agreed to be responsible for its
establishment and to provide much of the money and organizational
backing, she did not intend women to be allowed to become members.
'I am not going to show my own petticoat in it but will be represented
by a gentleman,' she told Tylor.[60] Her scheme was not realized until
after her death, with the formation of the Africa Society in 1901 at
the instigation of Alice Stopford Green.

Amelia Edwards also saw a society as the most efficient way to further
her professional goals. Alongside her vast number of contributions to
the press on the need to preserve and excavate scientifically the
archaeological heritage of Egypt, she drew up plans for the formation of
an Egyptological society with this specific purpose in view. At the
foundation of the Egypt Exploration Fund in 1882, Amelia Edwards
shared the Secretaryship with Reginald Poole and within twelve
months the Fund sent its first archaeologist, M. Naville, to Egypt. As
with Mary Kingsley's projected African Society, Amelia Edwards never
promoted or even suggested the employment of women archaeologists,
devoting her time and energy entirely to the furtherance of professional
interests independent of her sex. Her lack of sex-bias, however, was not
shared by her male colleagues. For although she worked in collabor-
ation with Poole in the formation of the Fund, she was soon ousted from
the decision-making process and excluded from anything more than a
merely secretarial role. She was restricted to the large but unrewarding
task of answering letters and subscription requests while the male,
academic members of the governing body formed policy and made

---

[59] Kingsley to John Holt 4 Mar. 1899, St Mary Abbot's Terrace, London.
[60] Kingsley to E. B. Tylor 10 Dec. 1898, St Mary Abbot's Terrace, London.

appointments.[61] While at the Annual General Meeting the committee would discuss academic and technical matters, Amelia Edwards as Honorary Secretary and the only woman officebearer, raised issues concerning American donors and subscriber numbers.[62]

Not all women fitted easily into the social networks the societies offered. Isabella Bird's awkward and unwelcome position as the symbol of the struggle for women's admission to the RGS hindered her incorporation into the Society's social activities. It was customary for speakers to be invited to dinner after their lecture, and accordingly the Secretary asked Isabella Bird to join the leading Fellows on the night of 10 May 1897, following her talk on 'A Journey to Western Sze-Chuan' – the first given by a woman before the Society. 'May I add,' she wrote tactfully in accepting his kind offer, 'that I hope that things will go on just as usual and that the invitation will not entail any trouble to anybody.'[63] But despite her wishes, a silent protest was launched. Only twelve Fellows sat down around the table that evening; the usual attendance was fifty.

This did not deter Isabella Bird from occasionally using the dinner table as a small but influential platform. While she was writing strongly worded articles for the *Contemporary Review* in defence of the Armenians and Syrians against alleged Kurdish maltreatment she had witnessed on her journey from Urmi to Trebizond, she met Mr Gladstone at her publisher's home where they discussed the atrocities. Her articles stirred further interest, and she was soon asked to speak in a Committee Room of the House of Commons on 'The Armenian Question'.[64]

Although Mary Gaunt shared Mary Kingsley's African interests, her political goals were less focused and, as a result, ultimately less successful. She bombarded the *Times* with correspondence on topics from the Jamaican mail service and white men in the tropics to the breadfruit tree, but also expanded her political views to men of power and influence behind the scenes. As with Mary Kingsley, the RGS Secretary was one of the first to receive her lengthy, argued correspondence. And despite getting only brief notes for replies,

[61] Philippa Levine introduction to Edwards, *Untrodden Peaks and Unfrequented Valleys*, pp. xxiv–xxvi.

[62] *Egypt Exploration Fund. Report of Second Annual General Meeting 1884.*

[63] Bird to John Scott Keltie 27 Apr. 1897, Huntingdonshire.

[64] Barr, *A Curious Life for a Lady*, pp. 262–3.

she would write back again at even greater length expounding on the importance of settlement in West Africa – and in particular the necessity for the settlement of white women – to the success of the British colonial endeavour. Like other women travellers, she reminded her correspondents that she had *been there*, and was therefore talking from a privileged vantage point of first-hand knowledge and not acquired, and implicitly biased, information gathered from secondary sources. 'Everybody has remonstrated with me, everybody has gone to the trouble to insinuate that, I, untrained and a woman, must be taking entirely wrong views and Gold Coast officials are inclined to be both angry and scornful,' she explained to John Holt. 'But what I have seen, I have seen . . . and I came back a sadder and a wiser woman. For the life of me I cannot help noticing and drawing deductions.'[65] Like Mary Kingsley, she asked permission to use his information and quote Holt's opinion in her talks. 'If my idea was right vast tracks of land would be open to the British nation,' she concluded modestly in another letter.[66]

Edith Durham was also a petitioner, frequently writing to the Foreign and War Offices on behalf of Albanian national aspirations. As Honorary Secretary of the Anglo-Albanian Association, she had access to Members of Parliament and influential individuals interested in Eastern European affairs. From as early as 1908 she was recorded in Foreign Office files as a woman of formidable opinion, and would soon be consulted over this sensitive area about which long-lasting and far-reaching policy was being formed. When she spoke at the Royal Institute of International Affairs and the Near East Association, a member of the Foreign Office attended to note down her controversial views. Her determination to pin the responsibility for the Sarajevo assassination firmly on the Serbian government led her to publish a number of articles in the press – but also brought her into further heated contact with the Foreign and War Offices.[67] So while, like Mary Kingsley, she was excluded from holding any official position of power, she exerted influence on the colonial administration through lengthy and frequent contact with those instrumental in the decision-making process.

[65] Gaunt to John Holt 2 Nov. [1911?], Finborough Road, London.
[66] Gaunt to RGS 23 Oct. 1912, Brompton Square, London.
[67] Hodgson, 'Edith Durham', pp. 25–9.

When Edith Durham was making her first pronouncements about the Balkan question, May French-Sheldon was travelling through the Belgian Congo on a journey sponsored by William Stead, editor of the *Pall Mall Gazette* and influential journalist. Stead gave the traveller five hundred pounds 'to proceed with the utmost dispatch to the Congo Free State for the purpose of making a close, searching and confidential investigation into the present state of things in those regions.'[68] But while she agreed to contribute to his publication a series of articles on her findings, she privately boasted with a typical grandiose flourish of corresponding with those in positions of very high power. 'My reports *re* the Congo have been received and in some instances solicited by the American President, by Lord Landsdowne of the English Foreign Office, by the President of France and by the Emperor of Germany,' she wrote to her political opponent Edward Blyden, the Liberian scholar and outspoken member of the Congo Reform Association.[69] She soon became the leading apologist for Belgian atrocities in the region – for which she was rewarded with the *Chevalier de l'Ordre de la Couronne* by King Albert of Belgium.

Many women, like May French-Sheldon, saw their first hand knowledge as a powerful tool to be used in the colonial endeavour. Gertrude Bell realized that her close acquaintance with the Arab peoples was an invaluable weapon in the hands of the British administration. 'There is nothing easier to manage than tribes if you'll take advantage of tribal organization and make it the basis of administrative organization,' she explained.[70] It was careful, backroom handling in which Gertrude Bell excelled. When a friend, knowing her political ambitions, wrote from Britain suggesting that she might stand for Parliament, she replied, 'No, I'm afraid you will never see me in the House. I have an invincable hatred of that kind of politics and if you knew how little I should be fitted for it you would not give another thought.'[71]

Although Gertrude Bell held an official position as Oriental Secretary in Baghdad, this did not prevent her from engaging in behind-the-scenes politicking. Indeed, she felt most comfortable

[68] Stead to May French-Sheldon 22 Sep. 1903, quoted in François Bontinck, *Aux Origines de l'État Indépendant du Congo. Documents Tirés d'Archives Américaines*, (Louvain 1966), p. 454.

[69] French-Sheldon to Edward Blyden quoted in ibid., p. 456.

[70] Bell to Florence Bell 1 Mar. 1918, Baghdad, quoted in Bell, *Letters*, p. 447.

[71] Bell to Janet Courtney 4 Aug. 1925, Rounton Grange, Northallerton, quoted in ibid., p. 736.

From Trebizond to Tripolis
She rolls the Pashas flat
And tells them what to think of this
And what to think of that

Caricature and verse on Gertrude Bell by Sir Herbert Richmond, her brother-in-law.
Reproduced by kind permission of Lady Plowden.

when she brought men of power together in an informal capacity. But while her position in the colonial administration was officially recognized, her methods were not. For she used her knowledge of local people and politics, and her linguistic abilities – for which she had been employed – to create informal connections between leaders of Arab opinion. Like many other women, she exploited her female skills as a social hostess by frequently arranging evening dinners in her small Baghdad home to which members of the British administration and local rulers would be invited with the specific intention of talking politics. In 1920 she informed her father, 'I've begun weekly parties for young Nationalists in my garden. The first was well attended by about 30 young men and half a dozen of my colleagues . . . I have a lot of beautiful old Baghdad lanterns which I hang about in my garden – it looks lovely. I shall provide cold drinks and fruit and cake. It will be interesting to see if it is a success.'[72] Within a few months these contrived forums had already proved their use. 'There wasn't a moment without quite excellent, sometimes almost brilliant conversation,' the hostess wrote ebulliently after one particularly successful Wednesday evening. 'If you can preserve that atmosphere what can't you do?'[73] By November she was giving three dinner parties a week. 'I feel that the constant unofficial intercourse is very valuable,' she concluded.[74]

But while Gertrude Bell revelled in 'creating kings' and 'running the affairs of Mesopotamia' beneath her eastern lanterns, the administration was not so delighted.[75] When her much loved superior Sir Percy Cox left for Tehran in 1918 and Arnold Wilson replaced him as acting Civil Commissioner in Baghdad, friction soon arose between them. Gertrude Bell, in disagreement with Wilson over the future government of Iraq, criticized his policy in private letters to the India Office in London and even to opposition leader Asquith. She repeated her misgivings in conversations with British officials and Arab leaders in Iraq. The Secretary of State for India was forced to admonish her in a private telegram: 'If you have views which you wish us to consider I should be glad if you would either ask the Civil Commissioner to communicate them, or apply for leave and come home and present them,' Edwin Montague wrote. 'Political officers must be very careful of their private correspondence with those not at present in charge of affairs. Apart from all questions of usual practice and convention, it may increase rather than diminish difficulties.'[76] Wilson regarded Gertrude Bell as a 'born intriguer', and was anxious that she should not convey her opinion of him to Chirol at the *Times*, whom he knew

[72] Bell to Hugh Bell 16 May 1920, Baghdad, quoted in Burgoyne, *Gertrude Bell, 1914–1926*, p. 135.
[73] Bell to Hugh Bell 21 Aug. 1920, quoted in ibid., pp. 236–7.
[74] Bell to Hugh Bell 29 Nov. 1920, Baghdad, quoted in Bell, *Letters*, p. 576.
[75] Bell to Hugh Bell, 8 July 1921, quoted in ibid., p. 610; Bell, Oct. 1920, Baghdad, quoted in Burgoyne, *Gertrude Bell, 1914–1926*, p. 173.
[76] Montague to Gertrude Bell 6 Aug. 1920, India Office, quoted in ibid., p. 154.

to be her close friend. A colleague commented that this was 'a typically woman-like thing' to do.[77]

Women travellers' apparent isolation and uniqueness was further belied by the fact that they shared networks of interests across the political spectrum. Although there were few explicit contacts between the women travellers, there was an implicit community of interests and experience. Women might also share or inherit, unknowingly, one another's political networks. This is most explicit in the case of Mary Kingsley and Mary Gaunt, who never met. On her first trip to West Africa in 1908 Mary Gaunt precisely, though not necessarily intentionally, followed Mary Kingsley's 1893 route from Freetown to St Paul do Loando, even including a short trip inland to Matadi on the Congo. Mary Kingsley was a correspondent of John Holt, for long periods sending him lengthy daily letters. When Mary Gaunt returned from her second West African journey in 1910, ten years after Mary Kingsley's death, she too struck up a literary friendship with this influential trader. As with Mary Kingsley, they began to exchange newspaper cuttings and references, and Holt provided information for Mary Gaunt's lecture to the Royal Colonial Institute. 'Now when I have a powerful man like you writing such a letter to one of the leading papers I feel I have weight on my side,' she confided.[78]

The indirect links between the women travellers, often via men of high standing in the societies and professions, were numerous. The botanist Reginald Farrer entertained Mary Gaunt in China, and asked Marianne North's sister Catherine to illustrate his book.[79] Mary Kingsley's Uncle Charles, the renowned author and cleric, gave Marianne North letters of introduction on her first voyage to Jamaica and it was his novel, *At Last*, which, the botanical painter claimed, had inspired her to travel to the West Indies. Charles Kingsley's daughter Rose advised Isabella Bird before she left for her trip to the Rockies. Scott Keltie at the RGS was a correspondent of Mary Kingsley, Isabella Bird, Gertrude Bell and Mary Gaunt among a host of other women travellers. Gertrude Bell dedicated *The Desert and the Sown* to the colonial administrator-cum-Indianist Alfred Lyall (a

[77] John Marlowe, *Late Victorian; the Life of Sir Arnold Wilson*, (London 1967), quoted in Winstone, *Gertrude Bell*, p. 218.

[78] Gaunt to John Holt 10 Nov. [1911?], Finborough Road, London.

[79] Gaunt, *A Broken Journey*, p. 5; Reginald Farrer, *Among the Hills. A Book of Joy in High Places*, (London 1911).

voluble anti-suffragist), with whom Marianne North had stayed in Simla in 1878, who corresponded in academic detail with Mary Kingsley over the discussions arising from his book *Asiatic Studies*, and who entertained Isabella Bird to dinner.

But although women travellers could share a number of networks, they rarely met. When Isabella Bird sailed into the hollow burnt-out shell that was Hong Kong at Christmas 1878, little did she know that her friend Constance Gordon Cumming was already on the four-mile wide island fleeing the same flames.[80] Gertrude Bell holidayed with Alice Stopford Green, whom she described as one of the 'very few people about whom one can say "they told me this and that interesting and new" and still fewer whom one feels as if one knew better personally after each conversation.' But although this older woman historian became one of Mary Kingsley's closest friends, the two young women travellers, with only six years age difference between them, were never introduced.[81] It was not until 1882 that Marianne North met Isabella Bird; and while the popular press insistently complimented the tiny traveller on her small, neat, feminine frame, Marianne North noted, 'she looks much more substantive than I expected, and quite up to invading the land of Ainos and managing Mountain Jims.'[82] Isabella Bird herself conflicted with the romanticized, feminized press portrayals of travelling women when describing Annie Taylor. Her 'wonderful Tibetan journey, which throws the Central Asian travels of men completely into the shade, will be a new difficulty for the RGS,' she wrote to her publisher three months after the rejection of women's Fellowship. 'She is a remarkable person – very unkempt in appearance.'[83]

Even when the women did meet they rarely drew upon each others' experiences and expertise, and refrained from mentioning such friendships in their published works. Although Marianne North was in constant correspondence with Amelia Edwards, who encouraged her to travel and comforted her between trips, she is not credited for doing so in her friend's autobiography. And while Mary Kingsley was present at the important moment when Agnes Smith Lewis identified

[80] Bird, *The Golden Chersonese And the Way Thither*, (London 1883), p. 31; Gordon Cumming, *Wanderings in China*, p. 9–11.

[81] Bell to Flora Russell 11 Apr. 1891, quoted in Richmond, *Earlier Letters*, p. 239.

[82] North to William Thistleton-Dyer 15 July 1882.

[83] Bird to John Murray 25 July 1893, Keswick.

the ancient Syriac gospels, there is no indication in her published work that she knew this distinguished scholar and traveller.[84] Although Gertrude Bell included Edith Durham's *High Albania* among her extensive reading, she apparently never met the author. Marianne North's father shared a political platform with Tom Brassey, whose wife Anna had written the bestselling account of their voyage around the world in the *Sunbeam* yacht in 1878 – but the two female relations were kept apart from one another. Elizabeth Bisland stayed at the Grand Oriental Hotel in Ceylon at the same time as Lady Barker, but declined to introduce herself as a fellow travel writer.

For many women travellers at the turn of the century the area of informal politicking which they exploited and in which they flourished was a closing field. They had been almost unavoidably imperial agitators, since they personally benefitted from the freedom British imperialism gave them in distant lands as 'white men'. But the imperialism which had allowed them to act thus, and which they therefore largely supported, was informal imperialism. They looked back wistfully to this world which was fast fading away and being replaced by colonial intervention and administrative control. The establishment of colonial settlements, with a specific and delimited place for white women, destroyed their privileges gained as 'white men'.

With the consolidation of power in the Middle East, the role of Gertrude Bell's informal networking and gathering of information became less and less valuable. By 1926 she was writing home, 'I don't see at all clearly what I shall do, but of course I can't stay here forever; already I feel . . . I'm not at all neccesary in the office.'[85] On the same day in a separate letter to her father she continued, 'Politics are dropping out and giving place to big administrative questions in which I'm not concerned and at which I'm no good.'[86] With the consolidation and codification of imperial rule the scope for unofficial politicking was dramatically reduced and the arena in which women exerted their power and influence diminished. While Gertrude Bell felt she had been regarded as a man in her official capacity, now a

[34] Margaret Dunlop Gibson, *How the Codex Was Found. A Narrative of Two Visits to Sinai from Mrs Lewis's Journals 1892–3*, (Cambridge 1893), p. 76.
[85] Bell to Florence Bell 26 May 1926, Baghdad, quoted in Bell, *Letters*, p. 764.
[86] Bell to Hugh Bell 26 May 1926, Baghdad, quoted in ibid., p. 765.

particular place was being developed for women within the colonial endeavour. Wives arrived in Baghdad, began attending evening functions and Gertrude Bell, as a woman, found herself awkwardly and unhappily put among them. 'On Christmas day I went to an enormous dinner party given by A.T. [Wilson] to all the Political Service and their wives,' she wrote to her father. 'I came home early, when they began to dance. I dance no longer.' On Boxing Day she drove out to a camp in the desert where she felt more at home and at ease.[87] She became more and more of a recluse, and 'slipped back into the quiet ways of history and archaeology,' dedicating herself to work as the Director of Antiquities at the newly formed museum.[88] Edith Durham too, defeated in her attempts to persuade the political powers of the importance of establishing the blame for the murder of Franz Ferdinand, recoiled back into her ethnological work, writing up notes from her earlier travels.

The professionalization of previously amateur areas of interest also effectively narrowed women's informal place within them. Marianne North had been able to develop from female watercolourist to botanical painter because of the undetermined, semi-amateur nature of botany and its relationship to the scientific establishment. But with the founding of agricultural colleges and qualifications – a move to which Marianne North constantly expressed opposition – women began to be excluded from areas previously informally open to them. So while many women travellers sought recognition by professional men and societies, they also resisted the complete professionalization of their own area of expertise.

In February 1913, when Lord Curzon, ardent opponent to women's Fellowship at the Royal Geographical Society in 1893, spoke in his capacity as RGS President in support of female admission, he declared the informal role of the traveller no longer held the same importance it once had. As a leading member of the Anti-Suffrage League to which Gertrude Bell had personally recruited him, he found no inconsistency in now supporting women's Fellowship. 'For in the one case it is the grant of a political right that is in question, a share in the sovereignty of the country and the Empire,' he explained about suffrage. 'In the other case it is the concession to women of equal

---

[87] Bell to Hugh Bell 4 Jan. 1920, Baghdad, quoted in ibid., p. 476.
[88] Quoted in Courtney, *The Women of My Time*, p. 82.

intellectual and educational opportunities with men, and a voice, in all probability a very limited voice, in the control of the Society that exists for nothing more formidable or contentious than the advancement of a particular department of human knowledge.' Objections were inevitably raised which echoed the debates of twenty years earlier – female Fellows would use the RGS as 'a club-house, and whenever two or three women were gathered together there would be argument,' said one Fellow. Mr Aflalo moved an amendment for the exclusion of 'the third sex – the militant suffragists.' But the vote was passed by nearly three to one, and women were admitted once and for all as ineffectual Fellows of the Royal Geographical Society.[89]

While Edith Durham had dedicated herself to fighting for Albania, Mary Kingsley for her 'beloved South West Coast', May French-Sheldon for the Belgians in the Congo, Gertrude Bell for King Faisal of Iraq, and Amelia Edwards for her awe-inspiring Egyptian ruins, these fights, like their journeys, were increasingly undertaken against a tide of change. Tired, disillusioned, the women travellers' minds began to wander back once more to the lands and people for whom they agitated. Home is where the heart is, and when, they wondered, would they voyage back there?

[89] *Geographical Journal*, vol. 41, (1913), pp. 181–5.

Part IV

Fare ye well, for I am homeward bound
Sea shanty

8

The Voyage Home

Marianne North had been barricaded behind her lockless windows and doors for two days. A smallpox outbreak in the Seychelles had already killed thirteen, and when the mail boat refused to give her passage home she was forced into quarantine. Marianne reacted violently to this unwelcome imprisonment. Her cabin was cramped with the canvasses on which she had captured the mountained islands and the strong odour of the fresh oil paint invaded her voluminous clothes and sun-roughened skin. Stitched inside her long black tiered skirt and padded beneath her shawl were two hundred pounds worth of bank notes which crackled as she paced up and down her self-imposed cell. She neither undressed nor slept.

At fifty-three her deafness – her father's legacy – was acute. Worried by the barely distinct voices of the handful of other Europeans on the quarantine ship, she imagined overhearing them plotting against her through the partition. She detected the faint sounds of their reading out loud the recent biographical portrait of her in *Queen* magazine by her close friend Amelia Edwards, and screaming with laughter over it. They even caught rats, she confided to her diary, to let loose in her room at night, for no matter how tightly she shuttered her windows, the next morning she found them just a little forced open to let the rodents in. They thought the middle-aged lady painter shut day and night in her cabin insane, and recommended she be committed to an asylum. At least, this is 'what I thought the truth in Quarantine Island in the Seychelles but do not publish', Marianne wrote as she scribbled away at the manuscript of her autobiography. As she had once painted vistas which her eyes could not see, the same furtive imagination put words into others' mouths which had never been spoken.[1]

As aching limbs and mental fatigue wore down and wore out the women travellers, they began more and more to look inside themselves for the realization of their dreams. As they once took their internal visions and imposed them on the landscapes outside, now they took their perceptions of the distant lands through which they had journeyed and retreated with them into their own private, inner worlds. As their disillusionment with their political and professional achievements grew, so did their recreation of and longing for these Dark Continents and Savage Lands. Yet again, they were troubled by the conflict between the calls others made upon them and their own more intimate desires. While the outer forces had changed – now no longer family but public commitments demanded their service and devotion – the inner struggle continued unabated. Tied to their role as representatives and organizers of opinion within Britain, they longed to break free from these restraints as they had years before. Inside the professional protaganists, political campaigners and behind-the-scenes agitators were buried the women travellers who looked once more towards the continents of their dreams.

When Marianne North gathered together her painting materials for yet another journey to escape the damp winter in September 1883, she had been in England for a total of less than three years since her first voyage to America fifteen years earlier. Even then, her brief rests at Victoria Street were broken into visits of no more than a few months during the warmer seasons. Through Japan, Singapore, Malaysia, Ceylon, India, Australasia and South Africa, she had carried her oil paints, easel and canvasses, rolling them up and posting them home on her later journeys to help lighten her load. By the time of her departure for the Indian Ocean in 1883, her health, always a worry to her, was already beginning seriously to break down. Even while working on the catalogue for the gallery at Kew the year before, William Hemsley had noticed how her constant tiredness did not check Marianne from throwing herself into the work.[2]

---

[1] Manuscript of autobiography, pp. 1126–7.
[2] Hemsley, 'In Memory of Marianne North', (1890), pp. 329–34.

Marianne returned from Quarantine Island broken in body and spirit. But the botanical painter remained in Victoria Street for only the bright long days of the early summer months of 1884 before packing her canvasses again for yet another continent. Although she could escape Britain's winters and polite society, she could not leave behind the perplexing paranoid 'noise of polyglot tongues' which followed her to South America.[3] 'And the torture has continued more or less ever since,' she wrote on her return.[4]

Gertrude Bell was also pulled between the luxury of sedentary life and the lure of unknown travel. Weary of being constantly on the move, she sought a place to settle down and belong, but on settling, was soon itching to be padding once again through the soft desert on a horse's back. She wrote to her father of the conflicting pulls of her Baghdad home: 'You do realize, don't you, how the magic and the fascination of it all holds one prisoner.'[5] 'That's the trouble with wandering, it has no end', she summed up.[6] As early as 1914, after only ten years of lone oriental journeys, she was becoming a jaded traveller, and the crossing of the Hamad was an anti-climax for her. 'Delicious', the all-encompassing word that had pervaded the letters of her youth, began again to replace more detailed and evocative descriptions of her surroundings and experiences. The zest of her earlier diaries was gone; she wrote from the heat of a Baghdadi summer, 'the worst of the extreme physical weariness which is apt to attack one in this climate is the mental weariness, not to say desperation, which accompanies it. You feel as if you never again would lift a finger without exhaustion and for all the iron and arsenic you are taking three times a day you're persuaded you'll not get well – not that you want to get well, far from it.'[7]

Edith Durham had been unable to resolve her attraction to Albania, her 'truly wild heart of a wild region', her tiredness with travel and frustration at the failure of her national political goals for the country. On her last visit in 1921, she found herself at once enthralled and longing to leave. When the heads of the Kastrati and Hoti came to petition her for support, she recorded in her diary, 'Said

[3] North, *Recollections of a Happy Life*, vol. 2, p. 325.
[4] Manuscript of autobiography, p. 1100.
[5] Bell to Hugh Bell 15 Aug. 1922, Baghdad, quoted in Bell, *Letters*, p. 646.
[6] Bell quoted in Winstone, *Gertrude Bell*, p. 134.
[7] Bell to Hugh Bell 10 Aug. 1917, Baghdad, quoted in Bell, *Letters*, p. 420.

I was powerless. They would not believe me. Said in vain I was now old and tired. They persisted till I promised to "write something" . . . God knows what.' 'Must get away at all costs,' she added abruptly the next day.[8] A poem by Christina Rossetti was the very last entry in her Balkan diary:

> The hope I dreamed of was a dream
> Was but a dream; and now I wake
> Exceeding comfortless, and worn, and old,
> For a dream's sake . . .
>
> Lie still, lie still, my breaking heart;
> My silent heart, lie still and break:
> Life, and the world, and mine own self, are changed
> For a dream's sake.[9]

She did not return to her wild land again, but kept the memory alive by writing about it. *Some Tribal Origins, Laws and Customs of the Balkans*, published in 1927, recorded information and experiences gathered on journeys undertaken more than twenty years earlier.

By the time Mary Gaunt reached Petrograd after more than a year journeying through Asia, her attempts at motivating herself to go sightseeing floundered on inertia. 'I had seen too much,' she confessed. 'There comes a moment, however keen you are on seeing the world, when you want to see no new things, when you want only to close your eyes and rest.'[10] But no sooner had she sat down in the garden of her small Kent cottage, optimistically named Mary's Haven, than she was again planning to escape. 'Africa has gripped me,' she confided.[11] As with many women travellers, it was her first journey, her first continent, her first breaking of the link with the past and forging of an identity as an independent traveller which continually called her:

> Africa holds. The man who has once known Africa longs for her.
> In the sordid city streets he remembers the might and loneliness

---

[8] Diary May 1921, quoted in Hodgson, 'Edith Durham', p. 24.
[9] Ibid., p. 25.
[10] Gaunt, *A Broken Journey*, p. 266.
[11] Gaunt to Secretary of the RGS 20 Oct. 1912, Brompton Square, London.

of her forests, by the rippling brook he remembers the wide rivers rushing tumultuous to the sea, in the night when the rain is on the roof splashing drearily he remembers the gorgeous tropical nights, the sky of velvet far away, the stars like points of gold, the warm moonlight that with its deeper shadows made a fairer world. Even the heat he longs for, the white foam of the surf on the yellow sand of the beaches, the thick jungle growth densely matted, rankly luxuriant, pulsating with the irrepressible life of the Tropics. All other places are tame. The fascination that he has denied comes back calling him in after years.[12]

From the window of her West London attic flat with the clatter of the traffic on the busy Cromwell Road below her, Mary Kingsley took her pen in hand and dreamt too:

The charm of West Africa is a painful one. It gives you pleasure to fall under its sway when you are out there, but when you are back here it gives you pain by calling you. It sends up before your eyes a vision of dancing, white, rainbow-gemmed surf playing on a shore of yellow sand before an audience of stately cocoa palms, or of a great mangrove walled bronze river, or of a vast forest cathedral, and you hear nearer than the voices of the people round you, nearer than the roar of the city traffic, the sound of that surf that is breaking on the shore down there, and the sound of the wind talking in the hard palm leaves, and the thump of the native tom-tom; or the cry of the parrots passing over the mangrove swamps in the evening time, and then everything that is round you grows poor and thin in the face of that vision, and you want to go back to the Coast that is calling you, saying as the African says to the departing soul of his dying friend, 'Come back, come back, this is your home'.[13]

The isolated missionary Christina Forsyth, living without the company of Europeans for over thirty years in the interior of southeastern Africa, balked nervously at the prospect of being posted back to her native Scotland. 'I can't tear myself away,' she wrote to

---

[12] Gaunt, *Alone in West Africa*, p. 399.
[13] Kingsley, 'West Africa from an Ethnologist's Point of View', (1897), pp. 72–3.

the secretary of the missionary society. 'Often in my dreams I am at home, and I invariably say, "Why did I leave Africa – how can I get back."'[14] Margaret Fountaine had travelled to Australia in 1914 in search of land to build a farm and settle down after over thirty years of worldwide travel and butterfly hunting. But soon she began to suffer a depression unfamiliar to her. 'Maybe I am longing for that old life which was so sweet, for we have laid aside our butterfly nets now, and given up our life of wandering,' she wrote in her diary.[15] A year later she was again on the move, though like many women travellers growing old, an unhappy wanderer. It is 'only a sort of miserable persistance which compels me to continue the same old wandering life from force of habit,' she said.[16] It was, wrote Marianne North's stationary sister Catherine, her 'restless mind' that took Marianne to the Seychelles against doctors' orders and, eventually, her own tranquility.[17] Gertrude Bell began to live in her wandering past from the end of her last desert journey in 1914. Leaving Baghdad on a fortnight's outing to Karbala, she remembered her travelling life before she settled in the Iraqi capital: 'Though I haven't stepped out of the cage very far, or for very long, it's agreeable to be knocking about in a tiny corner of the world again . . . I found myself forever stepping back into a former atmosphere – knowing with my real self that it has all melted away and yet half drugged with the lingering savour of it . . . I could scarcely bear to turn away,' she wrote, but, as always, did. 'I get back to Bagdad tomorrow and feel very much like one going back to school,' she explained. 'I'm not sure that it's a good plan to get out of the cage for a fortnight and enjoy the illusion of days that were almost like a former existence.'[18] As the years passed, her writhing quickened, but not her ability to break the bars of her imprisonment. 'I want to feel savage and independent again for two days instead of being a Secretary in a High Commissioner's Office,' she wrote unhappily.[19]

These pulls within the women travellers were often expressed to those whom they hoped might be able to understand and help soothe

---

[14] W. P. Livingstone, *Christina Forsyth of Fingoland. The Loneliest Woman in Africa*, (Edinburgh 1914), p. 209.

[15] Fountaine, *Butterflies and Late Loves*, p. 28.

[16] Ibid., p. 124.

[17] Catherine Symonds' epilogue in *Further Recollections of a Happy Life*, p. 315.

[18] Bell to Florence Bell 3 Jan. 1918, Karbala, quoted in Bell, *Letters*, pp. 439–40.

[19] Bell to Hugh Bell 9 Jan. 1924, Baghdad, quoted in ibid., p. 679.

their conflicting calls. 'I cannot be a bushman and a drawing-roomer,' wrote Mary Kingsley of her male exploring and female social world to a childhood friend. 'Would to Allah I was there [in West Africa] now, with a climate that suited me and a people who understood me, and who I could understand.'[20] Whereas Marianne North felt no affinity or belonging to any one foreign domain, she knew that somehow the London she so often left no longer held her. 'Home is only half home now,' she wrote from Bombay, 'a mere empty shell though a luxurious one.'[21] 'I was now practically an exile from my own country,' Margaret Fountaine echoed.[22] 'I feel like a woman without a country,' wrote Alexandra David-Neel, surrounded by holy relics taken back from her journeys to her home in southern France, including her adopted son Yongden. 'I should have died in my tent in the Tibetan solitudes.'[23]

Gertrude Bell wrote to her confidant about her attempt to smother the two people battling inside her wizened body:

> You must try and civilise me a little, beloved Domnul. I think I am not altered for you, and I know that you will bear with me. But whether I can bear with England . . . I come back . . . with a mind permanently altered . . . . This letter is only for you – don't hand it on to anyone, or tell anyone that the me they knew will not come back in the me that returns. Perhaps they will not find out.[24]

As the colonial community in Baghdad expanded, Gertrude retreated from its representives who gathered about her – especially the newly arriving colonial wives. 'I have crept, on the whole, into a very long shell and seldom care to be pricked out of it by anyone's pin.'[25] Her non-European identity grew stronger, and she increasingly wrote how she was overcome 'with the sense of being as much an Asiatic as a European.'[26] A year later she expanded, 'it's shocking how the East has wound itself round my heart till I don't know which is me

[20] Kingsley to Hatty Johnson 27 Jan. 1898.
[21] North to Arthur Burnell 11 Feb. 1878, Adelphi Hotel, Bombay.
[22] Fountaine, *Butterflies and Late Loves*, p. 54.
[23] Quoted in Foster, *Forbidden Journey*, pp. 251 and 286.
[24] Bell to Valentine Chirol 5 Apr. 1914, Baghdad, quoted in Burgoyne, *Gertrude Bell, 1914–1926*, p. 143.
[25] Bell to Hugh Bell 29 Dec. 1917, Baghdad, quoted in Bell, *Letters*, p. 437.
[26] Bell to Hugh Bell 30 Aug. 1920, Baghdad, quoted in ibid., p. 497.

and which is it . . . I'm more a citizen of Bagdad than many a Bagdadi born, and I'll wager that no Bagdadi cares more, or half so much, for the beauty of the river or the palm gardens.'[27]

For many women travellers, as they grew older they longed more and more to have a place where they belonged, a place to call home. Returning again to her flat in the centre of busy London and within calling distance of friends and admirers, Marianne North began to look around for a country house to rent, writing to the Director at Kew, 'if you hear of any beautiful old garden with a small house in it that wants a mistress please let me know, I must get into perfect quiet – the noise here is killing me – it is worse every day now.'[28] She found Mount House in the village of Alderley, close to the Gloucestershire market town of Wotton-under-Edge. It was a location that made up the final corner of her English square; for from the Sussex coast at Hastings, to the family seat of Rougham Hall in Norfolk, to her London flat and now her Cotswold cottage, Marianne had lived in as widely apart places as her home country allowed. Nor was the rolling landscape of the West at all like the seaside of her young years, or the flat expanse and vast skies surrounding Rougham, or the hubbub of the capital. Her landlord Major General Robert Hale was tolerant of his tenant's whims; in her quiet defiance of convention, Marianne planned a terraced garden on top of the lawn-tennis court and trained the white tumbler pigeons to fly in through her bedroom window and feed from her hand. The overgrown unweeded lawns and beds surrounding Mount House, with a path to the front door buried beneath a tangle of autumn rain and summer dew, drenched her long skirts. She thought it 'the most perfect garden in England'.[29] But the mocking voices pursued her relentlessly to the haven of even her quiet country home.

Isabella Bird also sought a home away from the metropoles of London or Edinburgh, and off the main Waterloo and Liverpool Street rail routes to deter visitors.[30] From the heights of the Rocky Mountains to the awe-inspiring depths of the Yangtze gorges, through Kashmir and Tibet, Persia and Kurdistan, this tiny woman had proved

[27] Bell to Hugh Bell 30 Jan. 1922, Baghdad, quoted in ibid., p. 632.
[28] North to William Thistleton-Dyer 28 Apr. 1886, Victoria Street, London.
[29] North to William Thistleton-Dyer 20 Apr. 1887, Mount House, Alderley.
[30] Barr, *A Curious Life for a Lady*, p. 333.

an unfailing, unflinching, and unfathomable traveller. Even her five year long marriage, in which both husband and wife had been constantly invalid until John Bishop's death in 1886, had not deterred her. Abandoning the mourning of a widow, Isa had packed her bags with the declared intention of carrying on the late doctor's work in a special study of medical missions in Asia, in preparation for which she took a three month nursing course. She returned from the Far East for the last time in 1897. In her sixty-sixth year, she determined it was time to find a base of her own. Like Marianne, despite her now comfortable financial status she would only consider renting the ideal cottage for which she began to search. She found Hartford Hurst on the bank of the River Ouse, only a few miles from her childhood home. But restlessness soon attacked her, manifesting itself as it did with Marianne in multifarious illnesses, and she moved to the cottage at Tobermory, haunted by her sister's ghost. 'I am on this wild island for a winter of much needed rest,' she wrote from Tobermory. 'The temptation to sacrifice life which is all too short at the long set is great.'[31] She escaped again as far as her failing health would allow – to North Africa – and rode seven hundred miles through the Atlas Mountains on an enormous black charger which at once terrified and enervated her. But although alternated between depths of bodily weariness and the summit of physical exuberance, the general pattern of her health was one of steady decline. The fibrous tumour in her spine grew once more, thrombosis set in, and her weak heart began to fail. She gave up Hartford Trust, unable to run even the small house by herself, and moved back to Edinburgh where, in a sense, the clergyman's daughter who never lost her ladylike composure strangely if awkwardly belonged.

With her possessions in store and her trunks packed in London ready for a journey to China, she roamed from nursing home to nursing home, 'in a bad-smelling ambulance' she once complained, even in these fading years unable to settle. 'Eczema transforms my face,' she was writing to Alice Stopford Green by September 1903.[32] A month later she was already beginning to alot her possessions – unusual, if of little monetary value – to distant friends. Alice in London was to receive her black oak bureau, small gold pencil case

---

[31] Bird to Alfred Lyall 31 Dec. [1897], Tobermory.
[32] Bird to Alice Stopford Green 1 Sep. 1903, Manor Place, Edinburgh.

('so called . . . which I suspect is aluminium') and a Persian silver thimble. Of Mrs Green she was especially fond, because she knew she had been close to Mary Kingsley and Isa had shared condolences with Alice at her death in South Africa over three years earlier. 'Every glimpse you give me of your life is delightful,' wrote Isabella. 'You are following Miss Kingsley.'[33]

In the autumn of 1903, Isabella Bird found not only her body but her will had failed her. 'The doctors consider me still dangerously ill and without hope of recovering or prolonged life,' she wrote bluntly. Correspondents were spared no details, jotted down in an increasingly spidery hand. 'Some singular affliction of the veins and heart not previously known . . . broken blue chains and broken veins all over my heart and chest. Breath often nearly ceases and there is no strength. My brain is quite clear. I cannot think that the end can be far off.'[34] But her body would torture her yet one more year. By the spring of 1904 she could no longer write her own letters, but dictated them to her assistant, who added her own postscript – 'a life so trying to one so active and bright in mind as she still is.'[35]

Ella Christie had rarely spent a winter snowed in at Cowden Castle since sailing for Bombay in 1904. Through the Far East, Siberia, Central Asia and the United States, she had made a six month journey every other year. As she grew older, she grew shorter, her five foot nine inch figure shrinking as if worn down by walks over Asian mountains and tramps through Scottish hills. After the Great War she returned to the Middle Eastern retreats she had visited more than twenty years earlier – Beirut, Syria, Jerusalem. She ran around Europe, from Rhodes to Paris, touching down in London, visiting Cowden to give a talk in nearby Dollar, before starting again from the station for warmer terrain. Cyprus, Tunis, the world never seemed large enough to accommodate all the places to which the tough Scotswoman travelled. But as her sister Alice first lost her eldest son in 1926, then three years later her husband Robert, these long and lone journeys were replaced by shorter ventures to European spas in search of a cure for the younger sister's lameness. Khiva and Golden Samarkand were replaced by the Italian Alps and Montecarlo – the haunts of Ella's childhood journeys with her father. Separated by

[33] Bird to Alice Stopford Green, 18 July 1904, Ainslie Place, Edinburgh.
[34] Bird to Alice Stopford Green 25 Oct. 1903, Bruntsfield Links, Edinburgh.
[35] Bird to Alice Stopford Green, Mar. 1904, Bruntsfield Terrace, Edinburgh.

geography for over twenty years – allowing Ella to roam guiltless abroad while her sister led the opposition to women's ministry and eldership of the Church of Scotland at home – the two halves were melded together again. Jointly, they began to write their memoirs, interweaving their two divergent lives in a single biography. When, in the year of publication, Alice died, Ella, approaching eighty, was left with few contemporaries. She retreated to the security of her sister's sphere, unveiling a tablet for the fiftieth anniversary of the School of Cookery in Edinburgh, organizing Red Cross parties, and writing a cookbook herself. Her Fellowship of the Royal Geographical Society, of which she was so proud, was allowed to lapse. Ella Christie, who had travelled to horizons never reached before by a British woman, began to draw in about her an ever smaller world. The high-ceilinged draught-ridden Cowden rooms were sheeted and shuttered one by one, until only the cosy sitting room in which Ella sat huddled on the sofa with her dogs was kept warm.

Mary Gaunt had also touched on five continents – from West Africa to China, from Russia to the West Indies. But although prolific and relatively successful in both her travel and novel writing, she was constantly short of funds and decided in 1921 to leave England for the continent where the value of her sterling income, boosted by a small allowance from her brothers Ernest and Guy, might stretch further. She settled at Villa Camilla in Bordighera on the Riviera coast of Italy, a small cosmopolitan town housing an exiled and aspiring artistic community. Her relative wealth abroad enabled her to employ, for the first time, a housekeeper, and Anselma, later her husband and finally a baby moved into the small first floor flat. Here, unable to speak any local languages and far away from publishing houses and pressing invitations, Mary worked on completing half-finished projects begun many years before. But she was no longer the successful travel writer and novelist she once had been, and could not attract the advances from publishers which she needed to survive. 'I am sorry the book did so badly!' she wrote to Murray after *As the Whirlwind Passeth* was remaindered. 'I wonder what I could write that would pay. Clearly it's no good going on writing books that don't.'[36] In 1934, in her early seventies and an inhabitant of the Riviera for over ten years, she published her last fictional work, *Worlds Away* – set on the West African coast.

[36] Gaunt to John Murray 23 Sep. [1926?], Bordighera, Italy.

Mary Kingsley's frustration at the world of colonial politicking and intrigue in which she felt entwined could not be quenched. Feeling at the same time desperately needed by the anti-Colonial Office pressure group and yet that their cause was increasingly a lost one, she was infuriated both at others and at herself for being unable, for the second time in her life, to break a self-denying bond. Continually ill – complaining of neuralgia and rheumatism in her right hand which prevented her from writing – her low mental and physical states exacerbated one another. In contrast to her boasts of excellent health enjoyed in Africa – she claimed never to have suffered fever until her return to Britain – in Kensington she complained of the cold and inhospitable English climate. By January 1898, with no definite date of departure in sight, she deteriorated drastically and close friends gathered round her; soon even Mary admitted the seriousness of her condition, 'I am in a nasty, fractious, naughty, miserable, lonely state of mind,' she told a close friend, 'but it will pass off when I am stronger.'[37]

While the duty of serving the West African cause called her so strongly, it could only be countered by an equally strong pull applied to the same, self-sacrificing part of Mary's splintered personality. As the Boer War raged and the pages of the press were filled with horrific accounts of the suffering of the troops from the contagious diseases which flew along the water-sodden trenches, she secretly applied to nurse in South Africa. Here, in the sphere of medical work, she could excuse herself from her political duty for that of service to her fellow-countrymen. Her request, however, was refused – and only by persisting did the telegram from the War Office finally arrive, giving her little over a fortnight to pack her black waterproof bag once again. The call was not, however, to the duty which had made her feel able to desert her political allies. For her patients were not to be the young British soldiers, Gertrude Bell's brother Maurice among them, sent out in their thousands to fight a white war in a black continent – but Boers.

Mary Kingsley had not left British shores for over four years when she stepped aboard the *Moor* at Southampton docks bound for the Cape. In the rush of her departure she secured agreements with Fleet Street newspapers to cover the war. Although prepared to nurse in

[37] Kingsley to Alice Stopford Green 31 Jan. 1898, Addison Road, London.

practice, in spirit she was planning longer journeys across the Orange River and north to the lands in which she had first realized her dreams. Behind the apparent self-effacement of her volunteering lay the plans and means of satisfying her own ambitions. She concluded her last public address in England with the words of an old sea shanty, 'Fare ye well, for I am homeward bound.'[38]

On arriving at the Cape, Mary reported to the Chief Medical Officer and was posted to Simonstown as nurse to the Boer prisoners-of-war taken after their surrender at Paadeberg. One hundred and fifty of these typhus-ridden soldiers were crammed into the converted wards of the optimistically named Palace Barracks. By the time Mary arrived they were dying at the alarming rate of four to five a day. She wrote,

> It is no use attempting to describe the thing, the rows of narrow iron bedsteads with sackcloth sheets and mud-coloured blankets mixed up with the aforesaid; more or less on the bed a big bearded man, or a boy of 16–17, delirious – in a typical typhoid way moaning and muttering, and now and then talking to his people at home or fighting a fight over again . . . . Meanwhile there is an unutterable stench . . . . Then there are the never-to-be-forgotten bugs and lice. They swarm. 'The Palace' supplies the bugs free of charge, the patients the lice; they get on well together and make common cause on humanity, of course including you.[39]

While her days and nights were absorbed tending to the needs of others, her early life began to flood back to her – before she became the daring Miss Kingsley and returned from the 'white man's grave' to provoke parliamentary debates, government enquiries, and numerous attacks from politicians and press. Here, in the Palace Barracks, the days of isolation as her mother's nursemaid seemed closer than they had since her death eight years earlier.

Gertrude Bell, becoming more and more redundant in her post as Oriental Secretary in Baghdad, could see no equivalent escape route. Her health began to fail, exposing her to infection and fever, bouts of being bedridden and hospitalized, and unwelcome convalescence. In

---

[38] Lecture delivered to Imperial Institute 12 Feb. 1900, reported in *Imperial Institute Journal*, vol. 6, (1900), p. 97.

[39] Kingsley to Alice Stopford Green 11 Apr. 1900, Simonstown, South Africa.

contrast to the feeling of physical strength in which she had revelled, now tied to a house and garden, she experienced an illness for which there seemed no remedy. 'Do you know I've never been so ill as this before,' she wrote while suffering from recurrent jaundice in 1916. 'I hadn't an idea what it was like to feel so deadly weak that you couldn't move your body much nor hold your mind at all.'[40] In November she informed her father with little pleasure that illness and the intense heat meant she had just taken her first walk since the previous May.[41]

It was when settling down in one place and leading a rooted life that Gertrude began to suffer from 'anaemia of the brain' which, she claimed, made her 'half-witted'.[42] While absorbed in her political work throughout the 1910s and 1920s, being stationary nevertheless became increasingly painful. Although by 1922 her negotiating role had been cut back and her behind-the-scenes power all but faded away, she was still ignoring the well meant advice of family, friends and the medical profession to return to Britain. Increasing pressure only made Gertrude more resistant – for while she saw her usefulness and role diminishing in Iraq she still felt some purpose and prestige in her position there. When her Oxford contemporary Janet Courtney visited in the summer of 1925, she revealed the question that had been gnawing away at her – what would she do if she returned to Britain? When Vita Sackville-West knocked on the door of her backstreet Baghdad home a year later the same question jumped from Gertrude's lips – what would she *do*?[43] 'I can't pick up the thread where I dropped it,' she explained, 'I can't. And it becomes more, not less difficult. Oh if I could look forward and see a time when thought should stop, and memory, and consciousness, I'm so tired of struggling on alone. Still I'll do it, as you know. At least it's easier here than in England.'[44] In May 1926 she had still come no closer to an answer to her persistent plea. 'I don't see at all clearly what I shall do,' she wrote desparately to her stepmother. 'But of course I can't stay here forever.'[45]

Many women travellers discovered in their distant lands the

[40] Bell to Hugh Bell 20 Sep. 1916, Bait Namah, quoted in Bell, *Letters*, p. 387.
[41] Bell to Hugh Bell 4 Nov. 1916, Basra, quoted in Bell, ibid., p. 388.
[42] Bell to Hugh Bell 29 Dec. 1917, Baghdad, quoted in ibid., p. 437.
[43] Account of Sackville-West's visit to Bell quoted in ibid., p. 764.
[44] Bell to Hugh Bell 27 July 1917, quoted in ibid., p. 420.
[45] Bell to Florence Bell 26 May 1926, Baghdad, quoted in ibid., p. 764.

emotional fulfilment and almost intimate, special relationship they had been unable to find in another human being. 'I am happy in feeling that I have got the love and confidence of a whole nation, a very wonderful and absorbing thing,' wrote Gertrude Bell to her father. 'I remember your saying to me once that the older one grows the more one lives in other people's lives. Well, I've got plenty of lives to live in, haven't I?'[46] Mary Kingsley wrote less contentedly of her work around West African affairs, 'I have always been the doer of odd jobs, and lived in the joys, sorrows and worries of other people. It never occurs to me that I have any right to do anything more than now and then sit and warm myself at the fire of real human beings. I am grateful to them for letting me do this . . . . My people are the mangrove swamps and the sea and so on.'[47]

This emotional tie to a people and land might be specifically equated with romantic attachments. 'I have written of politics and of commerce, of steamships and locomotive engines,' wrote Gertrude Bell. 'But I have not pronounced the word which is the bynote of true Iraq. It is *romance*. Wherever you may look for it you shall find it.'[48] With such a vivid image of the continent of their dreams before them, for many women travellers this proved a self-fulfilling prophecy. Even before departing from Charing Cross station one winter's day in 1913, widowed, unattached and very single Mary Gaunt was writing, 'it is a little thing to do, to get into a train and be whirled eastward. There is nothing wonderful about it and yet – and yet – to me it was the beginning of romance.'[49]

Like an old and too familiar love affair, however, the zest of the once unknown, the once untouched, dimmed. Yet for many the continent of their dreams still was their first love; for many it was their longest, most passionate and perhaps their only affair, and as such became part of them. Their identities had been forged in these turbulent relationships, and even in breaking apart from their Savage Lands, they could never forget them. Talking of a traveller's compulsive attraction back to Africa, the continent of her first journey, Mary Gaunt wrote, 'this mistress . . . has spoiled him for all else.'[50] Only the exultancy faded, not the commitment. So while

[46] Bell to Hugh Bell 16 Feb. 1922, Baghdad, quoted in ibid., pp. 632–3.
[47] Kingsley to Matthew Nathan 12 Mar. 1899, St Mary Abbot's Terrace, London.
[48] Bell, Baghdad, quoted in Winstone, *Gertrude Bell*, p. 257.
[49] Gaunt, *A Woman in China*, p. 4.
[50] Gaunt, *Alone in West Africa*, p. 399.

feeling no less drawn to their first loves, some sought a second, almost adulterous affair which would rejuvenate that unparalleled feeling of being vital, of being alive. The most adventurous began to look for a human love. But as in their attempts to find a settled place to call their home, so in this quest they failed.

With increasing frustration and with what they perceived as others' lack of understanding, sympathy and real interest for their work, many women travellers began to feel the creeping return of the loneliness which had haunted them as young women. While Mary Gaunt sat playing solo bridge in her pretty Kent garden, Gertrude Bell asked her father to send her a pack of patience cards to deal out to herself on the small table in her Baghdadi compound. On their travels being alone had been a symbol of freedom and independence. But rooted in European society, solitude became again a constant reminder of their exclusion. Mary Kingsley's proud nickname of 'Only Me' in West Africa was replaced by candid admissions to close friends of the isolation she felt. She was, she said, 'lonely in spite of being in a crowd'.[51] Marianne North complained that people showed no understanding of her paintings – proved by the fact that in admiring and cooing over them they held them upside down. Social engagements she found alienating: 'I can travel, and cover paper with paint,' she wrote, but she could not throw parties 'which other people understand the art of giving and I don't'.[52] Mary Kingsley complained, 'none of my own friends and relations up here care for what I am interested in. All the people I meet here I have to talk about West Africa very carefully to, and very lightly and briefly. They don't understand.'[53] 'It is too lonely my existence here,' wrote Gertrude Bell to her stepmother after refusing to join in the Christmas and New Year celebrations of the European community. 'I can't go on for ever being alone.'[54]

It was while her health was seriously breaking down and her political campaigns floundering that Mary Kingsley first met Matthew Nathan – a handsome, dashing young man of the same age as herself. Ambitious and capable, he had risen through the Royal Engineers to the post of Acting Colonial Governor in Sierra Leone. Nathan was an

---

[51] Kingsley to E. D. Morel 20 Feb. 1899, St Mary Abbot's Terrace, London.
[52] North to Joseph Hooker Thursday [Spring 1882], Victoria Street, London.
[53] Kingsley to John Holt 14 Feb. 1899, St Mary Abbot's Terrace, London.
[54] Bell to Florence Bell 16 June 1926, Baghdad, quoted in Bell, *Letters*, p. 770.

opportunist, and from their initial meeting around the dinner table of the prominent Jewish banking family the Montagus, he felt it would serve his career well to cultivate Miss Kingsley's acquaintance. A few days later he visited her flat to 'talk West Africa with her'.[55] Realizing that the apparently strong and invincible Miss Mary Kingsley in private felt lonely and defeated, he feigned attraction for the continent to draw her still further.

Mary needed but little encouragement to fall in love with Nathan. He was a Jew and therefore, she believed, an insider who would understand what it meant to be an outsider, a colonial officer but a Jew, 'a bushman and a drawing-roomer at the same time'. For wasn't he interested in Africa, her continent, and in particular her beloved West Coast? While Nathan was reading Mary's new book, *West African Studies*, on his voyage out to Freetown and jotting down unflattering comments in his meticulous diary, in London Mary began to write a twenty five page letter to him of extreme candidness and self-effacement. On reading it in the West African heat, Nathan recorded in his diary, 'letter from Miss Kingsley (her open soul)'. He did not reply.[56] Mary continued to write to Nathan at length, offering him advice and background information on West African affairs, from nursing to Muslim education. She only occasionally received a response in the form of a note of thanks.

At the age of forty-four, Gertrude Bell began an unconsummated affair with Major 'Dick' Doughty-Wylie who she had first met while digging at Konia. A nephew of the orientalist Charles Doughty, like Matthew Nathan he was a military man who had turned to diplomacy and shared a history rich in both heroic exploits and eastern travel. Their time together was snatched briefly and greedily at the Bells' country home and in London at his old bachelor quarters, for Dick was married and devoted, in a sense which perhaps Gertrude could not begin to understand, to his unsuspecting wife. The same embarrassing surrender of her independent mind and determined will was as eagerly embraced by Gertrude as it had been by the black-clad Miss Kingsley for the colonial officer. The 'that which is me, which womanlike is an empty jar' which, she had once told her cousin Horace Marshall, was filled with the excess of experiences and sensualities of the East, now

---

[55] Entry 20 Feb. in Nathan's 1899 diary.
[56] Entry Thursday 30 Mar. in Nathan's 1899 diary.

overflowed with a new human content.[57] 'You fill my cup, this shallow cup that has grown so deep to hold your love,' wrote Gertrude to her lover from Basra.[58]

But as distant lands called her, so did distant lovers, and Gertrude was attached to the unobtainable in Dick as much as the seemingly impossible challenge of crossing the Syrian desert. As early as 1907 she had excused herself from attending her younger half-sister's wedding – an awkward occasion for the older single woman – by appealing to the urgency of her archaeological work. Highly emotional letters to her father and stepmother written into her fifties – in which she calls her father Darling – are belied by the three-year long intervals between her visits to their home. She wrote excusing yet another postponement, 'I know I couldn't have left Iraq at this moment. I should always have felt that I had left my job at a moment when I might and very likely would be needed if anything untoward had happened, though I know I couldn't have made much difference, I should have imagined that just the little I could have done might have helped to turn the scale.'[59] For Gertrude, it seems, loved the unknown, the distant, the untouchable in humans as well as in geography, and created images of her beloved family and passionate lover far away from any of their arms. 'Do you know this is the eighth Xmas I've been away – 1913 Arabia, 1914 Boulogne, 1915 Egypt, 1916 Basrah and all the rest Bagdad,' she wrote to her father in 1921 with a strong sense of relief.[60] With her lover, too, their relationship was as firmly in the realm of fantasy as reality. 'I cannot tell you how much it moves me to hear you say – No, not that – to see it written by you, that you might have married me, have borne my children, have been my life as well as my heart,' wrote Dick to Gertrude, their commitment and future always expressed in the conditional, unrealizable tense.[61] When Dick Doughty-Wylie died at Gallipoli, one among thousands slaughtered in April 1915, she mourned a man who was already little more than a ghost.

As they were unable to take themselves back to the continent of their dreams, many women travellers attempted to recreate these land-

[57] Bell to Horace Marshall 18 June 1892, Gulahek, quoted in Bell, *Letters*, p. 25.
[58] Bell to Dick Doughty-Wylie 1914, Basra, quoted in Winstone, *Gertrude Bell*, p. 154.
[59] Bell to Florence Bell 10 May 1922, Jerusalem, quote in Bell, *Letters*, p. 638.
[60] Bell to Hugh Bell 30 Jan. 1921, Baghdad, quoted in ibid., p. 585.
[61] Doughty-Wylie to Gertrude Bell, 1914, quoted in Winstone, *Gertrude Bell*, p. 141.

scapes wherever they found themselves alone and growing old. Before, arriving at new continents, they had projected their inner lives on to the outer world; now they took these outer worlds inside and lived within their private domain. At the ruins of Philae, Amelia Edwards had stood alone and made a silent pact. 'I look; I listen; I promise myself that I will remember it all in years to come – all the solemn hills, these silent colonnades, these deep, quiet spaces of shadow, these sleeping palms. Lingering till it is all but dark, I at last bid them farewell, fearing lest I may behold them no more.'[62] Like many women travellers, she never saw the continent of her dreams again, but held that lingering image with her for the rest of her life. 'Always there is that in life, for good or evil, nothing can take away what we have done. We have it with us, good or bad, forever,' wrote Mary Gaunt.[63]

Just as they had done when young, the travellers took both imaginary and physical elements of their distant lands and transplanted them on to European soil. And as they had also done in their youths, they abandoned the damp, dull, dissatisfying country surrounding them and lived in spirit, if not in body, in these inner visionary worlds. Mary Gaunt left distant lands for the last time in 1921 when, aged sixty, she sailed back to Europe from the Caribbean. Within a few years she had returned to writing about West Africa in her novels – the first place where she had realized her 'longings after savage lands'. From there she crossed the continent on a psychological journey to the east coast and Arabia, as she wrote fiction set in these distant lands. Mary Kingsley spent her few years back in Britain writing up her West African travels, and in writing them living them too. While the walls of Gertrude Bell's room were covered with maps of Mesopotamia, Mary Kingsley sat surrounded by objects she had brought back with her from the Coast – Benin bronzes, tall wooden drums, and a yard-high nail fetish she called Mavungu. And while in public she insisted on dressing like a 'maiden aunt', in private she donned African bangles and jangled around her compact West London terraced house.[64] Like Mary Gaunt, throughout her travel books she confused the past with the present tense, and says 'here' when she means to write 'there', so involved was she in recreating her journeys. 'Just behind where I am sitting writing, a bare two miles

[62] Edwards, *A Thousand Miles Up the Nile*, p. 389.
[63] Gaunt, *Alone in West Africa*, p. 313.
[64] Bullen, 'Some Memories of Mary Kingsley', (1900), p. 570.

'Mavungu', Mary Kingsley's Congolese nail fetish.
Pitt Rivers Museum.

from the town of Montego Bay there is a swamp which breeds nothing but large and fierce mosquitoes,' Mary Gaunt had written of Jamaica – while sitting in the French town of Sainte Agnes where briefly settled in search of a continental home.[65] Isabella Bird called the book of her final journey to the East, *The Yangtze Valley and Beyond*, 'child of my old age'.[66]

Ella Christie, who in her no-nonsense manner was never given to the luxury of introspection, read and reread the detailed journals of her travels which she kept neatly marked and stored.[67] She had closed her stern Scottish heart after her father's disinheritance, and never opened it again for the next forty years, becoming the brusquely titled 'Miss Christie of Cowden' she insisted on being called and treating her tenants with a hardness and lack of generosity which appalled her relatives. Only her younger sister Alice kept the place in her affection which she had held before Ella shut the door. But now Alice was dead and Ella retreated even more into the pages of her journals.

Like many other women, Ella also sought to create a more concrete environment in which would evoke her earlier travels. First she had to convert the interior of her white stone manse into an exotic eastern palace. She replaced the plain bannisters with a gigantic elaborately carved wooden staircase imported from Burma at the exorbitant cost of one thousand nine hundred and fifty pounds. At almost eighty years old, she described her interior world:

> As I glance around the rooms at Cowden my eye lights on article after article – coins, china, beads, bells, bracelets, and much else – serving to remind me of a score of journeys about the world.
>
> That spray of bamboo, for instance, which I see on the smoking-room mantlepiece, its pale green leaves of jade outlined with seed pearls, is a trophy of a visit to Shanghai made during an eastern trip in the year 1907. The sight of it is enough to recall the joyful sensation one experiences when, after many weeks journeying in perils of waters, the vessel is at last firmly anchored, and a fresh country waits to be explored.[68]

[65] Gaunt, *Where the Twain Meet*, p. 58.

[66] Bird to Ella Blackie Dec. 1899, Tobermory, quoted in Barr, *A Curious Life for a Lady*, p. 335

[67] Ava Stewart to John Murray 21 June 1953, Murdostoun, Scotland.

[68] Christie and Stewart, *A Long Look at Life*, p. 188.

Ella Christie in her Japanese Garden, Kinrosshire, 1934.
Reproduced by kind permission of Robert Stewart.

Next Ella turned to the estate immediately surrounding this over-ornamented home, and here she faced her greatest challenge. She had written to her sister from Kyoto in 1907 of her enthralment with the gardens and flowers. It is 'a dream of beauty' she exclaimed.[69] And on returning to the mists and ceaseless winter rains of Kinrosshire she set about building this dream of a Japanese garden. 'In a sheltered foothold of a grassy range of hills that stretch from sunrise to sunset lies the garden of my dreams,' she wrote. 'After the fierce volcanic agencies that upraised them, and the long eons of time that had moulded their undulating lines, the softly rounded hills encircle "Sha-rak-uen", "the place of pleasure and delight".' This name was painted in Japanese characters on the wooden board which hung creaking in the hillside breeze.[70]

The size of Ella's project was daunting, for the site she chose covered over seven acres. First she imported the people to inhabit and supervise the realization of her vision. Taki Honda was a tiny young Japanese gardener from the Royal School of Garden Design at Nagoya, and it was she who was the main executor of Ella's plans. Matsuo arrived as head gardener in 1925, and proved as great an attraction to vistors as the exotic plants. Professor Susuki, worldwide expert on Japanese gardens, made frequent visits from Kew to advise on design and the care of the shrubs and trees. Next Ella had to import the plants, but here the ancient Scottish landscape proved irrepressible; between the oriental spruce, the Himalayan Cedar, the Korean Pine and the Japanese dwarf trees stood defiantly the hardy Weeping Douglas Fir.

By the mid-1920s a visitor could walk through the small wicket gate at the east end, duck under a thatched entrance hung with wooden lanterns, and enter Ella's oriental world. The 'place of pleasure and delight' surrounded a large lake crossed by stepping stones or a zig-zagged wooden bridge to the island tea house. It was here that Ella entertained her guests with traditional Japanese teas on Sunday afternoons, and with nieces and nephews gathered about told stories of her journeys spanning three decades and as many continents. Although a dry and pedestrian writer, she was a vivid raconteuse, and could keep the young eyes glued on her scrubbed round face. On the

[69] Christie to Alice Stewart 3 May 1907, Imperial Hotel, Kyoto, quoted in Stewart, *Alicella*, p. 210.
[70] Christie and Stewart, *A Long Look at Life*, p. 234.

west side of the garden, the gentle curves of the foothills of the
Ochils were renamed the Slopes of Fuji, and here as elsewhere Taki
Honda arranged groups of stones in the traditional Japanese style.
Under the trees on the imaginary mountainside stood a special
arrangement for the five virtues – Patriotism, Loyalty to Family Life,
Obedience, Faith and, most tellingly, Obedience to Parents.[71]

Marianne North also uprooted plants if not people from tropical soil
to the cooler climate of the Cotswolds. She ordered a forty by fifteen
foot greenhouse and here tended the cuttings sent to her from Kew.
'Her feeling for plants in their beautiful living personality was more
like that which we all have for human friends,' wrote Marianne's
sister.[72] Early each morning Marianne walked slowly and shakily down
the three steps from the front door, hose in hand, to water her friends.
Inside her home too, she collected together the trophys and triumphs
of her travels. Stuffed exotic birds stood chirpily in glass cases – her
father's paroquet long dead. Julia Margaret Cameron's photograph of a
younger Marianne waving a banana leaf and draped in shawls on her
Ceylonese balcony hung on the wall. A stuffed Australian bear,
lyrebird, platypus and hornbill made a mummified zoo, and shell and
crystals the beaches on which she had collected specimens to paint.
These mementoes surrounded her as she worked on new paintings –
'my children', as she called them – of Asian mountains and palm-
fringed beaches.[73] 'It is such a delight painting these things,' she
wrote to a woman watercolourist from an English winter. 'I feel as if I
was there all the time, breathing the warm air and talking to the funny
people and children. I believe the very idea of it helps to keep the cold
out.'[74] While she tried to recreate physically the worlds to which she
had travelled, her mental world had been occupied for some time with
writing up the journals of her journeys. 'When it is dark and yellow
fog, I scribble,' she told Burnell. 'I am writing "Recollections of a
Happy Life" and putting all my journals and odds and ends of letters
together – it is most amusing work even if it never comes to anything
more – it is curious how new and fresh some years of my life come

---

[71] Information on the Japanese garden from 'The Japanese Gardens at Cowden. A Brief
History and Description by Mr Robert Stewart of Arndean' produced by the Episcopal Church of
St James, Dollar, 28 May 1955; Christie and Stewart, *A Long Look at Life*; and personal visit.

[72] North, *Recollections of a Happy Life*, vol. 1, p. vi.

[73] North to Joseph Hooker 21 Aug. 1879, Lynmouth, Barnstaple.

[74] North to Barbara Bodichon 21 Jan. 1880.

back . . . I suppose it is a second childishness approaching.'[75] On cold Hampstead nights, Margaret Fountaine would sort through her collector's cabinet. 'A few brilliant *Preponas* from the forests of Matto Grosso, which struck me as being more lively than ever, and give me such a longing to be back in Brazil. The contents of the next drawer took me back to India and Java, for there were the *Kalimas*, then come the *Charaxes*, full of hot, African sunshine.'[76]

In these recreated Savage Lands, women were faced with the most poignant of all choices and expression of their freedom – the decision how to die. For many, death became the symbol of the final incarceration which had to be avoided as had all attempts to bind their physical and mental worlds. They looked towards the lands of their travels for this final journey.

At Abou Simbel, Amelia Edwards sat at the foot of the statues of the Gods in the inner sanctuary. Suddenly, in the imposing silence, she clearly saw in her mind the great mass of the mountain which stood above her head and felt the threat of it falling. She tried to scream, but could only whimper; she tried to run, but her feet were frozen. And although she walked slowly out and returned to the upper world, she wrote 'it would have been a grand way of dying, all the same; and a still grander way of being buried.'[77]

Gertrude Bell always rose early, still at fifty-seven overflowing with the unbounded energy which was intoxicating to all those with whom she came in contact. Sitting at her desk in her summer-house home reached through a door in an otherwise blank wall along a Baghdad street, surrounded by messy piles of papers on antiquities, archaeology and the political machinations of the Middle East, she lit one harsh Turkish cigarette from another in a long holder as spindly as her gaunt figure. The unceasing twirls of grey smoke resembled the now thin wisps of her long grey hair pinned neatly on top of her sculptured head. As her narrow upturned nose became exaggerated on her drawn face, she was now more than ever a cartoonist's gift. Outside her room, a white Arab pony pawed the ground in the corner of the garden which also served as a tea and drawing-room on cooler summer evenings. The children of her small household staff played in the

---

[75] North to Arthur Burnell 17 Jan. 1880, Victoria Street, London.

[76] Fountaine, *Butterflies and Late Loves*, p. 140.

[77] Edwards, *A Thousand Miles Up the Nile*, p. 305.

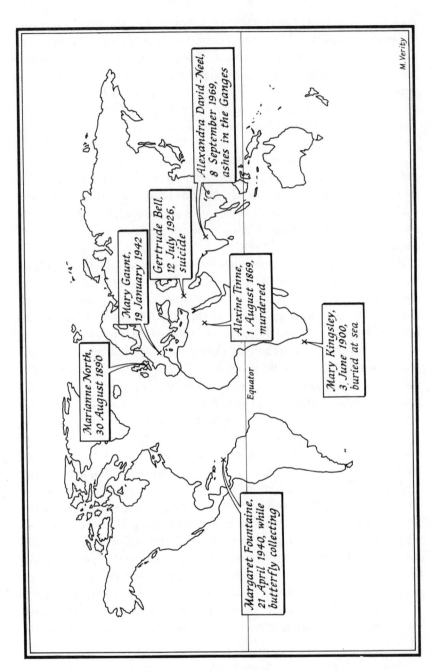

Alexandra David-Neel, 8 September 1969, ashes in the Ganges

Gertrude Bell, 12 July 1926, suicide

Mary Gaunt, 19 January 1942

Alexine Tinne, 1 August 1869, murdered

Mary Kingsley, 3, June 1900, buried at sea

Marianne North, 30 August 1890

Equator

Margaret Fountaine, 21 April 1940, while butterfly collecting

M. Verity

The Voyage Home.

courtyard too, and a tame partridge hopped about the small verandah between the pots of pink carnations – Red Barns and Baghdad meeting. Yet amid all this young life and animal vitality, Gertrude's jerky movements and constant curiosity rushed like a whirlwind about the crowded compound.

To quell her agitated body and mind, Gertrude took sleeping pills, keeping them in a small bottle beside her in the spartanly decorated bedroom. Early, too early, on Monday morning, 12 July, she awoke from her brief and fitful sleep and, in the rank darkness of the eastern night, reached out for the phial she knew would be next to her. Her long slender fingers found its shape and curled about the cold glass.

It was only a few hours later when her cool body was found lying lifeless in bed, her long grey hair almost down to her waist framing a colourless face. The death certificate recorded poisoning from her pills. She was buried the same day – in over a hundred degrees of heat human corpses are soon disposed of – with the military honours and fine thoughts she had wished. The High Commissioner said, 'At last her body, always frail, was broken by the energy of her soul. Her bones rest where she had wished them to rest, in the soil of Iraq.'[78]

In her late fifties, Marianne North was already suffering from severe rheumatism when she developed an acute liver complaint. 'No medicine affects the disease,' she wrote, 'and my doctor has left off amusing me with any. I merely exist from one operation to another, and may cease that existence any day. I do not dread it.'[79] Female relations, towards whom she felt little sympathy though some gratitude, flocked about her. At least her now total deafness spared her their polite and concerned conversation. First her niece Kay, offspring of her sister Catherine's unhappy marriage and bearing a striking resemblance to her aunt, stayed with Marianne over the damp English winters. By the spring of 1889 she had employed a fulltime nurse who helped her around the garden. 'I feel still that life hangs on a very thin thread,' she confessed.[80] By the spring of the following year she was writing in a very shaky hand, partially stilled by hot brandies, 'bleeding comes on if I walk much'.[81] The next day the maid telegraphed her sister, and for two months her immobility worsened.

[78] Quoted in Bell, *Letters*, p. 780.
[79] North to 'W. R.' quoted in *Hastings and St Leonards Observer*, 6 Sep. 1890.
[80] North to William Thistleton-Dyer 19 Mar. 1889, Mount House, Alderley.
[81] North, *Recollections of a Happy Life*, vol. 2, p. 334.

Like many women travellers, despite influential and prominent friendships cultivated during years of fame and moderate fortune, it was to her older, single woman companion, to whom she encharged her estate in case of death, that she turned. In August she sent for Mary Ewart – but by that time could speak no longer.[82] Ten days later her racked body was buried near the garden in which she had made her last imaginary journey to the tropics she had dreamed of twenty years before.

Mary Kingsley had been nursing only two months at the Palace Barracks, day in day out, when typhus fever struck. 'All this work here, the stench, the washing, the enemas, the bed pans, the blood, is my world,' she had written in her last letter home to her closest and older woman friend Alice Stopford Green, 'not London society, politics, that gallery into which I so strangely wandered – into which I don't care a hairpin if I never wander again.'[83] She rallied following an operation on her stomach on the first day of June, but Mary had seen too many men die to hold much hope. She asked to be left alone, perhaps with her dreams of moving up country, across the Orange River and through the desert to the swamps and rivers of her West Africa. On 3 June she died, and full naval and military honours, including representation from the Dutch community, accompanied her funeral. Her last request had been to be buried at sea. An empty lead-lined coffin awaited her in the family tomb amid the Victorian grandeur of Highgate cemetery, but above all she wanted to escape this final trapping of her indomitable body and spirit. Her body was washed away off Simonstown, and the Benguela current carried it northwards to her beloved South West Coast.

At the outbreak of the Second World War, Mary Gaunt was forced to flee her Italian haven, leaving behind the diaries of her life on which she had been working. Already infirm and approaching eighty, she took up residence at Vence in Southern France. Returning to Villa Camilla a few weeks later in September 1940, she wrote to her sister that Anselma, her companion and family for eighteen years, had fled and her home been ransacked. 'I cannot walk at all now,' she added simply.[84] Thirty years earlier, caught in the turbulent surf on leaving Addah, she had imagined her death. 'I could hear the crashing

---

[82] Mary Ewart to William Thistleton-Dyer 19 May 1892.
[83] Kingsley to Alice Stopford Green 11 Apr. 1900, Simonstown, South Africa.
[84] Gaunt to Lucy Archer 22 Sep. 1940 quoted in McLaren, *Mary Gaunt*, p. xxii.

of broken wood all round me, and I thought if I were to be drowned I would rather be drowned in the open.'[85] But for Mary Gaunt this final wish was not be granted, and on returning to France she was forced to live in a nursing home; the niece who had been her one family contact at Bordighera was now a colonial officer's wife in Africa, and Mary spent the last year of her life immobile and isolated, trapped in body and spirit.

It was a death feared most by those travellers to whom physical restriction meant mental suffering. Crippling disease was especially painful for women to whom strength and movement had meant mental as well as physical freedom. Many shared a horror of being busied on land, locked in the dismal grey vaults of Victorian Britain, decorated with posies and poems, symbols of the lives they fled. While Mary Kingsley asked to be buried in the waves off Simonstown, Alexandra David-Neel, at the age of 101, asked her devoted secretary to scatter her Buddhist ashes into the flow of the Ganges. Even in death, they wanted to be travellers, on the move. When May French-Sheldon enquired after someone who had died she was told, 'he has gone on safari.'[86] From the confinement of their homes to the continent of their dreams, death, for many, was just another journey. Death, for the fortunate, was the voyage home.

[85] Gaunt, *Alone in West Africa*, p. 307.
[86] French-Sheldon, *Sultan to Sultan*, p. 224.

Biographies of Victorian Women Travellers

Gertrude Margaret Lowthian Bell was born on 14 July 1868 in County Durham to a wealthy industrial family. Her mother died in childbirth two years later, and her stepmother Florence Olliffe became her closest female relative. At sixteen, Gertrude attended Queens College for young women from where she advanced to Lady Margaret Hall, Oxford, reading History. Her first trip to the East came in 1892, when she visited her uncle, then ambassador to Tehran. She returned to the area in 1899, and undertook her first desert journey to Jebel Druze; from then on trips climbing in the Alps and round-the-world Cook's tours with her brothers were gradually replaced by travel to the Middle East. Her journey through the Syrian desert to Asia Minor was recorded in *The Desert and the Sown* (1907). Already a skilled linguist and translator of Persian poetry, in 1907 she worked in Asia Minor with the archaeologist Sir William Ramsay, writing up her findings in archaeological journals and books. In 1913 she undertook a journey to Ha'il which earnt her much fame and drew her into work with Military Intelligence in Cairo during the war. In 1916 she moved to Basra as Political Secretary to Sir Percy Cox, and a year later to Baghdad which became her home. She was intimately involved in the negotiations over the dismantling of the British mandate in Iraq and a supporter of Faisal in his claim to the throne. A founder member of the Anti-Suffrage League, she was politically conservative on all issues relating to women's rights. Rarely and briefly returning to Britain, she died in Baghdad on 12 July 1926 of a drug overdose.

Isabella Lucy Bird was born on 15 October 1831 in Yorkshire to an Anglican clergyman and clergyman's daughter. Suffering from spinal problems from an early age, she was ordered for health reasons to take a trip to America in 1854 and wrote an anonymous account of her experiences, *The Englishwoman in America* (1856). On her father's death, Isa, her younger sister Hennie and her mother moved to Edinburgh, and Scotland became her adopted homeland. In 1873 she set out for Hawaii via Australasia and from there on to the United States and Rocky Mountains. Her experiences, recorded in letters to her sister published as *A Lady's Life in the Rocky Mountains* (1879), confirmed that her life would be one of travel. In 1881 she married the doctor who had nursed her dying sister, John Bishop, but was widowed within five years. She travelled on to India and Persia (1889), Korea and Japan (1894), and China (1896) described in *The Yangtze Valley and Beyond* (1899). In 1899 she moved to Huntingdonshire but, unable to settle, left again for Morocco in 1901. She died in Edinburgh on 7 October 1904.

Elizabeth Bisland was born on a plantation in Louisiana on 11 February 1861 and educated at home. After launching her journalistic career through working for the New Orleans *Times-Democrat*, she became an editor of *Cosmopolitan Magazine* for which she undertook the assignment of a voyage around the world; she left America in November 1889 for the Far East, writing up her 76-day journey as *A Flying Trip Around the World* (1891). In 1891 she married Charles Wetmore. Her writing career continued with the editing of a collection of letters, the production of political pamphlet, a novel and biographical portraits of men of history in the East. She died on 6 January 1929.

Lilian Mabel Alice Richmond Brown came from a wealthy Guernsey family and was educated at the local St Joseph's Convent. In 1906 she married Sir Melville Richmond Brown of Hampshire, but soon found sedentary country life stifling and offered to part-finance Frederick Mitchell-Hedges' trips to Central America in the early 1920s if she was allowed to accompany him. For the next ten years, until her divorce in 1931, Lilian and 'Mitch' went on several expeditions to Central America and made a large ethnological collection from the Chucunaque Indians, presented to the British Museum. A Fellow of many learned societies, Lilian was a founder member of the Pacific

Geographical Society. She died in Sussex on 4 October 1946, aged sixty-three.

Fanny Bullock Workman was born in Massachusetts on 8 January 1859 to a political family. Sent to finishing school in Europe, in 1881 she married Dr William Workman and had one child, Rachel, three years later. After poor health forced Dr Workman to retire from practice in 1889, the couple took to travelling around Europe using Germany as their base. Their journeys around North Africa and the Middle East in the mid-1890s led to the first of many joint travel books, *Algerian Memories* (1895) describing a bicycle trip over the Atlas mountains to the Sahara. During the next two years they pedalled nearly 20,000 miles around China and the Indian subcontinent. In 1899 they made their first trip to the Karakoram range of the Himalayas, and their passion for bicycles soon gave place to mountaineering. During the next seven expeditions to the Himalayas, Fanny twice broke the women's altitude record, including reaching 23,300 feet on Nun Kun peak (1906), recorded in *Peaks and Glaciers of the Nan Kun* (1909). Her final major expedition to the Srachen Glazier in 1912 was supported by the Royal Geographical Society. A campaigner for votes for women, although she took her husband with her on her travels and they joint-authored their climbing books, Fanny commonly insisted she was the leader of their expeditions. From the First World War onwards she lived in France, and died at Cannes on 22 January 1925 after a long illness. Her ashes were taken back to be buried in her home town of Worcester, Massachusetts.

Isabella Robertson Christie, known as Ella, was born on 21 April 1861 to a wealthy Scottish mineowning family. From a young age she had a close relationship with her only living sibling, her younger sister Alice, who married at seventeen. Her father suffered from mental illness which made him violent and paranoic, and at his death in 1902 he denounced his daughters and left his considerable estate to two orphanages. Ella and Alice challenged the will, and when the court decided in the sisters' favour Ella immediately sailed for Bombay. From that time on she was an inveterate traveller, claiming to have visited every European country except Ireland. In 1907 she went to China, Japan and Central Asia, returning on the Trans-Siberian Railway. She visited Samarkand (1910), Russian Central Asia (1912), the

United States and Cuba (1914). Although keeping detailed diaries of all her journeys, she published only one book of travel, *Through Khiva to Golden Samarkand* (1925). She spent the First World War in France running a canteen for injured soldiers, after which she mostly confined her travels to Europe and North Africa. She wrote two cookery books and a joint biography with her sister. The love of the later years of her life was her Japanese garden recreated in the foothills of the Ochils. She died of leukaemia on 29 January 1949 in Edinburgh.

Constance Frederica Gordon Cumming was born 26 May 1837 at the family estate of Altyre, Morayshire, the youngest daughter of sixteen, with fifty first cousins. As a child she was sent to Hermitage Lodge private school for girls in London. Her first voyage out came in 1868, when she accompanied her sister and brother-in-law on a tour around India. As an unmarried daughter, she was left with no fixed abode and increasingly wandered. In 1872 she went to Ceylon for eighteen months, returning to Britain and leaving for Fiji less than twelve months later for a two-year stay. She voyaged to Tonga, Samoa, Tahiti and the West Coast of America in a French Man-of-War, and to Japan and China (1878). She wrote several volumes on her travels, including *At Home In Fiji* (1886) and *Wanderings in China* (1881), based on letters back to her extensive family. An accomplished watercolourist, she executed several hundred paintings which were exhibited throughout Britain. She was particularly concerned with missions to the blind in China. She died on 4 September 1924.

Alexandra Louise Eugenie Marie David-Neel was born in Paris on 24 October 1868 to a French journalist father and Belgian mother fifteen years into their unrewarding marriage. From a young age she became interested in eastern philosophies and travelled around the capitals of Europe as student to various schools of thought, sailing to India in 1891 in further pursuit of a spiritual home. From 1894 until the turn of the century she performed with a travelling opera company under the name of Madamoiselle Myrial. In 1904 she married Philip Neel who, although rarely seeing his legal wife, financed her travels until his death in 1941. Alexandra slowly journeyed through the Indian subcontinent (1911–12), Central Asia (1912–16) where she lived as a hermit in the Himalayas for two years, to the Far East (1917–18) to which she returned during the Sino-Japanese war. While studying with monks in the Himalayas she met Yongden, a Sikkimese, who became guide and companion on all her travels. In 1923 she set out for the closed city of Lhasa disguised as a pilgrim, recorded in *My Journey to Lhasa* (1927). Renowned for exaggeration and an inflated sense of self-importance, her claims to have reached her goal were continually questioned. She became not only an expert on but a leading practioner of Tibetan Buddhism, and wrote several scholarly works on Buddhist philosophy and doctrine. In 1928 she bought Samten Dzong in the South of France to which she retired and lived with Yongden. She died on 8 September 1969 at Digne, and requested her ashes be scattered in the Ganges.

Ménie Muriel Dowie was raised on a Scottish estate until in 1890, in her early twenties, she travelled through Poland dressed as boy, writing up her experiences in *A Girl in the Karpathians* (1891). In 1891 she married Henry Norman, and together they travelled up the Nile and around Europe, Ménie often breaking away from her husband and finding her own way home. They had one son, Nigel, born in 1897. In 1903 she married for the second time, to the traveller and mountaineer Major Edward Arthur Fitzgerald. She authored several novels and works of fiction, as well as a collection on women who dressed as men, *Women Adventurers* (1893).

Mary Edith Durham was born in 1864 in Hanover Square, London to a medical family. She received training as an artist from Bedford College and the Royal Academy of Arts, which she put to use in naturalist painting and illustrations for books. In 1900 doctor's orders sent her by ship from Trieste down the Dalmation Coast and her long relationship with the Balkans began. From 1903 to the outbreak of the Great War she made a yearly journey to this region, including the winding passage through Montenegro and North Albania recorded in *High Albania* (1909). She reluctantly nursed in Skhoder during the Balkan Wars, shocked by the misery she encountered but unfitted for caring work. She was Honorary Secretary of the Anglo-Albanian Society and became entangled in Balkan politics in Britain as the leading advocate of Albanian nationalism and constant petitioner to the Foreign Office. She wrote more than ten books on her travels and on Balkan politics, as well as continuing to photograph and paint on her journeys. Nicknamed the Queen of the Highlands, the Albanians saw her as symbol and proponent of their cause. She made her last journey to Central Europe in 1921, but hurried back disillusioned to Britain. She died on 15 November 1944 in London.

Amelia Ann Blandford Edwards was born on 7 June 1831 in London and was educated at home by her mother. Her parents' early and sudden deaths forced her to make a living through journalism and many-volumed popular novels. She initiated herself slowly into travel, and with her female companion first made a trip to Belgium, before venturing into the more rugged Dolomites in 1872. In 1873 they travelled to Egypt and Amy was introduced to the study of Egyptology which became her passion. Her journey on a *dahabeeyah* up the Nile was recorded in *A Thousand Miles Up the Nile* (1877). Although never returning to Egypt, she spent the rest of her life working for and writing about this ancient land. In Britain she agitated for the formation of the Egypt Exploration Fund, of which she became Honorary Secretary. Although awarded a large number of honorary degrees from American universities, she received no academic recognition in her own country for her unremitting work in this field. In 1889 she embarked upon a lecture tour of the United States to raise money for the Fund and published her talks as *Pharoahs, Fellahs and Explorers* (1891). At her death on 15 April 1892, a few weeks after that of the female friend with whom she had been living at her Westbury-on-Trym home, she bequeathed a chair of Egyptology to University College, London.

Margaret Elizabeth Fountaine was born near Norwich in 1862 to a clerical family. After chasing a reluctant lover to Ireland in 1890, she drowned her sorrows in journeying around Europe, soon giving up painting and singing for the more outdoor pursuit of butterfly collecting. In 1901 she travelled through Syria where she met Khalil Neimy, ten years her junior, with whom she soon became passionately involved. Together they spent the next fourteen years travelling the world to Turkey (1903), Algeria (1904), Spain (1905), Southern Africa (1908–9), the Caribbean (1911) and India (1912–13). In 1913 they sailed for Australia hoping to settle, but Margaret found herself increasingly restless with the new continent and her lover, and left for the United States. Supplementing her income through collecting, in 1919 she left for New Zealand via Fiji, and further travels took her to the Far East, West and East Africa, the Caribbean and South America. She made an extensive collection of over 20,000 butterflies and contributed to entomological journals. She died of a stroke on 21 April 1940 in Trinidad with a butterfly net in her hand.

May French-Sheldon was born in the United States in 1848 and educated in Europe. She married Eli Sheldon, and together they found a publishing house for her novel *Herbert Severance* and first translation of Flaubert's *Salammbô*. In 1891 she left for Zanzibar and East Africa, the account of which appeared as *Sultan to Sultan* (1892), shortly after her husband's death. A friend of the traveller Henry Morton Stanley, she imitated him closely in her large retinue and imperious attitude. In 1903 she travelled to the Congo and wrote in support of the Belgian King Leopold's policy and administration of the area. In 1905 she travelled to Liberia. Of strong opinions, she was an ardent supporter of women's rights. She died 10 February 1936 in West Kensington, London.

Mary Eliza Bakewell Gaunt was born on 20 February 1861 in Victoria, Australia and moved at a young age to the fading goldfields around Ballarat where her father was Commissioner. She was taught by a governess and attended boarding school before spending one year at Melbourne University. Encouraged by a sympathetic professor, she contributed to local newspapers and began her career as a writer. With the money she earnt, Mary made her first trip to Europe in 1890, via India and Aden, with the hope of developing a British market for her work. Her first romantic novel, *Dave's Sweetheart*, appeared in 1894. In the same year she married Dr Hubert Miller, but was widowed six years later. With little income, she left Australia for Britain, hoping to make a living as a writer, and was never to return. In 1908 she made her first trip to Africa along the West Coast, returning two years later to penetrate further inland. Her experiences were recorded in her first travel book, *Alone in West Africa* (1912). The following year she visited China and Siberia, resuming her travels after the war to the West Indies (1919) and around Europe. She continued to write both fact and fiction based on her journeys, producing more than twenty books and numerous articles. She settled in Bordighera, Italy, where she could comfortably live on her moderate income. She died bedridden on 19 January 1942 in a nursing home in Cannes, having been forced to flee her Italian home at the outbreak of the Second World War.

Mary Henrietta Kingsley was born on 13 October 1862, four days after her parents' marriage. Her father, a younger brother of the literary Kingsley family, spent long and frequent periods abroad and her mother, increasingly physically and emotionally crippled, became her only daughter's charge. When both parents died within two months of each other in 1893, Mary broke free from the Cambridge home and sailed to the Canaries. Here she saw people and cargo from the West Coast of Africa, and plans were laid for her first four month journey from Freetown to Luanda in 1893. After returning from a second West African journey, including a pioneering route through the Gabon and an ascent of Mount Cameroon, she wrote *Travels in West Africa* (1897) and *West African Studies* (1899), which embroilled her in colonial affairs in Britain. She eventually returned to the African continent in March 1900 as a nurse and newspaper correspondent during the Boer War, but soon contracted typhus. She died on 3 June 1900 and was, according to her own wishes, buried at sea off Simonstown. A year later the African Society was founded in her memory.

Agnes Smith Lewis and *Margaret Dunlop Gibson* were twins born in Scotland in 1843 and educated at Irvine Academy before attending finishing school in Kensington. After journeys to Greece and Egypt, in 1888 Agnes married Reverend Samuel Lewis, antiquarian and librarian at Cambridge. At his death three years later, the close relationship between the twin sisters was strengthened still further and they undertook all their travels and scholarship together. In 1892 they visited the monastery of St Catherine at Mount Sinai where they discovered important early Syriac manuscripts. A visit the following year identified their find as an early version of the Gospels, to become known as the Sinaitic Palimpest. Margaret was encharged with the writing up of their experiences from Agnes' journals, which she did in *How the Codex was Found* (1893). The Palimpest established the sisters as leading scholars, and they made several subsequent visits to Sinai, the last in 1906. Agnes authored many scholarly books and articles, and was awarded honorary degrees in recognition of her contribution to the field of ancient language. After Margaret's death in 1920, the elder twin spent the remaining years immobile and incapacitated, dying on 23 March 1926 at their Cambridge home.

Georgina Mary Muir Mackenzie was born in 1833 on her father's Delvine estate, Perthshire, Scotland, the eldest of nine. From her earliest journeys, she always travelled in the company of *Adeline Paulina Irby*, first across the Carpathians from Vienna to Krakow by cart in 1859. Together and anonymously, they published an account of their journey, *Across the Carpathians* (1862). After two years travelling about Europe, in 1861 the friends set out on the Balkan travels which would establish them as reluctant spokespeople for the Christian Slavs under Turkish rule. They published several jointly-undertaken accounts of their travels, in *Christmas in Montenegro* (1861) using the pseudonym of their combined initials 'I. M.'. They initiated a scheme for the education of Bosnian girls as schoolteachers in Sarajevo. While Adeline moved to Sarajevo in 1871 to look after the school, in the same year Georgina married Sir Charles Sebright, Consul General of the Ionian Islands, with whom she moved to Corfu. She never returned to the Balkans, dying on 24 January 1874 and being buried on the island. Adeline continued to dedicate herself to welfare work for Balkan refugees, until her death on 15 September 1911 in Sarajevo.

Marianne North was born on 24 October 1830 at the family home in Hastings where her father was twice elected Member of Parliament. When widower Frederick North died in 1869, Marianne took up oil painting and in the guise of a botanical artist travelled first to North America (1871), then South America (1872–4), the Far East (1876–7), South Asia (1887–8), Borneo, Australasia and North America (1880). In 1882 a gallery containing her extensive collection of paintings was opened in the Royal Botanic Gardens, Kew. In the same year she left for South Africa, then travelling to the Seychelles (1883). By the time of her last journey to Chile in the summer of 1884 her health was seriously breaking down and she sought solitude in a country home at Alderly, Gloucestershire. She died there on 30 August 1890 after many weeks of illness. Her autobiography, *Recollections of a Happy Life* (1892), and *Further Recollections of a Happy Life* (1893) was published after her death, having been severely edited by her younger sister Catherine Addington Symonds.

Ida Laura Pfeiffer, born in Vienna on 15 October 1797 the only daughter of the six Reyer children, claimed to have spent her first thirteen years dressed as a boy. In 1820 her family arranged her marriage to Dr Mark Anton Pfeiffer, a lawyer twenty-four years her senior, by whom she had two sons. Although separated from her husband, it was not until after his death (1838) and when her children were grown that Ida undertook her first major journey to the Middle East in 1842, published in translation as *A Visit to the Holy Land* (1851). Three years later she made a journey to Iceland and Scandinavia before in 1846 embarking on her first voyage around the world. She circumnavigated the globe twice more (1851–5 and 1856–8), writing popular accounts of these journeys. On her third and last round-the-world journey her main purpose was to visit Madagascar, where she contracted the liver disease which slowly killed her. Declining health prevented her travelling again, and on 27 October 1858 she died in Vienna.

Alexandrine Petronella Francisca Tinne was born in the Hague on 17 October 1835. When she came into a large inheritance at the age of thirty, she took to travelling around Europe and North Africa. In 1862, together with her sister Harriet and aunt Adriana, they traced the Nile to Bahr-al-Ghazal, travelling in grand style with an entourage of three hundred men, over one hundred camels, numerous cages of fowls and six sheep. Never returning to her homeland, Alexine sailed around the Mediterranean with her crew dressed in Arab clothes. In 1868 she set off as the first European woman to attempt to cross the Sahara, but was murdered by Tuaregs on 1 August 1869.

Bibliography

ORIGINAL DOCUMENTS CONSULTED

Bodleian Library, Oxford
  Nathan papers
British Library, London
  Bentley archive
  Macmillan archive
  Marianne North to Wallace family, correspondence
British Museum (Natural History)
  Günther papers
Dundee Museum
  Mary Slessor collection
Edinburgh University Library
  Mary Kingsley to Im Thurn, correspondence
Highgate Literary and Scientific Society
  Mary Kingsley correspondence
  R. E. Dennett, 'A Visit to Cabinda'
House of Lords Record Office
  St Loe Strachey papers
India Office Library
  Lyall correspondence
John Murray Archives
  John Murray correspondence, including letters from Isabella Bird
    and Mary Gaunt
London School of Economics
  Morel papers
National Library of Ireland
  Alice Stopford Green papers

National Library of Scotland
  Stewart-Christie papers
National Library of Wales
  Hartland papers
North Family
  Manuscript of Marianne North's autobiography
  Miscellaneous correspondence, including copies of letters from
    Marianne North to Barbara Bodichon
Rhodes House, Oxford
  Holt papers
  Mary Kingsley to Saxon Mills, correspondence
  Overseas Nursing Association archive
  Tylor papers
Royal Anthropological Institute
  Edith Durham photographs and drawings
Royal Botanic Gardens, Kew
  Marianne North correspondence, including to Thistleton-Dyer,
    Burnell and Hooker
Royal Commonwealth Society
  Mary Kingsley collection
Royal Geographical Society
  Gertrude Bell's notebooks
  Papers relating to women's admission
  Mary Kingsley to Violet Roy, correspondence
  Scott Keltie correspondence, including letters from Gertrude Bell,
    Mary Gaunt, Lilly Grove and Isabella Bird
Somerville College, Oxford
  Amelia Edwards papers
South African Library, Cape Town
  Hatty Johnson papers
Stewart Family
  Ella Christie correspondence, photographs and miscellanea

SELECTED BOOKS BY WOMEN TRAVELLERS

Bell, Gertrude, (anon.), *Safar Nameh: Persian Pictures*, London 1894.
—— *The Desert and the Sown*, London 1907.
—— *Amurath to Amurath*, London 1911.
—— *The Palace and Mosque of Ukheidir*, Oxford 1914.

—— and Ramsay, William, *The Thousand and One Churches*, London 1909.

Bird, Isabella, (anon.), *The Englishwoman in America*, London 1856.

—— (ed.), *The Revival in America, by an English Eye-Witness*, London 1858.

—— (anon.), *The Aspects of Religion in the United States of America*, London 1859.

—— *The Hawaiian Archipelago. Six Months Among the Palm Groves, Coral Reefs and Volcanoes of the Sandwich Islands*, London 1875.

—— *A Lady's Life in the Rocky Mountains*, London 1879.

—— *The Golden Chersonese, and the Way Thither*, London 1883.

✗ —— *The Yangtze Valley and Beyond. An Account of Journeys in China, Chiefly in the Province of Sze Chuan and Among the Man-Tze of the Somo Territory*, London 1899.

Bisland, Elizabeth, *A Flying Trip Around the World*, London 1891.

Blunt, Anne, *Bedouin Tribes of the Euphrates*, (2 vols), London 1879.

✗ —— *A Pilgrimage to Nejd, the Cradle of the Arab Race*, (2 vols), London 1881.

Brassey, Annie, *A Voyage in the Sunbeam. Our Home in the Ocean for Eleven Months*, London 1878.

Broad, Lucy, *A Woman's Wanderings the World Over*, London 1909.

Brown, Lilian Richmond, *Unknown Tribes, Unchartered Seas*, London 1924.

Bullock Workman, Fanny and Hunter, William, *Two Summers in the Ice-Wilds of Eastern Karakoram. The Exploration of Nineteen Hundred Square Miles of Mountain and Glacier*, London 1917.

Bulstrode, Beatrix, *A Tour in Mongolia*, London 1920.

Christie, Ella, (trans.), *Fairy Tales of Finland* by Zachary Topelius, London 1896.

—— *Through Kiva to Golden Samarkand*, London 1925.

—— *Ration Recipes*, London 1939.

—— and Stewart, Alice King, *A Long Look at Life by Two Victorians*, London 1940.

✗ Close, Etta, *A Woman Alone in Kenya, Uganda, and the Belgian Congo*, London 1924.

—— *Excursions and Some Adventures*, London 1926.

Cumming, Constance Gordon, *From the Hebrides to the Himalayas. A Sketch of Eighteen Months Wanderings in Western Isles and Eastern Highlands*, London 1876.

—— *At Home in Fiji*, (2 vols), Edinburgh 1881.

—— *A Lady's Cruise in a French Man-of-War*, London 1882.

—— *Wanderings in China*, (2 vols), London 1886.

—— *Memories*, (autobiography), London 1904.

David-Neel, Alexandra, *My Journey to Lhasa*, London 1927.

Dowie, Ménie Muriel, *A Girl in the Karpathians*, London 1891.

—— *Women Adventurers*, London 1893.

Duncan, Jane Ellen, *A Summer Ride Through Western Tibet*, London 1906.

Durham, M. Edith, (illus.), *Dent's First Latin* by Atkinson, London 1902.

—— *Through the Lands of the Serb*, London 1904.

—— *The Burden of the Balkans*, London 1905.

—— *High Albania*, London 1909.

—— *The Struggle for Scutari*, London 1914.

—— *Twenty Years of the Balkan Tangle*, London 1920.

—— *Some Tribal Origins, Laws and Customs of the Balkans*, London 1928.

—— *The Serajevo Crime*, London 1925.

Edwards, Amelia, (trans.), *A Lady's Captivity Among Chinese Pirates in the Chinese Seas* by Mademoiselle Fanny Loviot, London 1858.

—— *Sights and Stories. Being Some Account of a Holiday Tour Through the North of Belgium*, London 1862.

—— *Barbara's History*, (novel), (3 vols), London 1864.

—— *Debenham's Vow*, (novel), (3 vols), London 1870.

—— *Untrodden Peaks and Unfrequented Valleys. A Midsummer Ramble in the Dolomites*, London 1873.

—— *A Thousand Miles Up the Nile*, London 1877.

—— *Pharoahs, Fellahs and Explorers*, London 1891.

Forbes, Rosita, *Unconducted Wanderers*, London 1919.

—— *Secret of the Sahara*, London 1921.

—— (ed.), *Women of All Lands. Their Charms, Culture and Characteristics*, London 1938/9.

Fountaine, Margaret, *Love Among the Butterflies. The Travels and Adventures of a Victorian Lady*, edited by W. F. Cater, London 1980.

—— *Butterflies and Late Loves. The Further Travels and Adventures of a Victorian Lady*, edited by W. F. Cater, London 1986.

French, Evangeline and Francesca, and Cable, Mildred, *A Desert Journal. Letters from Central Asia*, London 1934.

French-Sheldon, May, (trans.), *Salammbô* by Gustav Flaubert, London 1887.

—— *Herbert Severance*, (novel), London 1889.

—— *Sultan to Sultan. Adventures Among the Masai and other Tribes of East Africa*, London 1892.

Gaunt, Mary, *Dave's Sweetheart*, (novel), (2 vols), London 1894.

—— *Kirkham's Find*, (novel), London 1897.

—— *The Uncounted Cost*, (novel), London 1910.

∝ —— *Alone in West Africa*, London 1912.

—— *A Woman in China*, London 1914.

—— *A Broken Journey. Wanderings from the Hoang-Ho to the Island of Saghalien and the Upper Reaches of the Amur River*, London 1919.

—— *Where the Twain Meet*, London 1922.

—— *Reflection – In Jamaica*, London 1932.

—— *World's Away*, (novel), London 1934.

—— and Essex, John Ridgewell, *The Arm of the Leopard: A West African Story*, (novel), London 1904.

—— *Fools Rush In: A West African Story*, (novel), London 1906.

—— *The Silent Ones*, (novel), London 1909.

Ghika, Ella, *Switzerland. The Pioneer of the Reformation or La Suisse Allemande* by Madame La Comtesse Dora D'Istria (pseud.), translated by H. C., (2 vols), Edinburgh 1858.

Gibson, Margaret Dunlop, *How the Codex Was Found. A Narrative of Two Visits to Sinai from Mrs Lewis's Journals 1892–3*, Cambridge 1893.

Hall, Mary, *A Woman's Trek from the Cape to Cairo*, London 1907.

—— *A Woman in the Antipodes and in the Far East*, London 1914.

Kingsley, Mary, *Travels in West Africa*, London 1897.

—— *West African Studies*, London 1899.

—— (ed.), *Notes on Sport and Travel* by George Kingsley, London 1900.

—— *The Story of West Africa*, London 1900.

Larymore, Constance, *A Resident's Wife in Nigeria*, London 1911.

Leith-Ross, Sylvia, *Stepping Stones. Memoirs of Colonial Nigeria, 1907–60*, edited and introduced by Michael Crowder, London 1893.

Lewis, Agnes Smith, *Eastern Pilgrims*, London 1870.

—— *The Life of the Reverend Samuel Savage Lewis*, Cambridge 1892.

—— *The Four Gospels translated from the Sinai Palimpest*, London 1894.

—— *In the Shadow of Sinai*, Cambridge 1898.

Mackenzie, Georgina and Irmy, Adeline, (anon.), *Across the Carpathians*, London 1862.

—— *Notes on the South Slavonic Countries in Austria and Turkey in Europe*, edited and with a preface by Humphry Sandwich, Edinburgh 1865.

Macleod, Olive, *Chiefs and Cities of Central Africa. Across Lake Chad by the Way of British, French, and German Territories*, Edinburgh 1912.

North, Marianne, (illus.), *The Autobiography of the Honorable Roger North*, edited by Augustus Jessop, London 1887.

—— *Recollections of a Happy Life being the autobiography of Marianne North edited by her sister Mrs J. Addington Symonds*, (2 vols), London 1892.

—— *Some Further Recollections of a Happy Life selected from the journals of Marianne North chiefly between the years 1859 and 1869: edited by her sister Mrs J. Addington Symonds*, London 1893.

Pfeiffer, Ida, *A Visit to the Holy Land, Egypt, and Italy*, translated by H. W. Dulcken, London 1851.

—— *A Visit to Iceland and the Scandanavian North*, translation, London 1852.

—— *A Lady's Travels Round the World*, translated by W. Hazlitt, London 1852.

—— *A Lady's Second Journey Round the World*, translated by J. Sinnett, London 1855.

Sykes, Ella, *Through Persia on a Side Saddle*, London 1898.

Talbot, D. Amaury, *Women's Mysteries of a Primitive People*, London 1915.

SELECTED MAJOR WORKS ON WOMEN TRAVELLERS

Barr, Pat, *A Curious Life for a Lady: The Story of Isabella Bird*, London 1970.

Bell, E. Moberly, *Flora Shaw (Lady Lugard DBE)*, London 1947.

Bell, Lady, *The Letters of Gertrude Bell*, (2 vols), London 1927.

Birkett, Dea, *Mary Kingsley*, forthcoming (Macmillan) 1989.

Burgoyne, Elizabeth, (ed.), *Gertrude Bell, 1889–1914, (1914–1926). From her Personal Papers*, (2 vols), London 1958.

✗ Callaway, Helen, *Gender, Ideology and Empire. European Women in Colonial Nigeria*, London 1987.

Carr, Helen, 'Woman/Indian: The American and His Others', in Francis Barker et al., (eds), *Europe and Its Others. Proceedings of the Essex Conference on the Sociology of Literature*, Colchester 1985.

Foster, Barbara and Michael, *Forbidden Journey. The Life of Alexandra David-Neel*, San Francisco 1987.

Frank, Katherine, *A Voyager Out*, Boston 1986.

Gladstone, Penelope, *Travels of Alexine Tinne, 1835–1869*, London 1869.

Goodman, Susan, *Gertrude Bell*, Leamington Spa 1985.

Gwynn, Stephen, *The Life of Mary Kingsley*, London 1933.

Hodgson, John, 'Edith Durham', unpublished paper.

McLaren, Ian F., *Mary Gaunt. A Cosmopolitan Australian. An Annotated Bibliography*, Melbourne 1986.

Middleton, Dorothy, *Victorian Lady Travellers*, London 1965.

Moon, Brenda E., 'Marianne North's *Recollections of a Happy Life:* How they came to be written and published', in *Journal of the Society of Bibliography of Natural History*, vol. 8 (1978), pp. 497–505.

Price, A. Whigham, *The Ladies of Castlebrae. A Story of Nineteenth Century Travel and Research*, Gloucester 1985.

Richmond, Elsa, *The Earlier Letters of Gertrude Bell*, London 1937.

✗ Stevenson, Catherine Barnes, *Victorian Women Travel Writers in Africa*, Boston 1982.

Stewart, Averil, *Alicella. A Memoir of Alice King Stewart and Ella Christie*, London 1955.

Stoddart, Anna M., *The Life of Isabella Bird, (Mrs Bishop)*, London 1906.

Wheelwright, Julie, *Amazons and Military Maids*, (Pandora) 1989.

Winstone, H. V. F., *Gertrude Bell*, London 1978.

SELECTED ADDITIONAL READING

✗ Adams, W. H. Davenport, *Celebrated Women Travellers of the Nineteenth Century*, London 1883.

Alexander, Joan, *Voices and Echoes. Tales from Colonial Women*, London 1983.

Allen, Alexander, *Travelling Ladies*, London 1980.

Allen, David Elliston, *The Naturalist in Britain. A Social History*, London 1976.

Ascher, Carol et al., (eds), *Between Women. Biographers, Novelists, Critics, Teachers and Artists Write about their Work on Women*, Boston 1984.

Baker, Colin, 'Nyasaland 1905–1909: The Journeys of Mary Hall, Olivia Colville and Charlotte Mansfield', *The Society of Malawi Journal*, vol. 35 (1982).

Ballhatchet, Kenneth, *Race, Sex and Class under the Raj. Imperial Attitudes and Policies and their Critics, 1793– 1905*, London 1980.

Blanch, Lesley, *The Wilder Shores of Love*, London 1954.

Bontinck, François, *Aux Origines de l'État Indépendant du Congo. Documents Tirés d'Archives Américaines*, Louvain 1966.

Callan, Hilary and Ardener, Shirley, (eds), *The Incorporated Wife*, London 1984.

Christian, Carol and Plummer, Gladys, *God and One Redhead. Mary Slessor of Calabar*, London 1970.

Cock, Jacklyn, *Maids and Madams. A Study of the Politics of Exploitation*, Johannesburg 1980.

Flint, John, 'Mary Kingsley – A Reassessment', *Journal of African History*, vol. 4 (1963), pp. 95–104.

Fowler, Marian, *Below the Peacock Fan. First Ladies of the Raj*, Ontario 1987.

Gaunt, Guy, *The Yield of the Years: A Story of Adventure Afloat and Ashore*, London 1940.

Golde, Peggy, *Women in the Field. Anthropological Experiences*, Chicago 1970.

Grosskurth, Phyllis, *The Memoirs of John Addington Symonds*, New York 1984.

Hancock, W. K. 'A Note on Mary Kingsley' in *Problems of Economic Policy 1918–1939*, vol 2., part 2. *Survey of British Commonwealth Affairs*, London 1942, pp. 330–4.

Heald, Madelaine, (compiler), *Down Memory Lane with Some Early Rhodesian Women, 1897–1923*, Bulawayo 1979.

Hobsbawm E. J. Eric and Ranger, Terence, (eds), *The Invention of Tradition*, Cambridge 1983.

Holmes, Richard, *Footsteps. Adventures of a Romantic Biographer* London 1985

Hunter, Jane, *The Gospel of Gentility. American Women Missionaries in Turn-of-the-Century China*, New Haven 1984.

Levine, Philippa, *The Amateur and the Professional. Antiquarian, Historian and Archaeologist in Victorian England, 1838–1886*, Cambridge 1986.

Livingstone, W. P., *Christina Forsyth of Fingoland. The Loneliest Woman in Africa*, Edinburgh 1914.

Middleton, Dorothy, 'Some Victorian Lady Travellers', *Geographical Journal*, vol. 139 (1973), pp. 65–75.

—— 'Women in Travel and Exploration', in Delpar, Helen, (ed.), *The Discoverers; An Encyclopaedia of Explorers and Exploration*, London 1980.

Oliver, Caroline, *Western Women in Colonial Africa*, Westport 1982.

Pearce, R. D., 'Violet Bourdillon: Colonial Governor's Wife', *African Affairs*, vol. 82 (1983), pp. 267–78.

Pratt, Mary Louise, 'Fieldwork in Common Places' in Clifford, James and Marcus, George E., *Writing Culture. The Poetics and Politics of Ethnography*, Santa Fe 1986, pp. 27–50.

Russell, Mary, *The Blessings of a Good Thick Skirt*, London 1986.

Said, Edward W., *Orientalism*, London 1978.

Scourse, Nicolette, *The Victorians and Their Flowers*, London 1983.

Simpson, Donald, *Dark Companions: The African Contribution to the European Exploration of East Africa*, New York 1975.

Stanley, Liz, 'Biography as Microscope or Kaleidoscope? The Case of "Power" in Hannah Cullwick's Relationship with Arthur Munby', *Women's Studies International Forum*, vol. 10 (1987), pp. 19–31.

—— 'Feminism and Friendship: Two Essays on Olive Schreiner', *Studies in Sexual Politics*, 8, n.d., Manchester.

Stevenson, Catherine Barnes, 'Female Anger and African Politics: The Case of Two Victorian "Lady Travellers"', *Turn-of-the-Century Woman*, 2 (1985), pp. 7–17.

Stocking, George W., (ed.), *History of Anthropology*, vol. 1, *Observers Observed. Essays on Ethnographic Fieldwork*, London 1983.

Thornton, Robert, 'Narrative Ethnography in Africa, 1850–1920: the creation and capture of an appropriate domain for anthropology', *Man*, vol. 18 (1983).

Urry, James, 'Notes and Queries on Anthropology and the Development of Field Methods in British Anthropology 1870–1920', *Proceedings of the Royal Anthropological Institute*, (1971), pp. 45–57.

Winston, Elizabeth, 'The Autobiography and Her Readers: From Apology to Affirmation', in Jelinek, Estelle C., (ed.), *Women's Autobiography. Essays in Criticism*, Bloomington 1980.

Index